ITHACA COLLEGE

Founded 1892

THE ITHACA COLLEGE STORY

by

John B. Harcourt

Ithaca College
Ithaca, New York

Library of Congress Catalog Card Number: 82-084-589
ISBN 0-96105560X

Printed in The United States of America
By W. F. Humphrey Press, Inc.

For

Mary

Katy and Alan

Jamie and Laurie

Contents

Plate Series

Preface

The pages that follow are, quite unabashedly, an *institutional* history of Ithaca College. Doubtless other kinds of history could have been written (and, some will say, should have been written) — for example, one developing in far ampler detail the personalities and contributions of those men and women who, for our students in particular, *are* the College. But I have been guided by the conviction that an institution has a life of its own, transcending the lives and work of the individuals who compose it. The biological analogy is obvious enough: an organism is something more than the summation of the behavior of its component cells. In this larger sense, Ithaca College can be seen as a kind of social organism, with its distinctive life pattern — its coming into being (as "accidentally" as in any conception), its struggles to survive in an often hostile world (with no guarantees of success), its varied, though far from unlimited, strategies of adaptation to a changing environment, its uncertainties, at every juncture, about its future (except for the certainty that it will not be immortal). All analogies break down, of course: a collegiate institution generally does not seek to replicate itself, to reproduce its kind, although sending successive generations of graduates out into the world is a kind of seeding. More important, Ithaca College — unlike, say, a starfish or even some other colleges, especially the denominational ones — has not developed in accordance with an initially defined nature or purpose. If the existentialists are right in asserting that man creates his own essence in the unpredictable decisions he makes hour by hour, day by day, as much might be said of Ithaca College. Our collective history strikes me as being not the gradual realization of an identity implicitly there from the beginning but rather the record of a series of identity crises (or if one prefers, of unforeseeable quantum leaps in a context of radical indeterminancy).

That, in broadest outline, is the story that I shall try to tell.

Any history is based on other histories, and I gratefully acknowledge my indebtedness to those who have preceded me. Three published works treat of Ithaca College in whole or in part: Isadore Yavits, *The Ithaca College of My Time* (Ithaca, N.Y.: Norton, 1965); George C. Williams, *This Is My Story* (privately printed, copyrighted 1969); and Lillian Speakman Vail, *Remembering: A History of the Ithaca Col-*lege Alumni Association (Ithaca, N.Y.: Ithaca College, 1978). All three have been used for the chapters that follow. Full-length unpublished accounts include John Mason Potter, *The First Seventy-Five: A History of Ithaca College 1892-1967* and Leonard B. Job, *Source*. Potter, the College's director of public relations in the 1960s, presents good material from his own era and from the earliest newspaper accounts of the Ithaca Conservatory of Music; at other times, he uncritically follows an early version of President Williams's highly inaccurate reminiscences. President Job's recollections of the twenty-five years of his administration, with comments on those who preceded and followed him, make lively reading. Briefer accounts appearing from time to time in College publications or in the *Ithaca Journal* —by Adrian Newens, Harold Jansen, Charles Chatfield, and Ben Light, among others — seem not to have been based on independent research. Helen Hood, former professor of biology and dean of women, deserve special praise for her early efforts to place the archives in order and for her contributions to oral history in her tape recordings of interviews with President Williams and with others important in the history of the College.

It has been my privilege to know four of the six presidents of Ithaca College — Leonard B. Job, Howard Dillingham, Ellis L. Phillips, Jr., and James J. Whalen. All four have read and commented upon all or part of this history, which was begun at President Phillips's suggestion. If I have had any advantage over my predecessors, it is because President Whalen has placed at my disposal every record or document that I have requested and throughout the writing of these pages has maintained a lively and informed interest in my work, without ever suggesting in any way the shape it should take or the conclusions it might reach. Without his encouragement and generous support over the past eight years, this history could not have been completed.

Other readers of the typescript, from whose criticisms I have benefited, have been Clifford A. Allanson, chairman of the Board of Trustees in the forties; Eloise Blanpied, assistant to the provost; the late Lynn Bogart, former professor of Music; Walter Borton, former director of college relations; John P. E. Brown, alumnus and trustee; Frank Falcone, former acting provost; Craig McHenry, longtime dean of the

School of Music; the late George Hoerner, professor emeritus and former chairman of the speech-drama department; Mary-louise Potter, for decades secretary of the School of Music; Celia Slocum, professor emerita of music; and Isadore ("Doe") Yavits, historian and professor emeritus of the School of Physical Education.

Administrators who have responded to my requests for information with unfailing graciousness include: John M. Brown, director of counseling; Earl E. Clarke, former dean of the General College and dean of students; Colonel Richard Comstock, who has served the presidents of Ithaca College in a variety of titles; Richard J. Correnti, vice-president for student and campus affairs; Frank W. Darrow, professor of chemistry and former provost; Eileen M. Dickinson, who was executive assistant to President Phillips; Warren L. Hickman, first dean of the College of Arts and Sciences; Gail F Hogan, director of institutional research and planning; William B. Koch, dean of the School of Health, Physical Education, and Recreation; Thomas C. Longin, former dean of the School of Humanities and Sciences; Charles G. McCord, Sr., former vice-president for college relations; Larry W. Metzger, institutional research analyst; Joseph D. Minogue, director of development; Robert M. Mueller, assistant to the president during the building of the South Hill campus; Lee Moss Scott, former editor of *Ithaca Horizon*; Thomas R. Salm, business manager; Carl E. Sgrecci, comptroller; John D. Stanton, registrar; Joel R. Stegall, dean of the School of Music; Marylee Taylor, former dean of women; Richard D. Vogel, director of alumni relations.

Staff members have cheerfully coped with my sometimes daily requests for documents — among them, Gladys Diemond, long connected with student counseling and the Egbert Union; Marguerite S. Dispenza, formerly executive secretary to the provost (who ransacked the attics of Job Hall for me); Jane DeWysocki, administrative assistant to the president; Nancy I. Gould, custodian of the minutes of innumerable campus bodies; Marjehne A. Hoefer, assistant to the dean of Humanities and Sciences; Inez Hensley, executive secretary to the president, who found for me files I hadn't known existed; Myrtle Mastroberti, who times without number dragged out the heavy volumes of Board minutes

for me to consult (and who taught me a much needed lesson in punctuation); Nancy J. Weitzel, whose familiarity with the resources of the registrar's office proved invaluable; Jane Wilcox, college relations, who has the foresight to preserve critically important materials from the Ben Light period; Linda Longwell, executive secretary for student affairs. Donna Freedline, secretary of the English department, and Susan Hernandez '81 rendered valuable assistance.

At every stage, I have depended upon the Library staff, especially those concerned with archival materials: Sandra Bascom, archivist; Gail Moore Miller, former archivist; Frances Andrews; Gisele Fae; Kathy Langerlan. At the reference desk, Everett F. Morse and Kurt W. Bogart provided expert answers to many difficult questions. Patricia F. Leach supplied useful materials out of her long association with the College. Mary Campfield, former librarian; Florence Pfanner, former assistant librarian; and Stella Grant, former librarian, all provided important details, especially concerning the early days of the Library on South Hill.

Other present or past members of the College community whose memories I have exploited include Roberta Barnett, founder of the speech department in its modern form; Willard Daetsch, professor of German, whose files are archives in themselves; George King Driscoll, pianist and former professor of Music; Harold Emery, professor of history; Elsie Hugger Erwin, professor emerita of physical education; Beatrice Goldman, professor of education; Joseph Hamilton, former professor of physical education; the late Evalyn Lynch, secretary to many deans; John Ogden, professor of English, who has permitted me to quote from one of his poems; Marguerite Rowland, professor emerita of history; Robert A. Ryan, professor of history; Fay Swift, distinguished alumnus of the School of Music; E. William Terwilliger, professor of English; Arnold Wilhelm, former professor of physical education. Many of these will be mentioned in the pages that follow.

Others to whom I have turned or who have volunteered information are Annita Andrick, of the DeWitt Historical Society; W. Robert Farnsworth, investment adviser and once a lecturer at the College; Anne G. Kramer for details about Max Gutstadt; Mary LeBeau '18, who talked with me during a visit to the campus and sent me important memorabilia; Mrs. S. Morton Giles, who filled in the history of the Martin Institute of Speech Correction after its removal to Bristol, R.I.; Jane MacInnes, who made available useful records from the files of her late husband, John B. MacInnes, professor of history; Anita Monsees, music critic; Randall E. Shew, whose journalistic career has brought him into close contact with the College; C. Hadley Smith, for long the College's official photographer; Robert B. Tallman and Thomas H. Canfield, architects of the South Hill campus.

Many specialists came to my assistance once the writing was completed. Carol Betsch, associate manuscript editor for the Cornell University Press, expertly edited the typescript. Barbara Hall, Barbara Rowan, Margie Sczepanski, and Mary T. Harcourt read the proofs of the pages set in type by Bea and Kim Davis of Davis Graphic Services, Lansing, N.Y. James P. Harcourt provided pictures and photographic assistance.

A special tribute is owing to Margaret I. Gibson, director of College publications and designer of this volume, who has worked with me at every stage of its preparation and upon whose professional expertise and artistic talent so many of us have long depended.

Finally, an expression of gratitude for which words are quite inadequate to Lillian Speakman Vail. Everywhere in the documented record of the College, I found evidence that Mrs. Vail had been there before me, patiently correcting errors, tracking down facts and dates long obscured by time. Her history of the Alumni Association is at the same time a miniature history of the College; it has been one of my principal resources. Mrs. Vail has generously made her files and her near-total recall of I.C. history available to me at every turn; she has read my chapters at least twice and saved me from many a gross error. In a very real sense, she is a co-author of this history.

J.B.H.

NOTE: Since this history is intended for the general reader, extensive documentation has been omitted. A fully annotated copy will be deposited in the College Archives.

I. The First Decade 1892-1903

WHAT to say when founding a college? What sentiments are appropriate for articulation at so solemn a moment? Ezra Cornell's words, immortalized on the Great Seal of his university, set something of a standard:

> *I would found an institution where any person can find instruction in any study.*

To be sure, Morris Bishop, attributing the canonical version to Andrew Dickson White, suspects that the original words were more like "I'd like to start a school where anybody can study anything he's a mind to."* But the late nineteenth century was a time propitious for rhetorical flourishes, and whether or not William Grant Egbert was aware of what his counterpart on East Hill had said or should have said, the founder of the Ithaca Conservatory of Music was not without his own kind of eloquence.

> *It is my plan to build a school of music second to none in the excellence of its faculty, the soundness of its educational ideals and the superior quality of instruction.*

---

*Morris Bishop, *A History of Cornell* (Ithaca, N.Y.: Cornell University Press, 1962), p. 74.

An expanded version, reflecting the subsequent development of the institution, added "then to surround it with allied schools, encouraging breadth of view and contact so often neglected by the young student." An early Catalog (1895 - 1896) attempted grander flights.

> *The aim of the founder of this institution has, from the very beginning, been to establish and carry on a Conservatory of Music and kindred branches of learning to meet the demand for an institution where thorough instruction can be obtained; which should foster and spread the highest known truths in the departments of art lying within its scope; and which should be an active agent in widening the field affected by their refining and ennobling influence.*

But twenty years after the founding of his Conservatory, Egbert remembered a more homely and sentimental impulse.

> *Many years ago when the writer was a small boy facing the problem of having to go away from home to avail himself of satisfactory instruction in music, he confided to his mother that some day he should establish a Conservatory of Music in Ithaca, so that small boys should never have to go away from home to study music.*

1

Described as a child prodigy on the violin, Egbert had been born in Danby, New York, on a farm located not so very far from the present site of Ithaca College, on December 28, 1867. He is reported to have given his first concert at the age of seven; he distinguished himself at Syracuse University, where he played first violin in a quartet in which his teacher, William Schultze, had felt obliged to yield that position to his pupil; and in 1890, he was one of five students selected, in a competition of some fifty violinists, to study with Joachim at the Koenigliche Hochschule für Musik in Berlin. There he remained until his funds were exhausted; in his second and final year, he had begun to think again of Ithaca, where he might "establish the dream of his boyhood, a real live Conservatory of Music, make his fortune in two or three years, wherewith he should pursue the study of his chosen instrument to his heart's content." Egbert was later to remark that the Conservatory was "founded on optimism," and the thought of making a fortune out of an educational institution in order to support a career as performing artist must seem naive in the extreme. The original plan, Egbert recalled, was "to establish a string quartette giving a series of concerts in Ithaca and elsewhere, which should be the nucleus of a Conservatory faculty." Thus, even in these earliest days of planning, we note the preeminence of the concept of a faculty who were musicians in their own right as well as teachers.

A letter addressed to "a prominent and wealthy Ithacan" having afforded only "meagre satisfaction," Egbert renewed his acquaintance with a friend from his Syracuse days, Max. M. Gutstadt, by then residing in Ithaca. Correspondence laid the foundation for the realization of Egbert's plan. Gutstadt busied himself selling $50 shares, which gave the subscribers the right to receive instruction and attend concerts at the Conservatory, and by the time Egbert returned to the United States in the summer of 1892, arrangements could be made to rent four rooms of a house now numbered 403 East Seneca Street. There, on September 19, 1892, the Ithaca Conservatory of Music opened its doors.

Here again, the concept of performance dominated. After a day given over to the formalities of auditions and registration, the faculty proceeded to give a concert in the old Unitarian Church. Egbert remembered that "every available seat and place to stand was occupied long before the hour set for the concert." The event was not only a huge success but, more significantly, "the educational beginning of an institution which has given elevating programs running into the thousands free of charge to its students and the public generally." (In 1900 - 1901, the Conservatory could claim to have offered some 514 "entertainments, recitals, and concerts" during that academic year, 204 of them outside of Ithaca.)

On a more mundane level, the presiding minister at that first concert worked in a plea for more subscriptions as a demonstration of "practical sympathy" for the fledgling institution. Quite evidently, not all, or even enough, of Mr. Gutstadt's certificates had been snapped up.

The original faculty numbered eight teachers and two lecturers. Egbert headed the violin department, assisted by his business partner in the venture, Gutstadt. His wife, Gertrude Walker-Egbert, directed the vocal department, and Fräulein Sophie Fernow, "a pupil of Von Bülow and Klindworth," took on piano, organ, and harmony. Instruction was also provided in the banjo, mandolin, and guitar. Cornell faculty members filled in for French, Italian, and German, and the two lecturers presumably provided background in music history and biography. It was further announced that Edouard Cerneau, "ex-army officer of France," would teach fencing for ladies and gentlemen — the prototype of later developments in physical education.

The Catalog of 1893 - 1894 (the first Catalog, certainly the oldest surviving one) lists 125 students for the academic year 1892 - 1893, most of them from Ithaca and upstate New York, but with a sprinkling from New York City, Washington, D.C., Cleveland, Chicago, and even Iowa and California. It is important to note that enrollment in the Conservatory could mean many things. Music lessons were provided for persons of all ages: we hear quite early of the preparatory department, and the earliest Catalog states that "beginners of both sexes from the age of four will be accepted." At the opposite extreme, those local citizens who had bought certificates were entitled to instruction up to the amount of their subscription, and special one-year courses were provided, at reduced rates, "for teachers and artists."

The Conservatory was organized around private and class lessons in instrument or voice; for $22, one might obtain one private and one class lesson a week for a ten-week term, with training in chorus, solfeggio, theory, harmony, history, ensemble playing, and an orchestral class thrown in, along with admission to lectures and recitals. But it is impossible to determine who was enrolled for what or for how long. The

Catalog disarmingly states that "no definite time can be fixed for completing a course of study" and "certificates signed by the Faculty will be given to the students who shall attain the requisite standard of proficiency in their respective branches, provided such students attended at least one entire school year." And even if proficiency was not attained, "all the students who shall faithfully follow one of the special courses during at least one year will receive a testimonial signed by the Faculty." To broaden the range of possible applicants, special inducements in the form of a lower price were offered beginners ("although it is less agreeable to teach those who know nothing of music, such pupils are preferable to those who have acquired a faulty execution"); and a 10 percent discount was given to the children of clergymen.

During this first year, the Conservatory undertook to make a major contribution to local culture by sponsoring an appearance of none other than Ignace Jan Paderewski, then on his second American tour. The entire fee of $1,500 being beyond the resources available to Egbert, an appeal was made to the community for $400, and on February 28, 1893, the Paderewski concert was held. Then, as now, Ithaca was difficult to reach: the pianist missed his connection in Buffalo, chartered a special train at the cost of $429, arrived twenty minutes before his scheduled appearance, performed triumphantly, and left after midnight for his next engagement in Chicago. The local citizens were reimbursed, and the Conservatory had left its indelible mark upon the musical life of Ithaca.

By the end of the 1892 - 1893 year, the Conservatory had "surpassed all expectations of its projectors" and increased its faculty to twelve. The Catalog was moved to lyric prophecy.

Nobly and beautifully situated; the lake stretching out its silver beauty before her; the hills rising about her to form a terraced amphitheatre; Ithaca is today fast realizing all that is meant by the term, "A University town."

The second and third years of operation are largely undocumented. The first Catalog, written in the spring of 1893, lists Egbert as musical director, a three-man finance committee, a to-be-named registrar, three lecturers, and eight full- or part-time faculty members, including George M. Chadwick for organ, piano, and music history. Spanish makes its appearance among the foreign languages taught, and two new "divisions" are announced — the school of oratory, elocution, and physical culture and the painting department. The "four small rooms" of the Day residence on East Seneca Street were proving inadequate; supplemental space was sought in the West Block on State Street and in a house at 312 North Geneva Street. Then certain developments in downtown Ithaca made possible a more permanent home. Gutstadt had transferred his half interest in the Conservatory to Egbert in March 1893 and had opened the Lyceum Theatre on Cayuga Street, between State and Green, to be for many years the focus for the dramatic arts in Ithaca. The much smaller Wilgus Opera House (over the original Rothschilds Department Store at the southwest corner of the State and Tioga intersection) was no longer needed for its original purposes and so became available for lease to the Conservatory in 1894 - 1895.

The Catalog for 1895 - 1896 reflects the exhilaration of this expansion. It is, for one thing, illustrated, although the illustrations will seem woefully inadequate to those used to the slick promotional brochures of more modern times. All the older publications of the Conservatory highlight photographs of Lake Cayuga and the adjacent gorges and waterfalls, and they are not above using scenes from the Cornell campus (properly identified, to be sure) to heighten the impression of a collegiate atmosphere. But it is the interior views of the Wilgus Building that most interest us: an entrance hall with sweeping staircase, unfurnished except for two fire pails; the second floor administrative offices, including a reception room set up for a staff or faculty meeting; two desolate corridors labeled South Hall and West Hall; the director's office, so bleakly furnished that it might serve for a Dickensian counting-house; a "Corner of Painting Room," with easels and sculpture casts; and, what must have been the pièce de résistance, the third floor Music Hall, with its balcony, its seating capacity of 500, and (not illustrated because possibly not yet installed) its "beautiful two-manual organ." There were approximately nine classrooms on the third floor and three more above them, plus some unfinished areas. Surveying these assets, the Catalog reports, with evident satisfaction and some stretching of the facts, "probably no Conservatory in America enjoys a more complete home."

Along with this expansion of the physical plant, the finance committee has increased to four members, with two local banks prominently represented, and a Lew S. Chafer has been appointed special business manager. The faculty now numbers sixteen, not counting "assistants," and includes a name later to figure in the history of the institution, Bandmaster Patrick M. Conway, director of the department of band and orchestral instruments. The emphasis on performance continues undiminished.

> *From the start the teachers employed have been men and women who have not only devoted their lives to their art but who have the exceptional natural qualifications for success in their chosen career that enable them to be great public performers of the productions of the master minds of music.*

The curriculum unaccountably drops solfeggio, but adds violincello, zither, harp, canon, fugue, and conducting, each department being listed with its director (or directress in the case of Mrs. Egbert), faculty, and assistants. Descriptions of the courses (that is, the various curricula) are somewhat fuller than before, occasionally with an unmistakable recruiting orientation.

> *To those who find themselves with impaired respiratory organs, the study of Elocution offers an almost never failing remedy. Pulmonary diseases are found very rarely among elocutionists.*

The Catalog further notes the success of the piano kindergarten ("using the Parsons synthetic method," with sixty daily half-hour lessons, all for $10); indeed, this approach is to be extended to the violin department.

Another milestone in the history of the Conservatory is announced.

> *During the past year all musical work in Cornell University has been placed under the direction of the Conservatory, and a series of grand musical festivals inaugurated which is expected in the near future to develop into the most important and imposing musical event in this section of the country.*

Beyond this May Festival, the Cornell connection involved the cadet band (under Conway), the symphony orchestra and probably, to judge from later arrangements, responsibil-

ity for the music at Sage Chapel, plus a series of lectures in music appreciation.

Little emerges to illuminate the life of the students during these years. The large number of local students lived of course with their families; many commuted from nearby towns. For others, "We have a list of places carefully selected among Christian families, where pupils from abroad can obtain board with comfortable rooms with use of piano at very reasonable rates." As a charming concession to Victorian sensibilities, we are assured that "during the private lessons ladies may bring a parent or servant."

With the first commencement looming on the horizon, it was deemed necessary to spell out the graduation requirements for the class of '97 (that is, for all two members thereof). Piano students, for example, were expected "to prepare without aid and play on two hours' notice an accompaniment to a difficult vocal or violin solo or both in a satisfactory manner for concert, and also to finish within one week after notice and without any assistance, one composition for piano solo of the same grade of difficulty as in the first requirement, and to perform it in public in an artistic manner." Likewise, on one month's notice a standard selection from each of five eras in the piano repertory. In more general terms candidates for diplomas were expected to have studied diligently "in no less than three separate lines of work" during at least one school year of forty weeks. Some work in harmony, counterpoint, theory, and the history of music was mandated, with an essay on an aspect of music history. Candidates "wishing special mention as to ability as teacher" must submit a thesis "on the plan of work to be adopted in attaining the desired results in their specialties." A graduate must have demonstrated the ability to conduct four-part choruses from the score after two hours' study without instrument and unaided in any way. The study of German, French, and Italian must meet a standard of twenty class lessons of one hour's length in each language. And of course a recital — "performance in public of a recital of 1½ hours duration" — was the final demonstration of achievement. Finally, lest we worry about those four-year-olds enrolled at the Conservatory, it was decreed that "no individual will be allowed to graduate before reaching the age of eighteen years."

These requirements, the musical director claimed in his annual report for 1897 - 1898, were as high as those of any school of this kind in America.

Yet despite these auguries of artistic success, the Conservatory was in deep financial difficulties. Director Egbert was learning a bitter truth that was to beset the institution from its first days to the present time — that it is exceedingly difficult to operate out of tuition revenue alone, without benefit of endowment or public funds. Incorporation seemed to provide an answer. Immediately after the Conservatory's first commencement on June 19, 1897 (at which time Miss M. Ethel Nichols and Miss Kate Green, pianists, were graduated), the certificate of incorporation was signed by Egbert, his brother-in-law William L. Sykes, who was president of the Emporium Lumber Company in Benzinger, Pennsylvania, and seven prominent Ithacans. This certificate authorized a capital stock of up to $9,000, consisting of ninety shares each of the par value of $100; $2,000 was required to be on hand in order to begin business. (Subsequently, the capitalization and the number of shares were periodically increased.) The nine incorporators agreed to purchase a total of thirty-six shares, ten of them to Egbert and thirteen to Sykes. The Catalog of 1897 - 1898 listed twenty-nine stockholders and their professions, again most of them from the local community (two of them seem never to have purchased the stock they pledged to buy). About seventy shares were issued in 1897 - 1898 and in the next four years, three, six, eight, and none, respectively. Things picked up in the fall of 1902 - 1903 (before the typhoid epidemic struck) with twenty-three shares disposed of. The total sold in 1904 - 1905 was thirty, dropping to two the following year.

Incorporation therefore did not solve all problems. Some stock was given to Egbert in consideration of his interest in the Conservatory; other shares seem to have been used to pay for the new organ or even for advertisements in the *Ithaca Journal*. As early as September 10, 1898, the directors were apprised that the finance committee, appointed at the previous meeting, was unable to sell any additional stock and so was forced to sign a note for $500 to meet immediate debts. One suspects that for most of the buyers, Conservatory stock was more a charitable contribution than a business venture; Charles E. Treman in particular, with his twenty-one shares, should be signalized as a major benefactor.

The certificate of incorporation provided for nine directors, who were duly elected and who held a preliminary meeting on that same commencement day in June 1897. After arranging for contracts for Egbert and the principal teachers and giving authority "to order stationery, blanks, books, etc. necessary to do business," the Board adjourned until June 21, at which time by-laws were enacted and officers elected. They were Jared T. Newman, attorney, as president; John B. Lang, mayor of Ithaca, as vice-president; Frank D. Boynton, principal of the Ithaca High School, as secretary and treasurer; and William Grant Egbert as musical director. (In these early records, "president" signified what we would call "chairman of the Board of Directors"; although he was styled musical director, it is quite proper to consider Egbert as the first president of what was to become Ithaca College.) The duties of the business manager were spelled out (among other things, to "promote the interests of the Conservatory in every conceivable way"), for which services Mr. Boynton was to be reimbursed at the rate of $25 a week during his summers and an additional $500 for "giving all the time that was necesary" from September to July. The directors, who were paid for their services until that practice was discontinued in September 1898, met the first Saturday of each month at 9A.M.; the three-man executive committee every Saturday at 8:30A.M.; and, the Catalog informs us, Mr. Boynton could be found each day in the business office from 4:45 to 5:35P.M. Handwritten minutes of these innumerable meetings are preserved in the College archives.

George C. Williams, Egbert's eventual successor as president of the Conservatory, provides a melodramatic account of that first year as a stock company in his privately printed autobiography, *This Is My Story* (1969).

> *In the meantime, Dr. Boynton's management of the Conservatory was proving to be quite a financial failure. It is one thing to manage the Public Schools, where the money is raised through taxation, and quite another thing to conduct a Conservatory of Music which is entirely dependent on its tuition receipts for its existence. At the end of the school year, it was found that Dr. Boynton had spent, not only all the money received from the students, but also the $9,000.00 received from the sale of Conservatory stock. There remained less than $100 in the treasury, with about $900 of unpaid debts. As a result Jared Newman immediately resigned as President of the Board of Directors of the Conservatory and Charles Treman was elected in his place.*
>
> *As my department had developed more rapidly than any of the others, the Directors then turned to me with the proposal that I become the General*

Manager as well as teacher in the Conservatory of Music.

Unfortunately, the minutes of the directors do not substantiate these assertions. Boynton's periodic financial reports in 1897 - 1898 generally show a margin of a few hundred dollars, slightly better than Williams was to achieve the following year. On May 7, 1898, the total resources of the Conservatory (including pianos) were given as $6,907.75, the liabilities, $1,501.03. Boynton continued to serve as director until January 3, 1903, and Newman finished his term as president and was reelected at the annual stockholders' meeting on September 10, 1898. Treman did not become president until July 1, 1899.

The directors did discuss a proposal to appoint Williams as business manager for the year 1898 - 1899 at a meeting on May 14, 1898. The proposal seems to have been submitted by Williams himself and was approved on May 21. In all probability, it was felt that Boynton's duties as principal of the High School did not allow sufficient time to attend to the affairs of the Conservatory. There is simply no evidence of a major financial crisis, with Williams riding in to the rescue.

Like Egbert, Williams was a local boy, having been born in Dryden, New York, on July 23, 1874. His father operated a prosperous marble and granite company; there was much family reading of Dickens, and his lifelong passion for Shakespeare began at twelve when his mother presented him with a copy of the bard's complete plays. After high school, he served a year's apprenticeship with his father, but through the urging of his mother and of the superintendent of the Dryden schools, he relinquished the security of the family business for further education in Boston. There he enrolled in the New England Conservatory College of Oratory, largely because of its reputation in public speaking; he also learned to play the flute and pursued courses in Swedish gymnastics and fencing at Harvard. Throwing himself into the cultural life of a major city, he reveled in plays and concerts, but without neglecting the leading preachers of the day and developing his already active religious life through the Young People's Christian Endeavor Society. After graduation in 1893 (with an additional Bachelor of Oratory degree from Boston University in 1894), he accepted an offer to organize a drama and public speaking department at the Nebraska Conservatory of Music in Lincoln. Upon his arrival, this institution turned out to be

something less than its publicity had indicated: asking a man found varnishing a floor where the president might be found, he learned that he was speaking with the president. Williams's contract provided for his receiving 75 percent of the tuition paid by his students (an arrangement that was to have consequence for the Ithaca Conservatory), and when payment was not forthcoming, his students gave his share of the tuition money directly to him. From that, it was natural enough that he should take his students with him, when the Conservatory collapsed, in order to establish his own institution, the Nebraska School of Oratory.

This flourished, but Williams felt an urgent call to a vocation in the Presbyterian ministry. An offer from Egbert to come to Ithaca seemed to work in that direction: he could simultaneously take courses in Greek and philosophy at Cornell in preparation for enrollment at Princeton Theological Seminary. In the spring of 1896 - 1897, his assistant in Lincoln, Miss Mildred Gillum, was sent ahead to organize the elocution department at the Conservatory along Williams's model, and he arrived himself for the following academic year. In order to have "complete control of my time so that my hours of teaching at the Conservatory did not interfere with my studies at Cornell," he decided to forego a stated salary and work on a percentage basis: 75 percent for the first $800 of tuition, 70 percent of the next $700, and 15 percent of all receipts above $1,500. And crowded though his schedule was, he found time to marry a former piano student at the Lincoln Conservatory, Miss Ruth Robertson, on December 29, 1897. At the end of his first year in Ithaca, he was named business manager, as we have seen, and by November 1898, he had become a stockholder and was elected secretary-treasurer of the Board of Directors. The call to the ministry became less imperious and was eventually transformed into a concept of lay service, which remained central throughout the remainder of his ninety-seven years.

In his autobiography, Williams tells us that he accepted his new assignment on one condition, that he "be allowed to develop the Conservatory of Music into a State Teachers College." The importance of this new emphasis cannot be overstressed for the future development of the College. Williams further saw that "there could be no future for me or for the Conservatory unless it could be expanded into a state and national institution." "The Directors smiled condescendingly," he wryly reported, "and agreed to my terms."

Such a program led inevitably to extensive advertising; indeed, one of the most fascinating aspects of Williams's tenure as manager is the variety and ingenuity of his publicity efforts. For the Ithaca Conservatory of Music, advertising had to be free or virtually so; there simply were no funds for such a purpose. Noting that those were the golden years for the Lyceum and Chautauqua performances, Williams hit upon "a direct and practical means of advertising the Ithaca Conservatory of Music." The plan was to organize a "concert company," consisting of a pianist, a singer, a violinist, and a reader. A large four-page circular was prepared, prominently featuring the artists on page one and the program on the inner pages. The last page was left blank, so that any sponsoring organization could fill in with its own ads and so recoup the $25 fee. An enterprising student was designated booking agent, the receipts to be divided among him and the four performers. Intercalcated in the circular was "some very attractive information concerning the Ithaca Conservatory of Music," and during the program one of the members of the company took several minutes for a promotional spiel. In this way, the Conservatory had extended advertising with no expense beyond printing up the circulars. These companies continued down to the World War I years; as many as five at a time covered the Northeast and even ventured into Canada, the South, and the Middle West. One member of such a company, Miss Jessie Adkinson, has left an absorbing diary, with numerous pictures, of her tour through Ontario and New York in 1914.

By August 1897, 123 newspapers and magazines (including the *Ladies' Home Journal, Harper's,* and the *Review of Reviews*) were carrying either free or paid advertising for the Conservatory. A letter was printed in December for distribution to all Cornell students, touting Conservatory courses, especially in mandolin. In February 1898, the directors authorized an advertisement in the *Cornellian* provided that it could be paid for in tuition (the music lessons to be provided, one assumes, by an already overworked instructor); likewise, business agents were sometimes paid in tuition. A "Business Men's Circular" was approved for distribution, and in 1901, the Conservatory offered to provide music for the Pan-American Exposition in Buffalo — an offer that was declined. In sum, Williams could boast of a massive publicity effort, costing some $10,000 between 1898 and 1902 (mainly for the Catalogs, etc., and for extensive mail follow-up of prospective

students). Not every possibility was explored however: in July 1897, the directors decided "not to take advantage of the offer made by the Ithaca Street Rail Road for advertising in their cars," and in February 1898, they concluded that "the space offered on the curtain in the Farmer [later Covert], New York, Theatre was considered not desirable."

Another source of income was the Conservatory's relationship with Cornell, which had existed some years before Williams's arrival. By 1898 - 1899, if not sooner, the Conservatory was providing for the Sage Chapel services both morning and afternoon on Sunday and every Thursday afternoon, with daily vesper organ music for at least fifteen minutes on each other weekday, excluding Saturdays. The annual revenue for this activity was $1,000, and Williams was eager to expand the connection. At the request of President Jacob Schurman, he tells us, the Conservatory sought out a faculty member who might present courses of instruction in music history, harmony, and music composition at the University. After a recruiting trip to New York, Egbert and Williams engaged the services of one Sumner Salter, who turned out to be a disaster. By May 1901, the executive committee was requesting his resignation, and by June was offering him $500 to surrender his contract for the following year. With the wisdom of hindsight, Williams would conclude, in his autobiography, that the contemplated affiliation with Cornell might have resulted in a loss of institutional identity and thus the collapse of his vision of a Teachers College. But in 1902 - 1903, there were even plans to build on Cascadilla Gorge, adjacent to Cornell, and for many decades Williams remained convinced that "the Conservatory missed the opportunity of becoming an associated school with the University." The link with Cornell seems to have been completely severed some time around 1903 - 1904.

The impact of Williams's arrival was thus considerable and was duly noted in the annual report of the musical director for 1897 - 1898. After announcing that the Conservatory's enrollment had leaped from 125 to 374 in six years, Egbert described the growth of the elocution department as "nothing short of phenomenal": Williams had begun with one student in the fall and ended the year with seventy; two additional instructors had to be added in that department; twenty afternoon recitals and seven evening entertainments were given. Egbert went on to mention, among the Conservatory's "free advantages," a pantomime class and a "Tableau d'Art Company" — these, one feels sure, due to the stimulus of Williams's presence.

Williams had studied fencing at Harvard and was later to recall that at the age of fifty-eight, in the last year of his presidency, he had been able easily to defeat a Cornell student who had challenged him to a bout at a picnic on the proposed South Hill site of Ithaca College. Fencing therefore reappears in the Conservatory curriculum of 1897 - 1898, taught by M. Philip Brigandi, graduate of the National Fencing Academy of Naples, winner of the Gold Medal at the National Fencing Tournament in Naples in 1894, and formerly assistant fencing master of the New York Athletic Club. The rationale for the new course is interesting: few sports "appeal so strongly to the human love of a keen struggle for supremacy" and, without thought of women's liberation, "women who fence much believe that no other form of exercise tends so materially to improve their personal appearance." Williams's own enthusiasm burns through the Catalog copy: "How quickly can a thought be executed, not how violently, is the question; and in its solution lies the indescribable exhilaration which fencing offers."

Other new members of the faculty in 1897 - 1898 include Cornell's Olaf Brauner for painting, Esther May Wanzer from the Allen Gymnasium in Boston for physical culture, and Hollis E. Dann, supervisor of music in the Ithaca public schools, for chorus conducting. The Catalog notes an upgrading in the guitar, mandolin, and banjo department, which had apparently proved highly attractive, especially to Cornell students. The musical director sadly observed that although the piano department was one of the strongest in the Conservatory, there were relatively few students, because "the slipshod methods usually taught, leading to the performance of popular and very bad music, which, however, is apt to appeal more strongly to the musically uncultivated mind, still takes precedent with numbers of people over the thorough and painstaking method which alone will bring satisfactory results."

The Williams influence may also be apparent in a section of the 1897 - 1898 Catalog entitled "Artists for Entertainments." The Conservatory, we learn, is prepared to furnish vocalists, pianists, violinists, trios, string quartets, readers, with programs suitable for clubs and other organizations "at prices guaranteed to be safe and satisfactory, for towns, villages and cities" — only high-grade entertainments to be given. This Catalog further includes more specific details about the day-to-day activities of faculty members and students: reports are to be sent quarterly to parents or guardians of pupils under legal age; the faculty is to meet each Friday at 5 P.M.; smoking and liquor are prohibited on the Conservatory premises (although the proviso "the use of tobacco in any form must be discontinued when used to such an extent as to become a cause for complaint" may seem to countenance chewing tobacco). The new organ gets a full-page illustration (Williams was later to describe it as a "miserable failure," with fantastic repair bills), and there is reference to a gymnasium, presumably one of the larger classrooms, equipped with the apparatus necessary for exercises "accompanied by bright and appropriate music rendered by a competent pianist." Provision is further made for the use of advanced students to supervise practice at the rate of fifty cents an hour. The Catalog concludes with a list of some seven hundred students who have studied at the Conservatory since 1892.

The next surviving Catalog (1900 - 1901) affords further evidence of Williams's role in the Conservatory. He had been complimented for his successful work as business manager at the annual stockholders' meeting in June 1900. But his efforts were not limited to the business affairs of the Conservatory. The Catalog presents a new introduction to the elocution and oratory section, which seeks to ground the arts of speaking in a larger philosophical context — to develop "not the voice alone, nor the gesticulating powers in themselves, but the whole man, and then to teach him to express his thoughts, feelings, and convictions through his own individual and ideal character." Students are to be taught to be not readers merely but thinkers as well. In addition to the courses previously announced, the department now provides instruction in voice culture, gesture, dramatic art, lyric art, Delsarte, physical culture, psychology, home reading and a "Juvenile" course. The Pantomime Club and Tableau d'Art Company ("composed of lady students . . . in Grecian tableau gowns") continue and are supplemented by a well-organized Dramatic Club, with two public presentations being contemplated for the academic year. General literature (that is, English literature) makes its first appearance in the Conservatory curriculum. A Fortnightly Club met every other week to discuss literary topics, and its counterpart, the Vanity Fair Club, was a secret organization of musicians, the precise activities of which the Catalog cannot describe, beyond the generalized conviction that it is a "wide-awake wholesome society."

Throughout, the Catalog suggests a more structured institution. The business staff includes six persons besides Williams; courses are more clearly articulated as four-year programs; a table of required studies for graduation is printed. The concept of "loyalty" (which is to have a long history at Ithaca College) makes its appearance: "Upon connecting themselves with the Conservatory, all students pledge themselves to a loyal observance of the school regulations." As in the previous Catalog, any student can be dismissed "whose presence in the school would, in the judgement of the Management, be detrimental to its interests."

The entertainment bureau, the Ithaca Conservatory concert company, the teachers' bureau, and the choir agency get extended coverage and attest a due concern not only for Conservatory publicity but also for the professional experience, financial aid, and post-graduation placement of students. Two agents, we are told, assist in the booking of such events. The May Festival, one of Egbert's earlier dreams, was inaugurated by an impressive program at Cornell on May 22, 1900. A Conservatory Library has been started (a dubious claim); at least there is a reading room with a collection of books on musical and literary topics plus leading magazines, papers, and current literature. We note, however, that students are still being referred to the city and university libraries for serious reading. For the first time, an estimate of the cost of tuition, board, room, and all expenses is provided — $475 for a full course.

But the big news in the 1900 - 1901 Catalog is the opening of the Conservatory Home for Lady Students at 312 North Geneva Street (where some classes had been held as early as 1893 - 1894), with Mrs. Esther B. Egbert, the mother of the musical director, serving as preceptress. Described "as one of the most beautiful buildings in Ithaca" (although the illustrations, exterior and interior, seem not all that grand), the Home was to be conducted "on principles which give it a special atmosphere of culture and good order, and at the same time [it] is free from the temptations and dangers that often surround school life." At a cost of from $5 to $7 a week, the management will assume "full responsibility for the mental, moral, and physical development of its lady students." True, other lodgings are available, but, the Catalog darkly hints, "the Conservatory will not hold itself responsible for the care of students residing outside of the Conservatory Home."

The records for 1900 - 1901 attest to a growing body of alumni. In his report, the musical director lists the names of thirty-eight alumni, with their majors. In May 1901, the

directors resolved "to look into the expense of organizing and entertaining the Conservatory alumni on some date in the coming Commencement Week." For many decades, alumni activities were to be scheduled at that time in the academic year.

No Catalog for 1901 - 1902 seems to have survived. The faculty minutes of that year refer to a school of opera and announce, with a list of the cast, a first performance of *Powhatan,* scheduled for October 1901.

The eleventh annual Catalog (1902 - 1903) gives prominence to activities rather than to buildings — the chorus in Sage Chapel is pictured, as are the orchestra at the Lyceum Theatre, the Mandolin Club, a class in opera, a scene from *Martha,* two scenes from plays, a concert company, and the Tableau d'Art Company peering through floral hoops. The piano department proclaims the success of the "Virgil Clavier System," which involved classes of four to eight pupils "reciting the exercises simultaneously." The orchestra is fully described, and offerings in band and orchestral instruments are significantly expanded. Music theory courses are more numerous, and a new department inaugurates a two-year curriculum in "Music in Public Schools," under the direction of George Goldsmith Daland ("a pupil of Francis Fisher Powers, of New York City, and William Shakespeare, London, England," a former supervisor of music in the public schools of Rhode Island and New Jersey). The curriculum for elocution and oratory has been completely reorganized, especially for oratory. The idealistic approach continues — "the voice, when free and unrestricted by habits, defects, or misuse, is a true reporter of the soul." Shakespeare loomed large in Williams's teaching, and the commencement play for 1901 was *As You Like It.* Scholarships, with which the Conservatory was unusually generous considering its straitened finances, are now formalized: a board of inquiry, composed of the mayor of Ithaca and six Protestant clergymen, will screen applicants for an examination to be conducted by five judges, three of whom shall have no connection with the Conservatory. There are both scholarships-at-large and scholarships assigned to each of the congressional districts of New York State. Egbert would later estimate that in the first twenty years of its existence, the Conservatory had awarded approximately $100,000 in scholarship aid. And by 1902 - 1903, the average student was spending three years in residence.

A Conservatory magazine, the *Key Note,* had been

created at a mass meeting of students on October 4, 1901. This publication was extensively used for recruiting; unfortunately there are no extant copies dating before June 1904 (III,4). Among organizations, Vanity Fair and the Dramatic Club are not mentioned, although the main work of the latter, the commencement play, is continued. The major additions are a fraternity (the Delta chapter of Sinfonia) and the Alpha Tau sorority.

Alpha Tau (which would become Sigma Alpha Iota), was a local creation, the work of several members of the Vanity Fair Club who felt the need for a new organization to do for the women students what Sinfonia was doing for the men. This sorority, it was hoped, would become in time a national organization, dedicated to "a furtherance of the highest art, the promotion of friendship and loyalty to Alma Mater." Sinfonia, already a national, has a more interesting history. In April 1900, Williams had visited the New England Conservatory while on a business trip to Boston; there he had met with a local organization called the Sinfonia. Sensing the value of such a group for the male students of any conservatory, he joined in the efforts to arrange a convention to organize Sinfonia into a national fraternity. This convention was held in Boston the following spring. The Ithaca Conservatory was thus one of the original chapters, and Sinfonia, later to become Phi Mu Alpha, would eventually number more than four hundred chapters throughout the United States. The Catalog refers to "a very pleasant chapter room" in the Conservatory building, with plans for a chapter house already in formulation.

The 1903 - 1904 Catalog lists a new personality as head of the elocution department, Lakin Hannibal Richard, and some new curricular items also appear: a tuning department, courses in the "systematic study of violin literature," in "The Art of Conducting," and in parliamentary law. A certain stridency of tone can be heard in the announcements for foreign language study, which promise to give "a complete mastery of that fluency of speech and delicacy of accent which usually distinguish the native from the foreigner;" in French, the "Yersin Method" will successfully impart "an absolutely pure Parisian accent." The student body is now "a definite organization, with officers and a governing constitution," and all students shall attend chapel each morning, Monday through Friday, at nine o'clock, after which the regular periods of instruction begin.

One ominous note appears. Egbert is listed as being in Prague on a leave of absence that began on February 5, 1903. Behind this laconic announcement lay a personal tragedy — one which, in George C. Williams's words, "would have broken a man of less spiritual resistance." In 1900 - 1901 Mrs. Egbert had left for Europe in a move that portended the breakup of their marriage and a subsequent divorce. Egbert followed her abroad in an unsuccessful attempt at reconciliation; he soon returned to Ithaca but found himself unable to continue as musical director in the wake of such an emotional upheaval. Hence his request for a leave and his decision to return once more to Europe to continue his studies under Otakar Sevcik. He would be gone for three years, returning for the academic year 1906 - 1907. Williams for a while took over the duties of musical director, although Egbert did not immediately relinquish the title.

The financial difficulties continued. We have seen that the capital realized by the sale of stock begun in 1897 had never provided more than temporary relief. As early as February 1898, the directors were recommending fewer teachers, with heavier teaching loads. In October of that year, the Board was seeking a reduction in the rent paid for the Wilgus Building and attempted to pay for its local advertising by offering the *Ithaca Journal* a share of stock. The minutes of the executive committee for October 1, 1898, state glumly: "The report of the Business Manager for the year 1898 - 1899 was presented and examined. It was decided to withhold it for a time until we could accompany it with a more encouraging report." In September 1898, the directors had pledged the property of the institution as security for a note to cover current obligations. By November, resident stockholders were being offered two tickets for all faculty and student concerts — in lieu of dividends, one wonders, for there is no record that dividends were ever paid, although various proposals for doing so occur in the minutes. In February 1900, the fact that present stock had been practically disposed of prompted a resolution to incorporate for a larger amount ($12,000), which the stockholders approved in March. In July, the business manager was authorized to offer a 20 percent discount to any students who were instrumental in bringing new tuition money to the Conservatory. According to the minutes of February 6, 1901, the concert companies were "a greater success than ever before in an artistic way" but alas, they were losing money. By April, Williams was reduced to running a "special" — a trial offer at 50 percent discount for students not previously registered.

Things looked up a bit in 1902 - 1903. Williams was able to

report to the directors that the fall term had been the very best in the history of the school. But his sanguine hopes for the spring semester were destined never to be realized. An earlier Catalog (1897 - 1898), while enumerating the advantages of Ithaca as a college town, had boasted of its "excellent system of water works" (privately owned). A grim refutation of that claim came in the form of a devastating epidemic of typhoid fever. In Williams's words:

> *It struck in January [1903], just before the opening of the spring term. All students rushed for their homes. All public gatherings were forbidden. There were over 1200 cases and about 100 deaths. If we could have closed the Conservatory at that time, we could have weathered the storm; but, as it was, we had all the teachers' salaries to pay, besides rent and other running expenses. . . .*
>
> *After the epidemic was over, the Directors of the Conservatory met, found the Conservatory was practically bankrupt, and decided to close the institution. I gave the matter careful consideration. My dream was at stake and I would not allow it to fail. I met with the Directors of the Conservatory and told them that if they would turn in their Conservatory stock, which was now worthless, I would assume all financial obligations of the Conservatory.*

Or so it seemed to Williams sixty years after the event. The minutes of the Board of Directors read somewhat differently. Nothing indicates impending bankruptcy; there is no recorded discussion of closing the Conservatory; and the only direct reference to the calamity is in the minutes for March 7, 1903.

> *The members of the faculty expressed through Mr. Williams their willingness to make up lessons, both private and class, or extra time, for those students who have been absent from the Conservatory during the present epidemic.*

Williams's own report to the Directors (September 5, 1903) gives only two paragraphs out of fifteen to the effects of the epidemic and concludes, "In reality, despite our great reverses during the Second Term, no loss has been sustained this year." The stockholders continued to be the legal owners of the Conservatory, duly electing or reelecting their directors, until April 23, 1908, at which time eighteen holders of 110 shares of outstanding stock surrendered their interests to Williams, Eric Dudley, and W. Grant Egbert, who then assumed the debts of the institution.

Nevertheless, the spring of 1903 marked the end of an era. The first decade was over; it had been duly celebrated on February 10, 1902, at Sinfonia's first public concert. The institution, though shaky, had survived. It was now called upon to face an uncertain future without the guiding presence of its founder.

II. Consolidation of Control 1904 - 1918

WITH Egbert removed from the Ithaca scene for three academic years (1903 - 1906), Williams was able to effect some major changes in the operation of the Conservatory. In accepting control, he tells us, he had stipulated that the teachers would have to "cooperate with me and do away with salaries entirely." Instead of an annual stipend, each teacher was to receive 50 percent of the tuitions received from his or her pupils. Williams himself, as general manager (the title he seemed to prefer over the official business manager), would likewise work without salary but with 75 percent of the revenue brought in by his students in elocution. Later, as administrative duties reduced the amount of teaching he was able to do, the annual salary was restored — $800 in 1905.

Williams claimed that this arrangement was highly profitable to the faculty, and the evidence certainly suggests that such was the case for the general manager and for a handful of master teachers. His explanation is disarmingly simple.

> *When the teachers were giving instruction on a salary basis, each new pupil meant to him merely more work. But on this commission basis, each new pupil meant more money in his pocket. Thus both teachers and pupils were satisfied, and they made every effort to increase the enrollment of the Conservatory.*

Just how the system proved educationally advantageous to the students is not clear. There is some evidence of infighting among the faculty vicious enough to require the directors to act, to say nothing of growing hostility between the Conservatory teachers and local music instructors in competition for the market (students were still being accepted at all ages). Eventually the directors found it necessary to decree that faculty members "take at least one monthly vacation each year, or a full term's vacation every other year" (supplying a substitute for such periods of enforced absence). But Williams's "piece-work" approach to education was to continue, in one form or another, up to the time when Leonard B. Job assumed the presidency in 1932. The minutes from the Williams years are full of elaborate computations for the distribution of tuition money.

Williams preferred to remember this innovation as the perfect solution to the financial problems of the Conservatory.

> *Thus the Conservatory, with 50 percent of the tuition receipts, was able to meet all financial obligations and keep a reserve fund for further expansion.*

But again, the record suggests something less than a fiscal millennium.

First of all, the Conservatory was experiencing some difficulty in paying the rent for the space leased in the Wilgus Building. A move to cheaper quarters seemed indicated, and on February 20, 1904, the directors appointed a committee to investigate available quarters for the following year. These were found in the West Block, on the north side of State Street, between Cayuga and Tioga Streets. The *Key Note* lists its office as being in that building for 1904 - 1905; the Ithaca City Directories for 1905 - 1906 and 1907 - 1908 give 136 East State Street as the address of the Conservatory. The *Key Note* was again being published from the Wilgus Building by April 1908, and the June issue celebrated the move back to the Conservatory's former quarters, with considerably expanded facilities.

In May 1906, Williams was forced to announce a deficit of $1,300 for the current year and, predictably, was ready with another "Co-operative Plan." Under this, the principal teachers (Williams, Mr. and Mrs. Eric Dudley, Stanley Olmstead, Linwood D. Scriven, and, on his return, Egbert) were "to become responsible for the financial success of the school." After all operating expenses and current debts were paid, the balance was to be prorated among these six in accordance with their respective tuition receipts. But should this plan prove too profitable to the individuals involved (that is, if they were found to be making 25 percent or more above their income at the time the plan was initiated), 50 percent of the coverage would revert to the Conservatory, "to be used as stock dividends." This plan was to continue for some time, with occasional changes in the beneficiaries.

But the external stockholders were not to be numbered among those who profited from the Co-operative Plan. On April 23, 1908, the eighteen persons then holding shares met to sign an important document.

> *WHEREAS, the Ithaca Conservatory of Music has indebtedness in excess of its assets, and*
>
> *WHEREAS, Eric Dudley [musical director since 1904], W. Grant Egbert and George C. Williams have agreed to provide for taking care of the indebtedness in consideration of the transfer to them of all the stock of the said Ithaca Conservatory of Music,*
>
> *NOW THEREFORE, we the undersigned ... do hereby consent and agree, each for himself, to transfer all our several right [sic] title, and interests in and to the stock standing in our separate names on the books of the said Ithaca Conservatory of Music*

> *to Charles E. Treman, Trustee, to transfer the same to the said Eric Dudley, W. Grant Egbert, and George C. Williams, upon their fulfillment of their agreement to provide for the taking care of the total indebtedness of said Ithaca Conservatory of Music.*
>
> *IN WITNESS THEREOF ....*

The triumvirate thus established was to be increased by one additional member. Herbert Berton Hilliard had come to the Conservatory in 1904 as director of the piano department; in 1905, he left to establish his own School of Music in Binghamton. He returned in 1907 - 1908 in a part-time association with the Conservatory; then, in the spring of 1909, he appeared before the directors and was permitted to buy into the newly reorganized corporation — a quarter interest in the Conservatory for $1,500 (or possibly $1,200) and a guaranteed annual income for his work in revitalizing the piano department. The capital brought in by Hilliard was used to pay off "the entire indebtedness of the school."

Thus, as of July 1, 1909, four men constituted the stockholders, the Board of Directors, the officers of the corporation, the executive committee, and the administration; they also held key faculty positions. This tidy oligarchical structure still operated under the amended By-Laws of 1897, but obviously only the formalities of the originally separate functioning groups were being observed. The executive committee was the real locus of power, meeting endlessly and even voting to fine its members ten cents for every tardiness and twenty-five cents for every absence. No matter was too small for its attention: it met with parents of misbehaving students; it solemnly debated the authorization of the purchase of "a bow for the double bass viol at a cost not to exceed $4"; it weighed the pros and cons of buying individual volumes for the Library (not many appear to have been bought) and devised ways of financing such items as Grove's *Dictionary of Music* on the installment plan. But such arduous labors were not without their rewards. In March 1911, it was voted that members of the executive committee should receive 90 percent of their tuition returns in the summer session (ordinary faculty members received 50 percent) with an additional cut of the surplus (if any) after operating expenses had been met. In November 1916, a flat payment of $50 a month was ordered.

And it was apparently possible for the executive committee

to bail out a fellow director in financial difficulties. However welcome Hilliard's cash may have been in 1909 and however distinguished his professional achievement, he was to prove a financial embarrassment to the institution. The Conservatory saw fit to endorse his personal notes, sometimes with strict warnings that he regularize his affairs and "agree in the future to pay cash for everything he purchased and to run no further accounts." The amount thus covered was $3,150 by December 1915. The directors discussed the possibility of asking for Hilliard's resignation in February 1916; two months later, he collapsed in a nervous breakdown and fled the scene. In September, he was presented with an ultimatum: either pay up or surrender the Conservatory stock which had been offered as security. By November, Dudley, Egbert, and Williams were dividing those thirty shares among themselves. The oligarchy tightened when Mrs. Dudley was elected to fill Hilliard's place on the Board (April 25, 1917).

There had been signs of a power struggle within the Board even before the Hilliard affair. In June 1910, Egbert had briefly reassumed part of the duties of musical director, only to relinquish them to Dudley in the following September because of extensive teaching commitments in Rochester. In February 1911, the responsibilities of the position were distributed among Egbert, Hilliard, and Dudley, and the salary for the position was abolished. This arrangement can hardly have proved satisfactory, but the real difference appears to have been between Egbert and Williams. At the Board meeting of December 5, 1911, Egbert

> read a list of criticisms of the work of the Manager for the present year and Mr. Williams presented his resignation as General Manager of the School.

The resignation was tabled at this morning meeting. Williams was apparently wooed and soothed during lunch, and when the Board reconvened in the afternoon, he begrudgingly reconsidered. He would agree to be "merely an intermediary between the Executive Committee and other officers of the school," but not responsible for their services. The waters were still roiled on February 7, 1912.

> Moved by Mr. Williams that the Business Manager contribute his services for the second term without salary on condition that at the end of the school year a manager be engaged in his place.

The motion was carried, and Egbert was prompt to suggest that a Mr. Will of Rochester be interviewed for the position. But Williams's survival skills were considerable. By August 13, he was not only still in office but negotiating a three-year contract that defined his rights in painstaking legal detail: a salary of $2,300; a substantial share of the tuition money he generated; and the right to book fifty "entertainment engagements" each year, with the income for the first twenty-five of these to be entirely his, but with some compensation to the Conservatory for his absence during the remainder.

Sometime in the next five years, the battle lines were to be redrawn. As we have seen, Mrs. Dudley had been appointed in 1917 to fill the vacancy left by Hilliard's resignation. Dudley immediately presented a resolution terminating all contractual relationships between the Conservatory and Egbert and Williams. The latter countered by resigning their faculty positions. Williams then resigned as business manager, director, and a member of the executive committee, and a Fordyce Cobb was elected to take his place (Cobb's name was typed into the minutes at some later time, either in a blank space or, more probably, over some other deleted name). Egbert's resignation as director was then accepted.

On April 28, 1917, the Dudleys and Cobb met, appointed Dudley treasurer of the corporation, and authorized him to draw and sign checks. They met again on May 10, at which time Egbert was reinstated as president; S. E. Banks was also elected director. Cobb thereupon resigned, and Mrs. Egbert (Mabel Green Egbert, who had married Egbert in 1914) took his place. Mrs. Dudley then tendered her resignation.

Another meeting appears to have been held later that same day. Not only was Dudley absent, the minutes describe the Egberts and Banks as "sole directors of the said corporation." Williams was brought in, in Dudley's place; Banks resigned on cue; and Mrs. Williams was elected to succeed him. And last, "on motion, duly seconded, George C. Williams was elected Secretary and Treasurer," with full authority over Conservatory funds.

In just over two weeks, the membership of the Board of Directors had changed some thirteen times, with a total cast of only eight persons. Whatever the unrecorded offstage maneuverings, the net result was clear. The Dudleys were out, the Egberts and the Williamses in. And with the death of Mrs. Egbert in 1918 and her husband's prostration and consequent ill health, it was only a matter of years before Williams would be solely in control.

Meanwhile, Williams's ingenuity in devising schemes to keep the institution solvent compels our admiration. In 1910, the Conservatory was attempting to secure stenographic assistance through the offer of music lessons; a similar arrangement was proposed to a fencing master; the minutes contain a curious reference to "trade tuitions." In 1915, Williams proposed a "Dramatic Presentation Fee": each student participating in the mid-year or commencement play was to be charged $15 to underwrite the costs of the production (the students could recover their investment by selling the $15 worth of tickets they were given). In 1914, he was offering the Students' Aid Society of Chicago a 25 percent commission on any students they might send. When, in the following year, enrollment slumped, the faculty could receive a 10 percent dividend if they were willing to canvass for students. "To instill enthusiasm," Egbert told them, "see that students get twenty dollars' value for ten dollars." And by March 1918, the directors were considering the possibility of charging all graduates a commission of 5 percent if the Conservatory was instrumental in placing them in teaching positions.

When not preoccupied with the business concerns of the institution, Williams was actively promoting his own professional interest — elocution. Elocution had been part of the curriculum almost from the beginning, and Williams had set about restructuring that department according to his own model even before his arrival in Ithaca in 1897. Administrative duties, including even those of the musical director after Egbert's departure for Europe, certainly preempted his energies for a number of years. But in 1904, Eric Dudley was named musical director after a year as head of the vocal department, and the resignation of Lakin Hannibal Richard in November 1904, after two years as director of the elocution department, brought Williams once more into that area of concern. By November 1908, he was proposing a separate entity, to be called "The Williams School of Expression, Associated with the Ithaca Conservatory of Music." The directors agreed, with the prudent stipulation that Williams pay personally for all advertising for his new school, perhaps because Williams had already issued a brochure — the most handsomely printed in the history of the Conservatory — for "The School of Expression and Dramatic Art," the establishment of which he backdated to the time of his arrival in Ithaca and now described as "one of the leading schools of Expression of this country."

This brochure (undated but before the resignation of S. Edwin Banks as president of the Board of Directors on July 1, 1907), is lavishly illustrated with scenes from the dramatic activity of the school — the Anniversary Week play of 1905, the commencement plays of 1905 and 1906, plus some even earlier offerings. Quotations praising the high worth of oratory decorate the bottom of the pages: Emerson provides the words for Williams's own philosophy in "There is no true eloquence unless there is a man behind the speech." Indeed, the descriptions oscillate wildly between the highest flights of idealism and assertions like "The instruction is from the first to last practical." Public speaking, we learn, molds societies and upholds humanity, patriotism, and religion; but it is also noted that "of the thirty-six graduates from the School of Expression, twelve are holding teachers' positions, eight have chosen the Lyceum profession, four have accepted good positions on the Theatrical stage, eleven have married, and one has died."

The curriculum is divided into seven major groupings of courses: forensic oratory, voice training, physical exercise (still the "Swedish System of Physical Culture"), literary interpretation and general literature, dramatic art, platform art, and pedagogy (the "Normal Course"). Great stress is placed on performance.

> *Not only are short plays, or selected scenes from standard plays, presented once each month in the Conservatory Hall, but twice each year, during Anniversary and Commencement weeks, an elaborate production is presented in the Lyceum Theatre.*

It is projected that in the coming year, "a stock company with a repertoire of standard plays will be organized from the students of this department and sent on a tour of several weeks throughout the East." In the area of platform art, the concert companies continue: "For seven years the Conservatory of Music has sent Concert Companies on tours of from ten to twenty weeks in length through twenty-two different states." Likewise, individual tours are booked for monologue readers. Students further benefit from a "fine reference library" (this is egregious puffery), with "practically all of the papers, magazines, and periodicals published in the interest of the Dramatic or Platform Art" (eight are mentioned by name). A Dramatic Club is flourishing, and Ithaca affords the opportunity of seeing the very best dramatic productions and noted actors and actresses, such as Richard Mansfield, Julia Marlow, Maude Adams, Otis Skinner. These stellar attractions at the Lyceum Theatre are supplemented by "Interpretive Recitals" given by members of the faculty: *A Doll's House, Man and Superman, Ben Hur,* Dickens and Shakespeare, to say nothing of *Enoch Arden* and an *Evangeline* complete with musical settings.

Williams was also immensely interested in establishing links between the Conservatory and other schools of music in the vicinity. The *Key Note* of June 1908 reports that "branches are being established in voice and all other departments at Owego, Trumansburg and Candor;" the Dudleys were largely responsible for this activity. When Hilliard returned full-time in 1909, the directors considered operating his school in Binghamton as a branch of the Conservatory. In 1912, the possibility of cooperative action with the Cortland School of Music was discussed; the next year, a scholarship arrangement was worked out with the Conservatory in Trumansburg and also with one in Interlaken. In 1917, the school of Mrs. Warburton and Mr. Frost in Geneva was granted permission to announce itself as affiliated with the Conservatory. But no permanent branches appear to have been set up. For the most part, these arrangements were with "feeder" schools, mostly small groups of music teachers working together in nearby towns — more nearly studios than schools or conservatories.

More significantly, Williams initiated a drive to secure recognition of the Conservatory by the State of New York. In November 1909, he was authorized to "draft a petition to the Regents of the University of the State of New York for the registration of the Conservatory as a professional school." In the following year, he was able to report that "it would be necessary that the school first receive a charter from the Board of Regents [supplemental] to the one already held from the Secretary of State." He was instructed to proceed in that direction, but sometime in 1912, difficulties arose. Egbert and Williams met with a Professor Bristol, whose services had been engaged to assist in obtaining "more satisfactory arrangements with the State Department in Albany," and after Bristol had done the spadework, Egbert and Williams were to go as a deputation to Albany. The Catalog of 1911 - 1912 had already announced that "the Regents of the University of the State of New York have granted the Ithaca Conservatory of

Music a Special Certificate of Registration as giving approved instruction in Music and Elocution" — that is, graduates could accept teaching appointments within the state without further examination. In 1913, the Conservatory somewhat reluctantly agreed to comply with an order to adjust its schedule of courses to the requirements of the Department of Education and to use the examinations furnished by the Regents.

The major event of the second decade of the century was the move to a new location in the DeWitt Park area, which was to be the home of the Conservatory and of Ithaca College from 1911 until the construction of the South Hill campus in the early 1960s. The Conservatory had moved back from its cramped quarters in the West Block to a refurbished Wilgus Building in 1907 - 1908; as the *Key Note* described it:

> *Music Hall in the conservatory has been refitted and equipped that it can be used for theatrical as well as musical purposes. For this purpose the stage end of the hall is shut off from the auditorium, framing a proscenium arch, for which front tableau curtains have been made by the H. J. Bool Company. The stage has been fitted with electric footlights and other special stage lighting devices.*

On February 22, 1910, the directors agreed to a three-year lease with Rothschild Bros. (now owners of the building), to extend until July 1, 1913, with provisos for certain renovations. Some subsequent improvements were in fact made: the dramatic society received money to purchase curtains and scenery, and the owner agreed to extend the stage some six feet into the Hall. But in April 1910, the directors were debating the advisability of "obtaining the Schyler [*sic*] property corner of Spring and Buffalo or the Boardman property on Seneca Street." Judge Douglass Boardman's handsome town house was located at 120 East Buffalo Street, and its purchase was authorized on November 1, 1910, with a mortgage of $11,400. After appropriate renovation, the Conservatory was established in its new quarters by the academic year 1911 -1912.

We are often told that the move was made necessary because the Rothschilds were eager to expand their store into the entire building at State and Tioga. Nothing in the record suggests any such urgency. Rather to the contrary, the directors were casting about to find ways to wriggle out from a lease that bound them until 1913. On December 6, 1910, "Mr. Egbert and Mr. Williams were appointed to meet with Rothschild Bros. and endeavor to effect some adjustment favorable to the school in connection with the remainder of the lease." In the following May, the business manager "read a letter from Rothschild Bros. offering to cancel the conservatory lease in Rothschild Building on July 1,'11 providing School pay the regular rental to that date and $1,200 on the date of July 1st." This seemed a high price for lease breaking, and "the matter was referred to Mr. Egbert for further arbitration." We are not informed of his success, but the Music Hall in the Wilgus Building continued to be used until a new auditorium was constructed adjacent to the Boardman property, and the preparatory school remained there for some time. In all probability, the momentous decision to purchase property was made not so much from external pressures as from the growth of the Conservatory itself.

The *Key Note* of June 1908 had been ebullient in its survey of the academic year just completed — "in every sense, artistic, financial, and social, by far and away the most successful the school has ever enjoyed." The return to Wilgus had been itself a signal for expansion.

> . . .it was seen that the rooms originally used by the Conservatory in that block would be quite insufficient to meet the present needs of the school. It was therefore considered advisable to add to the rooms formerly occupied by the Conservatory, an additional 4,000 square feet of floor space, consisting of a suitable reception room for students — a thing long needed by the Conservatory, — a fine elocution hall, capable of seating 320 people, fitted with a stage having all theatrical appliances for use when the Lyceum Theatre is not available, and a large vocal studio large enough to hold singing classes of from 50 to 100 students.

All this space generated a flurry of professional activity — a violin department reinvigorated by Egbert's return; a permanent orchestra; tremendous growth in the elocution area; the good work of Hilliard and Nordin in the piano department, plus the purchase "at great expense" of five new grand pianos, to be placed in every studio, "a unique feature, as no other conservatory in America is entirely fitted out with Grand Pianos." The Dudleys had broken all previous records in the number of local students and had expanded their operations to Owego, Trumansburg, and Candor. Choruses of all sorts were functioning or about to be formed. Certain scholarships were now tenable for an entire year rather than for one term, and, the report triumphantly concludes "every teacher employed last year has been reengaged and several new ones added to the list."

Williams's career had also entered into a new phase. His increasing popularity as an elocutionist was taking him to many towns and cities, including an eminently successful recital in Rochester, after which he was invited to join the faculty of the University of Rochester as professor of public speaking, with a free hand in developing the department there. He was later to recall this offer as being made in 1914, but the *Key Note* of June 1908 records its satisfaction that he had successfully resisted the temptation to relocate. In 1909 he addressed the New York State Association of Elocutionists at an annual meeting in Schenectady, and his speech was so favorably received that he joined the organization and became its president two years later.

> . . . something happened that changed my entire attitude toward public speaking. . . . I thus became ardently affiliated with a fine group of teachers, all striving for the same goal, namely, to so develop and promote the teaching of public speaking that it would merit and receive equal recognition and prominence with all other courses of instruction in our colleges and universities.

Hence, by 1910, the Conservatory had consolidated its management and was ready to expand: the directors even considered engaging someone "to canvass the city for prospective students." Nothing could be more agreeable than a permanent home, in one of Ithaca's finest buildings, fronting a park that could serve as ready-made campus. To further that illusion, it was voted on April 18, 1911, to "remove the board fence on the west side of the lot and extend entrance from the park if possible both to the Conservatory and the Fraternity House."

Judge Boardman's mansion had thus become the new "Con," and the Sinfonia fraternity was at last installed in its chapter house — a small frame building north of Boardman, next to the Baptist Church. It remained to provide adequate facilities for concerts and plays, and that meant the construction of a new building. On December 21, 1911, the directors sent Williams to New York to interview Cady and Gregory, architects, who were eventually commissioned to build the Conservatory Hall (later known as the Little Theatre), using local contractors and at a cost not to exceed $20,540. This "New Music Hall" was used for a formal reception of the students by the faculty in the fall of 1913. A brochure, *Student Life at the Ithaca Conservatory of Music* (probably published in 1917 - 1918), provides handsome illustrations of the new facilities — the reception room, the reading room, the offices and studios as well as the new auditorium, and (beneath it, later to be called the Green Room) the Elocution Hall.

In July 1914, Williams reported that the total cost of building Conservatory Hall and remodeling the Boardman property had amounted to $27,128.83. The Conservatory had long since learned the art of signing notes with the local banks to meet operating expenses, especially during the lean summer months. Now it was learning that the acquisition of real estate permitted borrowing on a far larger scale. The same report acknowledges an indebtedness to the Ithaca Savings Bank and the Ithaca Trust Company of $33,900, not to mention another $1,800 due on piano purchases, $1,777.64 to the local contractor, C. J. Swartwood, and $25 in estimated unpaid accounts. In sum, the liabilities of the Conservatory had reached $37,502.64.

Williams was quite undaunted by these figures. He could estimate that the "Present Worth" of the institution ("not including its greatest single asset, its Name and Good Will") was now about $28,000.

We pause to consider that four years ago a similar statement would not have credited the school with a Present Worth of over Five Thousand Dollars. . . .

So gratifying a situation could only prompt the projection of further expansion.

Our present indebtedness of this [the Music Hall] and the old building [the Boardman mansion] should be paid as soon as possible, for it is only a question of a few years, with the continuation of the

present rapid growth of the school, when it will become necessary to build another annex to the present building, in order to furnish additional studios.

This addition was to duplicate the present frontage on Buffalo Street to the east, with a driveway at the eastern extremity of the property and an inner court between the existing buildings and the projected annex.

Such a building, costing approximately twelve thousand dollars, would furnish the school with an enlarged Reception Room, about fourteen new studios and a large Basement Space that could be used to good advantage.

Williams was bursting with plans to accomplish these objectives — an expansion of the entertainment bureau, a more effective advertising campaign (he was later to conduct surveys to determine what brought students to the Conservatory), the acquisition of a small printing plant to turn out publicity materials, an expanded scholarship program (but with strict limitations on renewal), and massive encouragement of activity among the 241 alumni of the school, now ready to "lend a hand" in some practical way.

This interest should be carefully fostered and developed, for as the years pass, the Alumni of our School may become, — as it has with many another school, — one of the greatest factors in its growth and development.

Alumni fund-raising entertainments were already being planned in New York City, he noted, and could well be extended to Rochester, Buffalo, Elmira, and elsewhere, "in each case one or more prominent members of the faculty being present." A happy wedding of fund-raising and local advertising was contemplated.

But mostly Williams pinned his hopes on the new school calendar, to begin in September 1914.

Too much, financially and otherwise, must not be expected from this change for the first two or three years; but it is certainly poor business policy to allow a sixty thousand dollar plant to lie idle and on expense for ten weeks, or one-fifth of each year. I am convinced that if we all do our utmost to make the Third, or Summer, Term as big a success as possible for the first four or five years that it will thereafter be quite as big as either of the other terms, and the revenue of the school will be increased by from one-fourth to one-third.

Later, other administrators would entertain that delusion. Williams's sanguine hopes were doubly doomed by the fact that as he wrote those words, the unpleasantness at Sarajevo had already occurred.

But before considering the impact of the Great War on the Conservatory, we should look more closely at the people who made up the college community during these years.

Around 1909 - 1910, the Conservatory published a brochure given over entirely to pictures and biographical sketches of its faculty, with copious extracts from press reviews of their public performances. The *Key Notes* of this period likewise contain much material on faculty members; after all, this publication played an important role in the recruiting effort. A surviving copy of the brochure on the faculty attests to its original usefulness: an unknown piano student had certainly studied the write-ups of possible instructors and penciled in their rates — $2 for Mr. Hilliard, $1.50 for Miss Nye and Mr. Nordin, and $.75 for Miss Holmes (a 1904 graduate, who joined the faculty the following year and who would remain for more than four decades).

British-born Eric Dudley, we learn, had studied at the Royal Academy of Music in London, where he won a gold medal for singing and a bronze one for elocution. Later, the Hampstead Conservatoire of Music awarded him a substantial scholarship without examination, solely on the basis of a public performance. He had made numerous appearances in concert, oratorio, and opera, both in England and in America. The *Ithaca Daily News* concurred in the judgment that his career had been "one continuous success."

He was splendid in "The Rebel," the defiant notes of which rang out like a bugle call, and fine also in the Freebooter's "Cradle Song," which calls for tenderness but also for depth of feeling to which he is peculiarly adapted.

Dudley's greatest triumph had come during Cornell's annual Music Festival in April 1906. This three-day event, with five concerts, included Haydn's oratorio *The Creation* on the first evening, with a chorus of 165 voices under Hollis E. Dann, plus the fifty-member Boston Festival Orchestra, conducted by Emil Mollenhauer. The major attraction was to be Dubois' *The Seven Last Words of Christ*, starring "the famous baritone Emilio de Gorgoza." But de Gorgoza failed to appear, and his place was taken "at almost a moment's notice by Mr. Eric Dudley, the Music Director of the Ithaca Conservatory of Music." According to the *Daily News*,

The absence of Mr. Gorgoza was disappointing for a time, but Mr. Dudley did as well, taking the missing baritone's place and evoking storms of applause.

The *Daily Journal* reported that Dudley "was given an ovation after the Fourth Word." It was generally concluded that, thanks largely to him, the festival proved to be "the greatest musical success that the city of Ithaca has ever known."

Mrs. Eric Dudley (Lilian), born and trained in Wales, later a student in Germany and also at the Royal Academy, had received three medals for the excellence of her work. The *Call*, of Paterson, New Jersey, proclaimed that

we have had fine singers here before but no one save Albani has so thoroughly captivated a Paterson audience.

The Dudleys had come to Ithaca to take charge of the vocal department in 1903.

The brochure adds further details about Egbert's musical career. While on leave from the Conservatory, he placed himself under the direction of "Sevcik, teacher of Kubelik":

This great master was so pleased with Mr. Egbert's progress that after six months of work, he appointed him Concertmeister and assistant conductor of his great string orchestra, which position he held during his three years of study at Prague. Mr. Egbert's popularity brought him the Presidency of the Prague Anglo-American Club where he had the honor of entertaining many of the notabilities of the Austrian court.

Egbert had left Prague with a gold medal, an engraved commendation, and Sevcik's testimonial that he was "a most gifted violin virtuoso . . . especially qualified as a teacher of the violin and my method."

Herbert B. Hilliard, whose financial relations with the Conservatory have been discussed earlier, is described as a Bostonian, a graduate of the Roxbury Latin School and briefly a student at Harvard. Seven years of study in Germany ensued: he was graduated with honors from the Royal Conservatory of Music at Leipzig and taught for a while in Germany. Returning to the United States, he opened a private studio in Boston and then was placed in charge of the piano department at the James Milliken University School of Music in Decatur, Illinois, before coming to Ithaca. The account passes discreetly over his two years' absence in Binghamton and contents itself with the affirmation that

> *after considering all the prominent and available pianists of America and Europe, the Board of Directors of the Ithaca Conservatory of Music finally called Mr. Herbert Bertron [his middle name is also given elsewhere as both Beeton and Berton] Hilliard to take charge of the Piano Department.*

Stanley Olmsted taught piano from about 1905 to 1907 and headed the department until Hilliard's return. The *Key Note* informs us that at seventeen he had composed an operetta, "The Astrologer," which had proved a "sensational success." Studying abroad under Leschetizky and at the Leipzig Conservatory, he had conducted a private studio in Washington, D.C., before coming to Ithaca, recommended by Edward MacDowell, Reginald deKoven, and "Knabe & Co., Piano firm." He is also credited with published short stories and a forthcoming novel.

Harry W. Nordin, a member of the piano faculty until 1909, had presented himself at the Conservatory as a student in September 1900. He held a scholarship for four years and served as assistant teacher before graduating in 1904. During his undergraduate years, he had composed the music for the Conservatory Alma Mater song, with words by Rosa K. Hamlin '03. After study in Germany, he returned to Ithaca and after his resignation was to go on to other colleges and eventually be decorated by the King of Sweden.

The violin department was headed during Egbert's absence

by Linwood D. Scriven. The *Key Note* of February 1906 published an article of his, "Success after Graduation," which distills much of the spirit of the Conservatory in these years. After dismissing mediocre students as "half-successes" — musicians likely "to degenerate in[to] a sort of Socialist and demand that he receive a certain sum for each note given to the world" — he went on to assure his readers that musicians could look forward to the rewards of diligence and hard work. True, "as a means of obtaining a steady income from year to year, teaching is, perhaps, the safest thing." But there is nothing grossly materialistic about that: "All true successes look out well for their financial condition." Beyond that, there are no limits to the aspirations of creativity. Never was there a time when musicians were expected to possess greater skills, including a breadth and depth of general culture. Music itself is only in its infancy; the promise of the future might be summarized in Carlyle's transcendental raptures:

> *"[Music] is a kind of inarticulate unfathomable speech, which leads us to the edge of the infinite and impels us for a moment to gaze into it."*

One potential appointment to the faculty was not destined to be actualized. In February 1915, the directors instructed Williams "to arrange an appointment with Miss Crane of the Potsdam Normal School, looking toward the possibility of securing her services at the Conservatory." But Julia Crane evidently preferred to operate her own School of Music, still flourishing as part of the State University College of Potsdam and one of Ithaca College's principal competitors.

That this was a hard-working faculty there is no doubt — Williams's Co-operative Plan would certainly have seen to that. Faculty meetings had been instituted early in the history of the Conservatory; hardly any minutes before 1913 have survived, and those after that date are largely preoccupied with the minutiae of scheduling and administering scholarship examinations. Committees arrived with vengeance in 1915: an alumni committee; a preparatory department committee; committees for student conduct, for the *Key Note,* for press and publicity, curriculum, Library; and a social committee. By 1917, these had been reshuffled somewhat — student conduct, student conduct for men, curriculum, concert and recital, publications, social, faculty, "adjutary," house, and housing.

Faculty, administration, and directors combined their efforts to safeguard the morals of the student. We have already mentioned the daily chapel, and by 1917, Williams, ever the frustrated preacher, was proposing a "two-week mid-winter inspirational course" — a kind of annual revival meeting for the student body. The directors' concern with student life would astonish any present-day Board. In 1909, it was decreed that Conservatory women could not live in any boarding house where male Cornell students also lived. After considerable faculty outrage over "modern dancing," the directors, on May 15, 1914, denied to the Sigma Alpha Iota sorority "the privilege of dancing the hesitation waltz at their annual ball." In 1915, it was voted that "students in the future should not be permitted to give dances charging five cents a dance." Curfews were endlessly discussed; usually, the Board rejected a petition to extend a dance beyond eleven P.M. By the end of 1916, guards were required at the doors of all dances, and it was ordered that "gentlemen should not be privileged to attend the same except accompanied by a lady." Far more wholesome than dancing were the "Wednesday Night Community Singing" assemblies: students were required to attend ten of these each year. And expulsion for breaches of decorum remained one of the more solemn functions of the executive committee.

Nevertheless, there is evidence that Conservatory students were not wholly passive under this officious paternalism. The curriculum was demanding; many were short of funds (as repeated Board actions regarding delinquent accounts attest) and combined jobs with study. Indeed, one of the official publications was *How I Worked My Way through the Conservatory*. But there was time for student government. Mass meetings, especially of the men students, were frequent, and formal organization of the student body came early. In 1907, the students were also organized by classes, with faculty advisers, and a Student Self-Government Association (for women students) emerged two years later "to supervise the students' general behavior when outside of the Conservatory and to deal with any indiscretions on the part of any student." A student council was formed, and by 1918, was showing some signs of independence: Williams was directed to meet with its members and explain "more clearly and in detail their responsibilities and the objects which the school hopes they may accomplish." The *Key Note* had been established by the students, and a number of copies of each issue were purchased from them by the Conservatory for publicity purposes. In 1913, the Mu Phi Epsilon sorority was assigned editorial responsibility; Sinfonia attended to the business concerns; and Sigma Alpha Iota took care of circulation. There was some measure of faculty or administrative supervision; yet in May 1915, the executive board decided "that the school could not accept [this issue] of the *Key Note* magazine in that the tone of the magazine was such that we could not make use of the same for advertising purposes." Unfortunately, the offending issue has not survived.

Fraternities and sororities continued to be central to the life of the Conservatory students. Sinfonia (later Phi Mu Alpha) dated from 1901, and Alpha Tau (to become Sigma Alpha Iota in June 1909) from 1903. Lambda Chapter of the Mu Phi Epsilon sorority had joined these two in February 1909. In 1908, an earlier Dramatic Club was revived by Williams as the Amards — *drama* spelled backwards — which was to become Theta Alpha Phi in 1934.

The Amards contributed enormously to the Conservatory scene. In the winter of 1898, a group of students had presented David Belasco's *The Charity Ball* at the Lyceum Theatre and had then taken their show on tour in several of the surrounding towns. This prolonged association had resulted in the Dramatic Club, with its constitution and by-laws, but eventually, a demand arose for "a more pretentious society organized along fraternal lines." Thus the Amards, with their strange monkish gowns, their elaborate initiation rituals, their quasi-Masonic degrees of membership. The *Key Note* of April 1916 describes them as having "entire charge of the presentation of all plays and the care of all social events in the school." Among the latter were to be numbered the October Hallowe'en masked ball, the Christmas festivities, the February sleigh ride, the March stunt fest, the May picnic and annual banquet. Beyond that, the Amards served as hosts to the alumni at commencement and organized the events of Alumni Day. With their own chapter room in the main Conservatory building, they contributed notably to the purchase of scenery, curtains, draperies, costumes, and wigs for the Conservatory Hall — all this without relying on dues, but wholly from the receipts of the plays and recitals.

An important Amards tradition was the "stage supper," described in the *Key Note* of June 1909.

Immediately after the curtain fell on the final scene [of the Commencement play] the stage hands quickly changed the setting from a library to a cozy dining-room, and the tables were loaded with eatables. It was indeed a happy party — many of them still in costume, though without their make-up — that surrounded the tables.

Visiting alumni were guests of the cast; the eating, toasting, and speech making continued until midnight.

Concerts, recitals, plays, festivals abounded; one of the most elaborate of these was the Drama Festival of May 1911. A combined effort of the entire school "to picture the past of the drama in its varied phases," the festival undertook to survey the history of the theater from Aeschylus to the present in three successive evenings. The series opened with *The Suppliants,* for which "special Greek scenery" had been obtained along with the appropriate costumes. This was followed by *The Festival of Adonis.*

Nothing can be more gay and natural than the chatter of these women, which has changed no more in two thousand years than the song of the birds.

This "Ancient and Medieval" segment continued with *Everyman.*

Particularly striking was the utterance of Dethe [Mr. Bell], when upon arising from an open grave, scythe in hand, he suddenly throws aside his cloak and discloses himself clad in a costume upon which nothing but the chalk white bones of a skeleton were visible. . . .

With some stretching of chronology, this dramatic marathon evening concluded with a fifteenth-century farce, *Master Pierre Patelin.* A Shakespearean evening followed, with the Lancelot Gobbo scene from *The Merchant of Venice*, a striking rendition of Lady Macbeth's sleep-walking scene by Mrs. Rose Broughton, the woodland meeting of Orlando and Rosalind, and Ophelia's mad-scene.

"Modern Drama" reached back into the seventeenth century to include Molière's *Les Précieuses Ridicules,* in which Williams, obviously the writer of this *Key Note* account,

starred as Mascarille. Then a scene from *The School for Scandal*; *The Contrast* ("the first American play ever performed in public by a company of professional actors"); and, to restore us to the present, a short piece by Henry Arthur Jones. Again, Williams "gave a very pleasing impersonation of the great engineer Sir Stephen Famariss," and, his account concludes, "the novelties of yesterday are pleasing but we live with the things of to-day."

But for all the excitement of these varied activities, commencement held its special place as the culmination not only of the school year but of the students' work at the Conservatory. Lasting a full week, the early graduations uniquely reflected the interests of the school — music, elocution, and drama. The program for 1909 is typical. There were twelve graduates, only three of them men and only four from outside New York. Beginning on May 25, each evening was given over to one of five senior recitals, the musicians in the group now, interestingly, outnumbered by the elocution graduates. On Monday, May 31, the juniors sponsored a reception and ball for the graduating class, and the following night, there was an "Advanced Students' Recital." The next two evenings were devoted to "Graduation Recitals," in which both music and elocution seniors combined their talents. And then, on Friday, the commencement play — *Judah*, by Henry Arthur Jones, performed at the Lyceum for what was described as the largest audience thus far to have attended a school presentation.

The boxes to the right and left of the stage were occupied by the members of the Sigma Alpha Iota Sorority and the Sinfonia Fraternity, as nearly every member of the cast belonged to one or the other of these organizations. All of the boxes were draped with the flags and colors of the sorority and fraternity.

Saturday saw the last of the graduation recitals. A baccalaureate service was held on Sunday, and commencement itself took place in the Lyceum Theatre on the evening of Monday, June 7.

The program for this, the seventeenth annual commencement exercises, was serious, even grim. There were an invocation and a benediction, but no commencement speech; instead, music and the spoken word. A piano student, with the Conservatory orchestra, rendered a movement from a Beethoven concerto, followed by a reading of "The Murder of Nancy Sykes." The latter, the *Ithaca Daily News* reported on the following day, "made a marked impression." Dickens's lugubrious episode was followed by a vocal solo ("Die Lorley"); then more piano, another reading ("Goats"), and a rousing chorus of "Come Sisters, Come." More music, more readings, and at last the presentation of the diplomas by Mr. Williams.

Much the same pattern obtained for the following year, though with a change in the baccalaureate service. Instead of worship in one of the local churches, where "with the exception of the presence of the senior class little else of the Conservatory spirit has been in evidence," the seniors were treated to yet another musical program in Music Hall, with brief sermon. The *Key Note* also describes the Class Day exercises of that year — the ever present music plus an address by the president of the senior class, the class history, the class presentation, the class oration, the class prophecy, and the class will. There were seventeen graduates, eight of them in elocution.

On this occasion Mr. Egbert saw fit to address the commencement audience, warning them that the road to greatness "may be a *Great Sorrow*" and that all things exact their price.

> *There seems to be an equitable law of balance — we must all buy — and all pay. For health you pay in self-denial and right living, for wrong you pay in sorrow. You may take about what you like in this life and the bill will be collected later. We must all buy — and all pay.*

He closed by asking the seniors to consecrate their lives to goodness, nobility, cheerfulness, inspiration, and hard work — "and at the end may your lives have all the beauty of pale stars as they fade to pearl at the hour of dawn."

After that somewhat chilling send-off, we are hardly surprised by the solemn sentimentality of the program, — a reading of "The Mallet's Masterpiece":

> *She impressed her hearers with the grief of the sculptor over the destruction of his masterpiece by an enemy. . . .*

Then a section of *Rebecca of Sunny-brook Farm*: "Humor and pathos abound in this selection. . . ." And finally the second act of Schiller's *Mary Stuart* (all of it? one wonders).

> *This was the strongest reading of the evening, and necessitated close insight. The haughty tones of Queen Elizabeth and the heart-broken cry of Mary Stuart were equally well rendered.*

Musical numbers enhanced the general gloom: Tchaikovsky's "Ah! Sad My Heart" and Schubert's "The Erlking." But the Conservatory string orchestra managed to end the occasion on an upbeat with Grieg's "Der Frühling," unless, of course, the Reverend Herbert W. Hutchinson succeeded in canceling that vernal impulse with his benediction.

Alumni activities formed an integral part of commencement week. There were the inevitable business meetings, followed in the afternoon by a boat ride on Cayuga Lake in the launch *Dana*, and, after the graduation recital in the evening, a dinner at the Hotel Ithaca, complete with innumerable toasts and seven readings.

> *After the final toast all arose and, forming a circle with clasped hands, sang fervently "Auld Lang Syne." So thoroughly enjoyable was this occasion that the following slogan was adopted for the coming year:*
> *"Again, again, in nineteen-ten! All out!"*

The number of alumni had gradually grown, from the two pianists of 1897 to more than a hundred by 1907 and 161 by 1911 (105 of them in Music, 56 in Elocution and Drama). In 1908, thirty-four graduates in Elocution were the first to organize, as the Alumni of the Williams School of Expression. By March 1910, the executive board of the Conservatory resolved "to secure a larger attendance of the School Alumni for the Commencement events of this year and to formally organize the Alumni at that time." This timetable was not adhered to, however, for in the following May, the *Key Note* was informing its readers that

> *the Alumni of the Ithaca Conservatory of Music are planning a general gathering of the graduates of the institution at Commencement time this June, with*

the purpose of forming a regular Alumni Association.

For a while, there appear to have been two different alumni groups, for we read, again in the May 1911 *Key Note*, that

the Alumni of the Williams School of Expression will not only join in the festivities of Alumni Day, June 13th, but will hold a meeting of their own, on June 10th.

The two alumni groups had coalesced by 1920.*

The Conservatory's new interest in alumni activity was soon to affect the corporate structure of the institution. In September 1914, a Board of Trustees was created, comprising the existing Board of Directors, the mayor of Ithaca, and, in addition to those other persons the Board of Directors might see fit to name, four representatives of the alumni. By 1917, faculty members could be elected as advisory members to the Board of Directors.

Up to this point in our history, there is little in the record to indicate an institutional awareness of any world beyond Ithaca, except for happenings in the world of music. But World War I inevitably left its mark. In 1915, we read of a Belgium Relief Concert, with proceeds going "to the local Belgium committee." In 1917, the "aviation boys" at Cornell were invited to Conservatory dances — the school must "do its bit," the directors decided, whatever the moral risks

involved. By the following year, concert companies were aiding the Red Cross to raise money "for strictly war purposes," and the Conservatory found it necessary to purchase a service flag. In October 1917, the faculty endorsed and supported the plan of providing musical instruments for the soldiers overseas, and the appropriate committee was formed. Some faculty members were sometimes absent from campus as they traveled to entertain soldiers in various camps, and Williams himself was placed in charge of the "Four-Minute Men" of Tompkins County — a group formed to deliver four-minute patriotic speeches in theaters, movies, and other public gatherings, and also to sell war bonds.

The most noticeable effect of the war was probably the disappearance of a large number of the male students and the consequent enrollment of more women. To accommodate them, part of the Egbert house at 404 East Buffalo Street (later to be Egbert Hall) was used as a women's dormitory. Thus the second Mrs. Egbert found herself not only with a house full of students but, with the outbreak of the influenza epidemic, with a makeshift infirmary of sick students. In Williams's words:

Our own dormitories were necessarily turned into hospitals with cots placed in all the hallways. Mrs. Egbert . . .worked ceaselessly day and night caring for the sick. As a result she was stricken and did not recover.

Mabel Green Egbert died on November 2, 1918.

This was yet another blow — one from which her husband was never fully to recover. Within six years, George C. Williams would succeed him as the president of the Ithaca Conservatory and its affiliated schools.

---

* A full account of the growth of the Ithaca College alumni may be found in Lillian Speakman Vail '21, *Remembering: A History of the Ithaca College Alumni Association* (Ithaca, N.Y.: Ithaca College, 1978), Mrs. Vail's volume is an essential supplement to this history.

III. The Affiliated Schools 1919 - 1932

FROM the beginning, William Grant Egbert's Conservatory had tended to grow by a process of fission, or, perhaps more accurately, by budding. The original curriculum had included a course in elocution as part of the instruction appropriate to a musician, and we have seen how, from the arrival of George C. Williams in the fall of 1897, this department had grown until in 1908 it had become the Williams School of Expression, with its own Catalog and a separate listing of its administration and its faculty. By 1926 - 1927, it would be appealing for a new building of its own —vainly, as it turned out.

Other departments were to develop along similar lines. The Catalog of 1902 - 1903 had announced a two-year curriculum in Public School Music, "to prepare students for positions as supervisors or special teachers in music in public schools." Here, the emphasis was on sight-reading, on the psychological and vocal development of the child, plus the usual methods course and a survey of the published material available to a teacher in this field. George Goldsmith Daland, organist, was in charge. After Daland's departure, the program briefly lapsed and then was reestablished under Eric Dudley in 1906 - 1907. It drops out of the Conservatory Catalog for 1911 - 1912, quite possibly because by then it had its own brochure, of which no copy has survived. In any event, later accounts date the establishment of the Institution of Public School Music as 1910 — the curriculum was registered in Albany in September of that year. Beginning in 1921 - 1922, the course was extended to three years, and the *Key Note* of June 1921 refers to a new director, R. H. Richards, who "has brought his department into greater prominence in the school than ever before" — so much so that

in the graduating class the highest percentage of graduates were from the Public School Music Department and many have already signed contracts for the coming year.

The demand for graduates from such a program continued to grow, especially after the arrival of Albert Edmund Brown as dean in 1924. Brown had been on the faculty of Boston University and for many years had headed the only department of public school music in New England (at the State Normal School in Lowell, Massachusetts). He had been active in Chautauqua, had been vocal soloist with the Boston Symphony, and, as a friend of Calvin Coolidge, had been chosen to conduct the music at the Republican national convention in Chicago in 1920. Within two years of his arrival in Ithaca, enrollment in the Institution had jumped to a hundred students, with a faculty of twenty-two. An important feature of the program was an arrangement for practice teaching in the classrooms of the local parochial school — an innovation credited to Ruth Blackman Rodgers '11.

American involvement in World War I had revealed,

among other things, shocking physical inadequacies in American youth, with a consequent emphasis on the need for physical education programs in schools and colleges. Williams had perceived the trend as early as the spring of 1917, when he received permission from the directors to go to Albany "to consult with Dr. Finegan concerning the proposed course in physical culture." We remember that fencing had figured in the curriculum almost from the first days of the Conservatory and that Williams himself was a lifelong advocate not only of fencing but also of "Swedish gymnastics." The minutes of a faculty meeting in 1917 apprise us of his success in securing the approval of the Board of Regents, and four students were graduated from the program in 1920.

In these early years, classes were taught in the gymnasium of the Ithaca High School, partly under Edgar E. Bredbenner, Sr., director of physical education for the public schools. But I.S.P.E (the Ithaca School of Physical Education, pronounced to rhyme with *wispy*) really came into its own in 1921 - 1922 when Albert H. Sharpe became its dean. Sharpe, a doctor of medicine as well as athlete, had been director of athletics at Yale, school physician at the Penn Charter School, and football, baseball, and basketball coach at Cornell. The former Star Theatre on East Seneca Street was converted into a gym, Percy Field (the present site of the Ithaca High School) was used for outdoor sports, a summer camp was acquired on Lake Cayuga near Stewart Park. The 1921 - 1922 Catalog outlined a two-year "Normal Course" (including two summer terms) and also a one-year course in coaching. An enticing future was sketched out for those who should enroll.

> *Perhaps in no other field of instruction has there been such rapid advancement during the past few years as in Physical Training Work. Every High School in New York State and several other states is obliged to furnish a course in Physical Training. Nearly all Private and Professional Schools, Normals, Colleges and Universities prescribe a certain amount of Physical Training in every course of instruction offered. This sudden and unusual interest in this important subject has created a great demand for properly trained teachers and as a result the salaries of Physical Training Teachers are considerably above the average.*

The program also included instruction in aesthetic dances, folk and national dances, and social dancing under Miss Elsie Hugger, who had joined the faculty in 1920.

Dean Sharpe announced his intention to return to collegiate coaching in 1928 - 1929 and was succeeded in the following September by Dean Laurence S. Hill. Hill came to Ithaca from the Albany school system, but for some years he had been operating a summer program in physical education for Cornell University and Cortland State Normal School. Indeed, one of his stipulations, on coming to the Conservatory, was that his private camp on Lake Champlain, Singing Cedars, be expanded and summer attendance made mandatory for I.S.P.E. students (with separate sessions for men and women). This arrangement continued into the early 1930s; the camp activities are vividly described by Professor Isadore ("Doe") Yavits in *The Ithaca College of My Time.** Yavits, also from the Albany school system, would come as Hill's assistant in 1930, with James ("Bucky") Freeman arriving the following year.

Williams's many interests extended to speech correction as an important branch of the voice culture work within his School of Expression.

> *The School offers corrective instruction for the following defects: Stammering, Clerical Sore Throat, Lisping, Muttering, Mouthing, Hoarseness, Nasal Tone, Palatal Tone, etc.*

By 1921, this single course had grown into another affiliated school, as Frederick Van Doren Martin arrived to found the Martin Institute for Speech Correction. Martin, the son of a physician, had himself begun the study of medicine only to find himself apparently hopelessly handicapped by his speech difficulties.

> *Dr. Martin became such an acute stammerer while in college that he soon earned the appellation of "Silent Martin." During the "Class Day Exercises" when he graduated — he was presented with a bottle of glue to paste his words together, and a tin whistle to help him start his speech.*

Finally suffering a complete loss of voice, he spent years traveling in search of a cure, finding it eventually with Cher-

---

**Isadore Yavits, *The Ithaca College of My Time* (Ithaca, N.Y.: Norton Printing, 1965), pp. 7-10.

vin in France. His own problems thus successfully resolved, he decided to devote his life to helping others through speech correction. In 1915, he organized, at the College of the City of New York, the first public clinic for speech defects in the United States. This and other professional appointments established his repute as a pioneer in the field, and after America's entry into World War I, he was chosen to train specialists to work in the rehabilitation of soldiers whose speech was impaired by shell-shock or injury. Martin had provided special care for the voices of Metropolitan Opera stars; he had also worked as an art expert in the J. P. Morgan Library and was once featherweight national amateur boxing champion and captain of the Columbia track team. His list of publications was impressive.

At Ithaca, Martin aimed at nothing less than total therapy.

Such an institute had given Dr. Martin [he had earned a Ph. D.] his long cherished wish, of a residential home — where he might have his cases under personal surveyance night and day — so as to thoroughly reorganize not only their attitude and conception of speech but their general mental and physical organisms as well.

The regimen was strenuous, to say the least. Williams had secretly registered for a summer session course with Martin at New York University in order to observe his work firsthand, and reported:

When a stammerer came to him, he was at once "placed in silence." For two weeks he was not allowed to use his vocal organs. He was given a paper-pad and pencil with which he was obliged to convey his wishes. At the end of this two weeks of absolute silence, he was given a first grade primer, and with it Dr. Martin proceeded to reconstruct his speech, as though he had never spoken before.

Once-A-Week (from October 1926, successor to the *Key Note*) reports on "A Day in Martin Hall" — which was located on North Tioga Street between Court and Buffalo.

By the time we arrive (8:30) all of the cases have had a cold shower, eaten their breakfast, made their beds, and straightened up their rooms. . . .

At eleven the morning session is over. Do they all go to their rooms and read or loll about? I should say not! All must go out for a fast walk or a run and another cold shower before lunch. . . . The afternoon session is much like the morning one.

A full day, yes and a full evening, too. Sometimes they go to the movies but generally they prefer to practice, they can go to the movies when they leave. Frequently Dr. Martin comes upstairs and corrects or suggests something about the way they are practicing. You see, his own apartment is in the same building, he feels the need of constant supervision over the cases. At nine-thirty lights are out.

There is a spirit at Martin Hall which is unequaled in any other institution in the country.

Before long, patients from all over the United States and Canada and even from Europe were arriving in Ithaca for treatment. The academic program was a one-year "Normal" course, with intensive summer programs. His Institute continued at Ithaca College until 1936.

Not all the affiliated schools took root. The *Key Note* of March 1925 ran a headline, "Operatic School for Grand and Light Opera Latest Addition to our Institution." Beneath a dashing picture of Andreas Dippel, it continued:

At last the Conservatory has a School of Opera and, best of all, we have as its head and personal director, the leading man in this line of work in the country — Andreas Dippel — formerly leading tenor, and, for two years, Executive Manager at the Metropolitan Opera, New York. Mr. Dippel's long and successful association with the foremost European and Metropolitan Opera companies has given him the widest possible experience, placing him in the front ranks of impresarios.

But little more is heard of this venture, and no mention is made of it in the listing of the affiliated schools in the Catalog of 1927 - 1928.

Another eventual failure was launched with considerable fanfare when Edward Amherst Ott arrived from Waukegan,

Illinois. Williams had earlier established an "Ithaca School of Lyceum Training" (more nearly what we would term a department), but in September 1922, the institution was ready for a full-blown School of Chautauqua and Lyceum Arts, with its curricula of one, two, or three years (plus correspondence courses) elaborately presented in its own Catalog. A full-page picture of Ott dominates this publication, and his prose is equally overwhelming. Chautauqua and Lyceum arts are peculiarly American, we read, as their motto, "Fire-side folk, fire-side programs by fire-side artists," would indicate. To succeed in such endeavors, the student must possess far more than technical proficiency in speech.

The question of appeal, authority, earnestness and magnetism all come back to the social purpose of the orator, that is to his background. For that reason, we correlate all technical training with a study of the fields of leadership and social movements, human needs and American problems. Rhetoric with us is not an abstract study, but a matter of program building, thought organization, and dramatization of ideas.

Williams must surely have applauded this latter-day Emersonianism, and Ott went on to describe the Ithaca Conservatory Schools as uniquely blending "high social purposes, with intellectual and emotional developments." He concluded with a demonstration of his concept of platform eloquence.

The world is alive. There is a natural urge to live spendidly and well. To the field of leadership for the orator, and for the musician and the entertainer, the fine arts give the opportunity for self-expression without which no full happiness can come. The educational plan that neglects the opportunity for developing and glorifying the individual life and not using and refining the emotions, is ignoring a great lesson in nature's economy. Neglected and undirected emotion is at the root of much unhappiness and nearly all vice and crime. The emotionally highly endowed are called to the arts to glorify joy, beauty, truth, and lead the social life of their age with gladness and reverence, grateful for the gift and opportunity.

Ott had reduced "personality development" to something of a science. A student not improving in this respect under Ott's regime "must either be perfect when he comes or fail to be graduated, as grading is done on a development basis." Since "it is obviously disappointing to educate students technically and leave them illiterate in the arts of living," Ott had devised, and copyrighted, a "Personality Development Record," with fifty-two categories for evaluation (merely scholastic attainments were relegated to the bottom of the form).

...the student is expected to make himself strong and to master his mind and body and impulses, as he would master his studies. By this plan, each student becomes an expert in character psychology, and can measure himself and others on a scientific basis. This chart is a blue print of a human soul. It is a yard stick of soul values.

If this plan were adopted in all educational institutions, we would graduate no more "smart rascals" or mentally developed weaklings. Successful careers are based on character and personality.

The student willing to submit himself to this intensive intellectual, emotional, and spiritual reconstruction might, if sufficiently talented, eventually command from $10,000 to $20,000 a year!

Ott's Catalog is an extraordinary blending of a highly individual educational philosophy and the most shameless self-advertising. He had completed twenty-five years with the Redpath Lyceum Bureau, had taught at Hiram College and served as dean at the College of Oratory at Drake University in Des Moines. He had also operated his own school of oratory in Chicago. As lecturer, he was best known for "his interesting and timehonoured lecture" entitled "Sour Grapes," which he had given some five hundred times and with which he had electrified his Ithaca audience in Conservatory Hall on March 31, 1922. The theme, the *Key Note* reporter felt obliged to explain, was not horticultural, as the title might suggest, but rather eugenic — "a powerful exposition of the doctrines of life." Ott propounded a simple solution to the problems of crime and abnormality.

Dr. Ott said that the only way to get rid of criminals is to allow abnormal people to die out, prevent, in the

PERSONALITY DEVELOPMENT RECORD

SCHOOL OF CHAUTAUQUA AND LYCEUM ARTS

(Copyright 1922 by Edward Amherst Ott)

Name_____ Department_____ Date_____ Number____

Age_____ Height_____ Normal_____ Sub-Normal_____

Weight_____ Normal_____ Sub Normal_____

Deductions are indicated in squares and totaled at right | Deductions

SELF MAN-AGEMENT (A)	A1 30% Time	A2 30% Initiative	A3 20% Care and use of money	A4 20% Moral Habits
WILL POWER (B)	B1 20% Concentration	B2 50% Self-Control	B3 10% Poise and Posture	B4 20% Action
MANNERS (C)	C1 25% Dress	C2 25% Courtesy	C3 25% Social usage	C4 25% Offensive Habits
LEADER-SHIP (D)	D1 30% Earnestness	D2 30% Salesmanship	D3 20% Tact	D4 20% Character Analysis
MENTALITY (E)	E1 20% Memory	E2 20% Logic and truth	E3 30% Imagination	E4 30% Alertness
SOCIAL INSTINCT (F)	F1 30% Humane Interests	F2 20% Loyalty	F3 20% Thought-fulness	F4 30% Sympathetic Listening
ORGAN-IZATION (G)	G1 20% Tasks	G2 20% Things	G3 20% Information	G4 40% People
HEALTH (H)	H1 30% Care of Body	H2 30% Care of Moods	H3 20% Eating	H4 20% Sleeping
EXPRESSION (I)	I1 20% Pleasing	I2 20% Forceful	I3 30% Purposeful	I4 30% Technique
ENTHU-SIASM (J)	J1 30% Joy in working	J2 30% Diligence	J3 20% Joy in perfecting	J4 20% Manifes-tations
ATTRACT-IVENESS (K)	K1 20% Friendliness	K2 40% Cheerfulness	K3 20% Magnetism	K4 20% Attitudes
VOCATION OR PRO-FESSION (L)	L1 30% Service or Program	L2 20% Control of People	L3 20% Dignity	L4 30% Reliability
EXTRA CREDITS (M)	M1 25% School Leader	M2 25% Religious Service	M3 25% Service to new students	M4 25% Service to School

Total Deductions ————

Love is the motivation of the social virtues
SCHOLASTIC CREDITS

Chautauqua and Lyceum History __ ———
Collateral Reading _____ ———
Community Events _____ ———
Company Management _____ ———
Company Rehearsals _____ ———
Debate _____ ———
Ensemble _____ ———
Extemporaneous Speaking _____ ———
Expression _____ ———
Health Culture and Physical Training _____ ———
Leadership _____ ———
Make-up _____ ———
Major Subject _____ ———
Oratory and Orators _____ ———

Band and Orch. Instruments _____ ———
Physical Expression _____ ———
Piano _____ ———
Platform Technique _____ ———
Program Building _____ ———
Recitals and Hearings _____ ———
Rhetoric and Thought Organization ———
Speaking Voice _____ ———
Thought Dramatization _____ ———
Violin _____ ———
Voice _____ ———
Miscellaneous
_____
_____
_____

meantime, marriages of abnormal persons, and people the nation with a clean, decent, normal population.

All defectives are to be institutionalized and prevented from procreating.

Normal people should never have to look upon the faces of abnormal or degenerate persons.

Ott also advocated a ninety-day waiting period before a marriage of even "normal" persons could take place: this "would prevent 75 percent of foolish and unwise marriages."

Ott held forth the highest expectations for the future development of his field. Writing in the *Key Note* for April 1922, he observed that the number of Chautauquas had doubled within four years: "the field is ever widening and the supply is not too great." Entertainment skills of every sort are eminently marketable, although he reminded his readers that talent counts only for 30 percent, with the remainder charged to "personality." His Catalog had taken passing notice of a potential threat to the lecture circuits, but only to dismiss it.

The stage and the "movies" have lost much of their hold on public confidence, by forgetting the cultural standards of American audiences, and using technically skilled artists, who are unwilling to learn "The art of living."

But for all that, the motion picture, radio, and the Model T had already come into their own. Chautauqua and Lyceum entertainments would markedly dwindle, and by 1928, Ott's school had disappeared from sight.

In January 1922, Williams announced that Patrick Conway, "noted director of the famous organization that bears his name," would be returning to Ithaca to establish the Ithaca School of Band Instruments (later known as the Conway Military Band School). Conway, whom many considered to be the successor to John Philip Sousa, had been associated both with Cornell University and the Conservatory in the 1890s and early 1900s and had first organized his band in Ithaca. After his departure for Syracuse, his national reputation had grown by leaps and bounds, both through extensive and prestigious engagements throughout the country and

through phonograph recordings. Now "Conway's Band" would be based in Ithaca once again, and the affiliated Band School, described as the only institution of its kind in the country, would serve as feeder.

Conway died in June 1929, to be replaced by Ernest S. Williams, bandmaster of the Kismet Shriner Band of Brooklyn and widely acclaimed soloist both on the trumpet and cornet; his wife was a member of a well-known group called the "Gloria Trumpeters." In the summer of 1930, Dean Williams, doubtless following the example of I.S.P.E., touted the band and orchestra camp which he operated — "situated in one of America's outstanding beauty spots in the foothills of the Catskill mountains near Saugerties, N.Y., on-the-Hudson." Cottages and bungalows, each "an architectural gem," with all conveniences were enthusiastically advertised, to say nothing of a Little Theatre seating four hundred and a spacious dining room with "an excellent cuisine." A complete athletic program supplemented the instruction provided by a distinguished faculty drawn from the great orchestras of the country, and it was announced that some of the world's foremost conductors were to appear as guests. This is inflated promotional copy, and the pictorial record suggests an establishment on a far more modest scale. In any event, Dean Williams left after two years to set up his own school in Brooklyn (he took with him all the records of the Ithaca Band School, including the applications of prospective students, which had to be recovered by legal action). By 1931 - 1932, the Band School had been absorbed by the department of music education. Jay W. Fay was listed as head of "the Band and Orchestra School" then, but clearly he was only a departmental chairman under Dean Albert Edmund Brown.

Around 1920, John Finley Williamson had established a fine choir at the Westminster Presbyterian Church in Dayton, Ohio, and, more recently, had created the Westminster Choir School in conjunction with it.

From a handful of students meeting in night classes three times a week, it has developed into a five-day-a-week school with classes in English, psychology, theory and ear training, history of music, church music literature, conducting and other related subjects, and attended by more than 100 students from 36 states of the Union.

In the autumn of 1928, President Williams had learned that the Choir School was seeking affiliation with a collegiate institution in the East in order to enrich a curriculum that was about to be extended to a four-year course. Accompanied by Dean Brown, Williams had journeyed to Dayton. The Williamsons came to reconnoiter in November 1928. Their schedule was filled with high-level conferences and a round of social events including a dinner with the faculty; in the background, Cornell University, the Chamber of Commerce, and the ministerial association were all at work to support the effort to persuade Williamson to relocate in Ithaca. And in fact, after considering offers from other leading conservatories, Williamson did opt for affiliation with the Ithaca institution.

It would take 10 years, a herculean amount of work, and a tremendous amount of money to give to my present and future students in the Westminster Choir School the advantages they will have next year.

The entire group received a gala welcome in March 1929, just before they set out on a three-month singing tour of Europe, under the sponsorship of such notables as President and Mrs. Hoover and Chief Justice Taft.

As dean, Williamson brought with him about one hundred twenty students and seven faculty members (their principal benefactor in Dayton, Mrs. H. E. Talbott, became a member of the Conservatory's Board of Trustees). Williamson, a crusader for the reformation of church music in America, derived his educational philosophy from an intensely religious conviction that "we must worship God not only in the beauty of holiness but in the holiness of beauty." Like President Williams, he sensed a vocation as a kind of lay-minister, and his school was created to produce nothing less than "ministers of music" for churches of all denominations.

First among the qualifications for entrance to the school is character. It is Dr. Williamson's conviction that the ministry of church music cannot be accomplished except through leaders of real moral and spiritual life. Next comes personality, with the element of leadership, and then musicianship, mental equipment, and voice.

The curriculum mandated a thorough acquaintance with Protestant, Catholic, and Jewish liturgical forms, links were established with a large number of churches in the surrounding area, and each student was required to organize and direct three choirs — a children's choir, a high school choir, and an adult choir.

The new school was welcomed as "the most significant addition to the local institution since its founding," and plans were projected both for a new building especially designed for its needs (complete with auditorium and large pipe organ) and for a new dormitory to house its women students. Nothing quite so grand actually happened: the Choir School was assigned studios in a converted rectory (a modest frame building on East Buffalo Street, between the Conservatory Building and Williams Hall), and the students were quartered in the far-from-new Westminster Hall at the corner of North Tioga and East Court Streets. In 1932, the Westminster Choir School elected to depart for Princeton, New Jersey, rather than lose its identity in the reorganized Ithaca College.

The older components continued to flourish during this era of new affiliations. After assuming the presidency in 1924, Williams could hardly devote much time to the school that still bore his name. But he had been favorably impressed by a book entitled *The Teaching of Public Speaking*, so much so that he traveled to Butler University to meet its author, Rollo Anson Tallcott. Tallcott, with a varied collegiate background and some twenty years' experience as public reader, actor, and producer, was accordingly named dean of the Williams School of Expression and Dramatic Art in 1925; with him came his wife, Jennie Witmer Tallcott, to teach English and pedagogy. In the spring in 1931, Tallcott resigned, in order to continue his studies for the doctorate at Cornell as it was officially announced. He would receive his degree, spend 1932 to 1936 at Slippery Rock College, and then return to Ithaca as professor of English (and, briefly, as dean of students). Mrs. Tallcott remained with the College throughout the period of her husband's absence; both retired in 1952. With Tallcott's resignation in 1931, Adrian M. Newens arrived, functioning at first as administrative head both of the Conservatory and of the Williams School of Expression.

The Conservatory itself could boast of a constellation of great names in the 1920s. Although the Catalog of 1921 - 1922 struck rather an isolationist note,

The management is very glad to be able to announce that every department of the Ithaca Conservatory of Music and each affiliated school is under the direction of an American who has received the very best preparation and experience both in this country and Europe

the headlines were made largely by distinguished faculty members from abroad. Léon Sampaix had arrived from Belgium to replace Hilliard as head of the piano department and was in turn succeeded by Oscar Ziegler, a Swiss pianist who had covered himself with glory at the Salzburg Festival and who came to Ithaca fresh from three triumphant concerts in New York. Ten years before Ziegler, Giuseppe Fabbrini had come to join the piano faculty: he had been admitted to the Royal Conservatory of Naples at the age of eight and among other things had been special instructor to the Khedival family in Cairo. Jaromir Weinberger, described as "one of the best known Czech composers since Dvorak," arrived from Prague to take charge of theory and composition.

But the strength of Egbert's Conservatory remained in his own chosen area, the violin. In 1920, he was moved to write an article, "Ithaca Conservatory of Music Gaining World Prominence," in which he noted that eminent conductors were recruiting among Conservatory students and that one of its graduates had been awarded the Federated Music Clubs of America prize for the best trained American violinist under thirty. He went on to make the triumphant announcement that Otakar Sevcik, his own teacher and "probably the greatest living teacher of the violin," would be joining the faculty. "The world will be coming to Ithaca to study the Violin," he concluded. Another virtuoso, César Thomson, was numbered among the violin faculty from 1924 to 1927. Thomson, admitted to the Conservatory at Liège at the age of seven, had enjoyed a brilliant concert career on three continents and had held important appointments at Liège, Brussels, and Paris. Adolph Pick had headed the violin department at the Conservatory of Berne and had conducted the symphony orchestra there. William Coad, born in Sidney, Australia, had become seriously interested in the violin when, at the age of three, he had heard a street musician; on his way from London to Sidney via New York (where his concerts were acclaimed), he was persuaded to swell the Conservatory ranks in Ithaca. Small wonder, then, that the *Violinist* should state that "there

is no school in the United States that deserves more credit for bringing great teachers to America than 'The Ithaca Conservatory of Music.' "

Not all the new additions were foreign-born. One of the Conservatory's own graduates, Lynn Bogart, became assistant to his teacher Egbert in 1924; for many years, Bogart's concerts would be highlights of the Ithaca musical season. Wallingford Riegger, already distinguished as a composer, came to head the department of theory and composition in 1926. The vocal department also had its luminaries: John Chipman, Ruth Blackman Rodgers, Herbert Witherspoon (later appointed to succeed Gatti-Casazza as general manager of the Metropolitan Opera) in 1921 - 1922, and, replacing Witherspoon as director in 1924 - 1925, Bert Rogers Lyon. "Dad" Lyon, as he would be styled in later years, was at first a self-taught musician. After a year at the University of Cincinnati, he spent five years working in a steel mill by day and taking vocal lessons in the evening; then he joined a vaudeville company in order to secure funds for further study in Europe. After his year in Paris and London, he opened his own studio in Cincinnati, pursued studies with Witherspoon, and came as faculty member to the Conservatory in 1922. Mr. and Mrs. Lyon would be notable campus figures for more than a quarter of a century.

A collegiate operation of such growing complexity required an ever expanding administrative superstructure. The Catalog of 1921 - 1922 listed Egbert as president, Williams as secretary and treasurer, and Benjamin Johnson as business manager, with eight additional "administration officers" including an "Adviser of Women" and her two assistants. Egbert's deteriorating health prompted him to announce his resignation as president at the alumni banquet in June 1924; he would continue as vice-president and musical director while Williams assumed the presidency. After Egbert's death in December 1928, the top administration was reduced to Williams and Johnson, but there were by that time no fewer than twenty-two other administrators. Miss Ida Powell was now dean of women; Gertrude Evans was publicity manager; and names of other persons destined for long and fruitful association with the College began to appear — Florence Howland, Nellie Van Dyne, Marylouise Potter.

The 1920s also witnessed an explosion in the publications of the institution. Not only the Conservatory itself but each of its affiliated schools issued catalogs and brochures; there were booklets on the faculty, on the residence halls, on the entertainment bureau, on scholarships. *The Program Book* collected the programs of the more recent concerts and recitals given by members of the faculty and their students. *The Proof of the Pudding* sketched the professional activities of graduates of the Williams School of Expression and Dramatic Art, and *Letters from Our Graduates* did the same for the alumni of the Institution of Public School Music; *Education an Investment* indicated "the large number of prominent positions held by Conservatory Graduates and Former Students." Some of the affiliates had their own professional publications. In 1925, the Williams School began to issue a *Service Bulletin* to bring public school speech teachers up to date with the latest developments in their field, and the Westminster Choir School announced that it was about to begin a *Music Journal* in October 1930. The first handbook for incoming freshmen was apparently the *Conservatory Bible* of 1918; other student handbooks followed in the succeeding years. There was even a *Boys' Activity Book* — "a booklet of illustrations confined to the activities of the male students" in the school (no copy, unfortunately, is extant). There are senior class books for 1912 (the first), 1913, 1914, 1916, and 1918; in 1923, it was called *The Conservatorian;* in 1925, *The Annual;* and, beginning in 1929, *The Cayugan.* By 1932, the last mentioned had proceeded to color photography.

The first campus newspaper was of course the *Key Note,* dating from 1901 and frequently cited in this history. It served many purposes — a source of news for the campus and of the larger world of music, an alumni newsletter, a student directory. Its successor, *Once-A-Week,* was published from October 15, 1926, to December 1930, after which the *Ithacan* became the student newspaper. The historian, reading the files of these student publications from the vantage point of the 1980s, is impressed by many things — by their journalistic competency and high standards of English prose, by their constructive concern for and pride in the institution, and, negatively, by the amount of space given to insipid jokes and to ethnically insensitive dialect humor. The first of an apparently unending series of short-lived alumni publications appears to have been the *Messenger* in 1926 - 1927.

There were even some signs that the Conservatory was prepared to move into the publishing business. The Catalog of 1928 - 1929 states that the school had published "several

textbooks used in the various courses of instruction" and available at the school bookstore. Five of these had been written by President Williams — ranging from *The Speaking Voice* and *Shakespearean Questionnaire* (in sixteen manuscript volumes) to *Introduction to Ethics* and *Problems of Religion.* And, by Dean Tallcott, *The Art of Acting and Public Reading.*

Up to this point in its history, the Conservatory awarded certificates or diplomas to its graduates (which were honored for teaching appointments), but it was not empowered to grant degrees. Partly because of the expansion of the twenties, partly because a degree was fast becoming a requirement for public school teaching, Williams was impelled, during his first summer as President, to initiate a move to secure for the Conservatory the right to confer degrees. He soon learned that New York State law required a minimum endowment of $500,000 before such a right could be given, and a fundraising campaign was started. The *Key Note* appealed for alumni support: $5 a year from every past, present, and future student "would assure the sum needed." The first student to have been registered in the Conservatory on September 19, 1892, Miss Flora Brown, had already contributed the first dollar, and an additional hundred had been pledged. But nothing remotely like $500,000 was ever raised. The noncompliance with state law would become a critical issue in 1931 - 1932.

Even so, Williams's push for recognition continued. In April 1925, the lieutenant governor and a committee of state officials visited the Conservatory, with apparently highly encouraging results. A week later, the Board of Trustees resolved

> *that the President and Secretary be authorized to make application to the Board of Regents for a change of name of the institution from the "Ithaca Conservatory of Music" to the "Ithaca Conservatory and Affiliated Schools," and further that the charter be so amended as to grant power to the institution to confer the following degrees:*
>
> *Bachelor of Music (Mus. B.)*
> *Bachelor of Physical Education*
> *   (B. Phys. E.)*
> *Bachelor of Oral English (B. O. E.)*

The new charter was granted on January 21, 1926.

Related changes in the legal identity of the institution had been in progress before the new charter became official, since more than a new name and new powers were involved. On December 7, 1925, the stockholders were summoned to a meeting "to consider and take action on a *proposed dissolution* of the corporation in the manner prescribed by Article 10 of the Stock Corporation Law." Copies of this notice were duly served upon the Egberts (William Grant Egbert and his minor son), the Williamses, and Benjamin L. Johnson (who had been appointed business manager in 1922 and who served as secretary and treasurer from 1924 until his death in 1932). The Certificate of Dissolution of the 1897 corporation was officially filed with the secretary of state on January 22, 1926.

The advantages of this last change were chiefly financial. As a private corporation, the Conservatory had been obliged to file tax returns; now, as "a public institution of higher learning under the official guidance of the Board of Regents," this was no longer necessary. Nor did the small group of stockholders lose by the transaction. True,

> *as an expression of faith in the new project, the owners of the Conservatory and Affiliated Schools have turned over to the newly chartered institution actual school equipment appraised at $300,000 as an absolute gift.*

But it was also true that the owners "preferred to the newly chartered institution our complete dormitory system at one-half the appraised value." That value having been determined to be $150,000, Egbert and Williams were to receive $75,000.

In 1921 - 1922, the Conservatory had had a seven-person board of trustees, plus five alumni members; a four-man board of directors; and an executive committee of two. Under the new charter, there were, in 1927 - 1928, eight trustees (including alumni) and a three-man executive committee. By the following year, there were ten trustees, and six in 1930 - 1931; in that year, the executive committee was replaced by a "Faculty Council" of ten — the president, the treasurer, the academic deans, the dean of women, and two faculty members.

A new charter, a new name, the right to confer degrees — so why not a new campus? In Williams's narrative:

> *We had now reached the point where, due to our very rapid expansion, we were "bursting at the seams." It became a grave question as to whether we should continue to develop here in the center of the city, or endeavor to secure a campus of our own outside the city limits. After much discussion, we invited about twenty-five of the most prominent and influential men of Ithaca to an evening banquet, and we plainly presented our problem to them and sought their advice. After a lengthy discussion it became their unanimous opinion that we should seek a campus of our own outside the city limits.*

Williams and Johnson had already selected a site on South Hill (approximately the present location of Ithaca College) and had secured options on the farm land there.

> *The plan is to build the new institution upon this site, one building at a time, until more than 14 modern college buildings stand on the new campus. Plans for the first increment of buildings are in the hands of architects. Ample acreage is provided by the new site for athletic fields, tracks, etc., and [it] affords one of the best panoramic views of the city, the valley, and Lake Cayuga.*

An endowment campaign for $1,500,000 was announced on April 13, 1926, with "representatives of well known college endowment campaigns" already working on the project. The "faithful faculty and student body" had already pledged $12,800 at an enthusiastic mass meeting; another such assembly was held in January 1927, with the *Ithaca Journal* reporting that "pledges of $22,000 assure a new campus for Conservatory."

The total plan was a far-reaching one, anticipating a new charter before the ink was dry on the current one.

> *An ultimate plan is to build a national university of Fine Arts, where students will receive the best available professional training, and while they pursue the subjects of collegiate grade that pertain directly to their chosen field of art, they may likewise create for themselves a culture from aesthetic values, comprehensive or limited, according to their talent, initiative, and capacity.*

There would be separate buildings for each of the affiliated colleges, a museum of arts and crafts, a little theatre and theatre workshop, dormitories, a student union, and all the appropriate auxiliary services.

> *We plan to have a college of music that will include the Conservatory of Music, Ithaca Institution of Public School Music and the Conway Band School; a College of Speech Arts including the Williams School of Expression and Dramatic Art, the Ott School of Chautauqua and Lyceum Arts and the Martin Institute for Speech Correction; a College of Physical Education with Dr. Sharpe's school as the nucleus; and a college of Arts and Crafts.*

Once-A-Week, in an October 1929 editorial entitled "A Glance into the Future," anticipated an expansion of unprecedented proportions. It ended on a note of exhortation.

> *Be not among those who criticise — or those who are nursing wrong feelings. Look forward — Help — both by your spirit and attitude. . . . A determined courage and optimism is guiding us toward this fine institution of the future.*

No such development was destined to occur of course, at least for many decades. The one surviving financial statement from the period lists total receipts for the campaign as $4,949.23, of which more than $4,000 had been expended on attorneys' fees, travel expenses, "excursions, dinners, and Misc." and on the options for the South Hill property. It would thus appear that a balance of $756.51 was on hand for the University of Fine Arts, now estimated to cost $2 million.

Williams had pinned his hopes on a single benefactor, the Ward Baking Company. Benjamin Johnson, the Conservatory treasurer, had connections with the president of that company, which had recently established "a Foundation for Philanthropic Purposes, into which the Company could place all otherwise taxable receipts." After President Kent had visited Ithaca, Williams had received the impression that the Ward Foundation would underwrite — or at least substantially contribute to — the endowment fund. He had therefore proceeded to put down money against the land

purchase and had even staged a picnic on the selected site for the students and a number of influential guests.

> *Then suddenly our glorious bubble burst. The United States Government indicted the Ward Baking Company for creating a monopoly. Mr. Kent was forced to resign and the Company was dissolved of its many affiliated units. And we were left with mere options on property which we ardently desired but could not purchase.*

And so, however crowded they may have been, the Conservatory and its affiliated schools were forced to remain in downtown Ithaca. According to the Catalog of 1921 - 1922, property holdings then included the Conservatory building, with adjacent Music Hall and the Sinfonia Chapter House to the rear, plus the dormitories — Williams Hall, Egbert Hall, DeWitt Hall, Griffis Hall, the S.A.I. House, and, also listed for good measure, the Y.M.C.A., where men students rented rooms. In the middle of the decade, work was begun on a new administrative annex, between the Music Hall and the First Baptist Church; the *Key Note* of the summer of 1924 boasted that "when this is accomplished, our school buildings will compare favorably with any in the country." And, as one by one the affiliated schools came into existence, makeshift locations were provided for their use. Around 1921, the Star Theatre on East Seneca Street was acquired and remodeled into a gymnasium, and a home for the Martin Institute was found at 311 North Tioga Street. By September 1928, the Public School Music building was at 123 East Buffalo Street (across from the main Conservatory building); within a couple of years, these premises would be turned over to the still miniscule Library and to various classroom and administrative uses as Public School Music moved into an imposing colonial mansion on the southwest corner of Cayuga and Court Streets. In 1929, the former rectory of Saint John's Episcopal Church at 128 East Buffalo Street became the studios of the Westminster Choir School (with some doubts as to the Conservatory's credit rating recorded in the minutes of the vestry). By 1930 - 1931, there were six residence halls for women, three sorority houses, and two fraternity houses. The infirmary was located at the corner of East Seneca and Spring (now Schuyler Place).

Thus Williams had relinquished his dream of modern functional buildings on South Hill. Ever one to make a virtue of necessity, he was prepared, in a 1929 "General Information" pamphlet, to revert to the copy of the 1921 - 1922 catalog.

The administration of the Ithaca Conservatory and Affiliated Schools after many years of study and experience has developed a dormitory system which is second to none in the country. It is the aim of the school to give these residence halls as much of a home appearance, and as many home accommodations as possible. . . . In accord with this policy the school has erected and planned a number of comparatively small residence halls, rather than the customary large building with stall-like rooms, and of one design and appearance.

That "the school has acquired whatever odds and ends of local real estate it could lay its hands on and converted them into residence halls for women" would be closer to the truth.

The achievements of these years were shadowed — for the institution as a whole but particularly for the Conservatory — by the death of William Grant Egbert on December 9, 1928. Memorial services paid quiet musical tribute to his work; his role as founder and moving spirit within the Conservatory was extolled in eulogy and in the press. The alumni, meeting in December 1929, commissioned a life-size portrait in oils to be executed by Egbert's friend, the artist Christian Midjo, "to be hung in a niche built expressly for it in the foyer of the new Auditorium Building to be erected . . . within the next year." No such building would be erected, but the portrait was completed and formally presented to the College at a memorial service held at the First Methodist Church on June 6, 1935. President Leonard B. Job presided; Leonard Liebling, editor of the *Musical Courier*, delivered the principal address; Mayor Louis P. Smith and Dean Albert Edmund Brown contributed their reminiscences; and the College choir and orchestra provided the musical selections. Perhaps Dean Brown said it best.

William Grant Egbert was a great man as well as a great musician. He maintained his independence of thought no matter what public opinion was. He was

quiet. He thought clearly, he spoke intelligently, he lived simply. He sought no praise and was never offended. He worked for the joy of it. He was simple and strong and believed that at last every man comes into his own. Truly he was a musicianly man and a manly musician.

Egbert's daughter Gladys and granddaughter, Miss Jane Beller, were on hand to unveil the portrait. The alumni, however, were not satisfied with the likeness, and in 1946, a new portrait would be painted by Professor Kenneth Washburn of Cornell, who worked from snapshots and from casts of Egbert's hands. This is the portrait now hanging on the third floor of Job Hall.

Student life reflected the complexities and the excitement of the decade of affiliation. The supervision of personal behavior continued to be strict, whatever the new freedom of the Roaring Twenties may have meant for America at large. In September 1919, the faculty issued a series of extraordinary decrees. No Conservatory women could attend Sunday movies; women might "walk out after dinner" until 7:30 (but not on State Street); they were forbidden to seek refreshment after that hour without a chaperone or escort or to dine at any hotel or attend evening movies without the same; and canoeing on Lake Cayuga was "strictly forbidden." Quite understandably, by January the faculty was hearing of "a spirit of unrest among the students," and some minor relaxations of the rules were enacted — by April 1920, the directors extended the curfew to 8:00, with some late permissions until 10:30. A baccalaureate sermon in 1924 fulminated against the Jazz Age. Even as late as the spring of 1931, the proprieties of the ballroom exercised the directors: it was resolved that "the so-called modern dances should be prohibited from all future Conservatory social affairs." And in the following autumn, students were apprised that they might not wear any kind of high school insignia; they must turn their sweaters so as to conceal the offending letters.

The students were strong on "traditions." An account dating from 1924 - 1925 enumerates many of these: Male Freshmen were required to uncover at the command "Spuds! Frosh!" — a "spud" being what would later be called a beanie; any freshman "known to be out with the same girl more than once a week from September 20, '24 to

April 2, '26 shall be dealt with severely." Freshman orientation had come into its own: in 1930 -1931, the theme of a "prescribed course for all new students" was "Right Attitudes" — "The Right Attitude toward My School," "The Right Attitude toward My God" (the second day was a Sunday); "The Right Attitude toward My Student Organizations," "The Right Attitude toward My Studies." There were rushing rules as early as 1919.

Inevitably, Conservatory students were singing students. The original Alma Mater song, "Ithaca, Thou Lovely City," dates back to 1904, and the College archives contain two early notebooks of George Daland with Conservatory songs. The advent of the School of Physical Education and of collegiate sports stimulated a demand for a new "Team Song"; around 1930, "The Blue and White" was written by Bob de Lany '30,

Conservatory Alma Mater

Music by HARRY NORDIN, '04

Ithaca, thou lovely city;
  Hill and Lake and Dell,
Home of our loved Alma Mater,
  Loud thy praise we'll tell.

CHORUS
I. C. M., dear Alma Mater,
  Hail to thee, all hail!
May the brightness of thy glory
  Never, never fail.

World wide go thy sons and daughters
  On their mission bent;
Cheering, blessing and uplifting
  As from Heaven sent.—CHORUS.

As the waters of Cayuga
  Smile beneath the sun,
May God's blessings smile upon thee
  While the years roll on.—CHORUS.
           ROSA K. HAMLIN '03.

with music by Roger Schwartz '30 and arranged for the band by Maurice Whitney '32. It concluded:

> *No such word as failure,*
> *With victory's flag unfurled;*
> *The Ispie game will win us fame*
> *Around the world!*

There were also some distressing cheers:

> *I scream,   You scream.   We all scream*
> *Ithaca   team   team   team*

and:

> *Alla   Behold me   Victory*
> *For whom   Ithaca   Team Team Team*

A later generation of students would surely have stumbled over the grammatical precision of that *whom*.

After the first indoctrination, the student was periodically checked against the "Personality Development Chart," at least as long as Dean Ott was on the campus. A Loyalty Council consisted of the president of the student organizations, the president of Amards, and a representative from each class organization. They met regularly with Williams and Dean Tallcott "in order that matters of mutual interest to the students and the school may have free and frank discussion, and a spirit of sincere co-operation may exist between the students and the Faculty." Such reciprocal amity seems not always to have prevailed, however. In November 1930, the students were so irate because a scheduled trip to Oneonta left no time to study for an ethics examination that they loudly demanded a dean of students to serve as mediator between them and the administration.

Much of the spirit of this generation of students is distilled in a "Creed for the Students of the Ithaca Conservatory and Affiliated Schools," printed in *The Cayugan* for 1926.

Student government had become more complex, as a direct mirroring of the developments within the institution at large. A student council had taken over from an earlier student governing committee by September 1919, and by the end of the decade, its membership reflected the growing number of organized student groups: The Women's Self Government

Association, Mu Phi Epsilon, Phi Delta Phi, the Amards, Phi Mu Alpha, Phi Epsilon Kappa, Kappa Gamma Psi, Delta Pi, Oracle, representatives of each of the classes and affiliated schools, of "Outside Girls," and of *Once-A-Week*. Sigma Alpha Iota sorority seems to have been somehow omitted from that list; in 1930, a Physical Education group, Iota Pi Alpha, sought national affiliation as the eighth fraternal organization on the campus. By January 1930, the school was moving toward an interfraternity council. The Newman Club for Catholic students was also organized in that year.

The inclusion of Oracle attests to an important development — the emergence of honor societies. Oracle was founded in April 1928 by the dean of women, Mrs. Phyllis Spencer; before long, it would become a powerful force within the college, in part through its sponsorship of *Scampers*. That annual theatrical event was born out of financial crisis. The publication of the 1927 yearbook had left a substantial deficit, and Mrs. Tallcott had suggested that each of the six fraternities provide a stunt or act, to be collectively called *Six Student Scampers*. The debt was paid off in full within four years, and there was no show between 1930 and 1934. In 1934, Mrs. Talcott, by then the faculty sponsor for Oracle, suggested that that organization undertake the revitalization of *Scampers* — this time without the idea of competition and with the proceeds to be used to create a scholarship fund. *Scampers* thus became one of the major annual events of the campus well into the 1960s; after 1940, it would become a unified musical review, written by a student or students and involving the cooperation of the three divisions of the College. A freshman honor society, Adelphi (later to be Zeta Sigma Nu), was created in 1929 - 1930.

The calendar of activities followed previously defined patterns. The Amards continued to add color to the social scene, especially with their Twelfth Night Revels, now a high point in the school year. The Revels began at four in the afternoon on January 6 and continued until midnight or after. *Once-A-Week* summarizes the proceedings in 1930. First, President Williams read "The Other Wise Man" to the Amards and the public at large. After that, the fraternity and its guests repaired to Elocution Hall ("lavishly disguised for the occasion") for a banquet that included Reveler's Salad and Twelfth Night cakes. The "Bringing In of the Boar's Head" was followed by carol singing, and then the "Bringing in of the Yule Log," with more singing. "The Lutterworth

Creed for the Students of the Ithaca Conservatory and Affiliated Schools

We believe in friendship between men, between women, between men and women---friendship which recognizes the value of individuality, friendship based on neither self-seeking nor on passing fancies, but on a firm basis of common interests and genuine affection.

We believe in art for life's sake.

We believe in well rounded knowledge to fit ourselves for life work.

We believe in an appreciation of the beautiful as found in Nature, the arts, and in bodily perfection.

We believe in Honor, expressed in every act and relationship of life.

We believe in obedience to the laws of Nature and of man, for in obedience we gain liberty for the body and the mind.

We believe in the establishment and maintenance of the highest social and moral standards.

We believe in and pledge loyalty to the ideals of our Alma Mater; and we believe in the expression of those ideals through unity and cooperation.

We believe that life is a gift to be used thoughtfully and reverently.

1926

Christmas Play" was next presented, "by the Strolling Play-ers, in form and manner as given at Christmas Time during the reign of Good Queen Bess." Then a reading from Dickens and the "Crowning of the King and Queen of the Bean; to be henceforth known as the 'Lords of Mis-Rule.'" More carols and readings, and many speeches. Later in the evening, the concluding Revels were held in the Little Thea-tre — readings and songs; a one-act play; "Twelfth Night Games under the direction and domination of the newly elected King and Queen of the Bean, — the Lord and Lady of Mis-Rule;" and finally "Twelfth Night Dances" — "Our revels now are ended."

The Conservatory, as before, dominated the musical life of the Ithaca community. It was deeply involved in such events as Cornell's Twelfth Annual Musical Festival (May 1920), held at Bailey Hall — four concerts included *Aida,* the New World Symphony, the Tchaikovsky Fourth, Elgar's *The Dream of Gerontius* (Part I), and Franck's *The Beatitudes,* with the Chicago Symphony Orchestra and the Cornell Festi-val Chorus. On November 13, 1922, the Conservatory repeated a triumph of its very first year: in observance of its thirtieth anniversary, it again presented Paderewski, this time at Bailey Hall (there was considerable protest in the public press over the price of the tickets). By 1924, a new series was inaugurated closer to home — the First Music Festival, under the direction of Bert Lyon, held April 24 - 26 at the Methodist Church. For that occasion, a chorus of 175 voices and an orchestra of 60 members, both "composed almost entirely of Conservatory students," presented Mendelssohn's *Elijah* and Rossini's *Stabat Master.* It was noted that of the nine soloists, three were alumni and two, faculty members. The record from this point on is studded with reports of Lyon's triumphs — Verdi's *Manzoni Requiem* in 1928, the *Saint Matthew Passion* in 1929, Franck's *The Beatitudes* again in 1932. A "Cosmopolitan Opera Company" presented *Carmen* and *Hansel and Gretel* at the Conservatory in 1932.

Major dramatic productions of the Williams School of Expression had come to number more than fifty, according to a tabulation in the Catalog of 1928 - 1929. Many of these were long-forgotten works of little significance, but Shakespeare loomed large, with six plays performed. The most recent of these, *Twelfth Night,* is illustrated in the Catalog, and earlier, in 1922, there had been a notable *Othello* at the Lyceum Theatre for the benefit of the George Junior Republic, with Williams alternating with Edward Royce in the roles of Iago and Othello on successive nights and with Lillian Speakman Vail as one of the Desdemonas. Modern drama was repre-sented largely by Pinero, Maeterlinck, and Galsworthy; Ibsen and Shaw were conspicuously absent. The arts of the elocu-tionist still found ample opportunity for development. Publi-cations of the 1920s are full of pictures of Williams in the various roles he assumed in his "entertainments," and clearly his students were encouraged to follow in his footsteps.

In 1925, the Conservatory was considering leasing the Lyceum Theatre, "dark since last fall" because of difficulties with the local Musicians' Union. But the musicians were no more inclined to negotiate with Williams than with builder Gutstadt (who died on February 9, 1925) or with Ithaca Theatres, Incorporated, who had acquired most of the stock. The Lyceum surrendered briefly to motion pictures and even-tually was dismantled, so that the Conservatory undertook to sponsor legitimate drama in Ithaca. The Conservatory Hall thus became the Little Theatre, with extensive remodeling, and a professional stock company arrived, under the direc-tion of "an able New York Directing-Manager, Mr. William Blair, and [with] six professional actors from New York City." Students from the School of Expression were afforded the opportunity of working with this group and were "expected to render cheerfully any service required of them incident to the production of plays" — scene shifting, lights and properties, set building, and costume making fell to the students. Two ten-week runs were scheduled for the spring of 1925 and the fall of 1926 and included "the most recent Broadway successes" such as *The Cat and the Canary* and *Outward Bound.*

This arrangement was of brief duration, however. Yet in 1930, we read once more of two professional actors on the campus, presenting three plays and expressing their com-mendations for the students who joined them in the minor roles. Even earlier than that, when Walter Hampden had played Hamlet at the Lyceum, he had found time to address the Conservatory students, with considerable effect.

Another much heralded annual event was the Little Thea-tre Tournament. Inaugurated by Williams in 1924 and under the direction of Gertrude Evans, the tournament had grown from a competition of only four schools to one that involved most of New York and Pennsylvania. In 1931, a luncheon for the visiting directors and principals was added, and Williams announced plans for a week-long conference of speech teachers in conjunction with the tournament. One-act plays were presented, and a silver trophy awarded to the winning school. A High School Public Speaking Contest was also held in May; the winning student received a trophy for his school and a $200 scholarship to the Conservatory.

The festive weeks of the school year continued to be "Mid-Week" (the last week of the fall term) and commencement week. The former featured a concert by the Chorale Club, the junior ball, a concert by the Orchestral Association, the Amards' dramatic presentation (at the Lyceum), the sophomore stunt fest, and a wide variety of fraternal activities. Commencement, according to the 1928 - 1929 Catalog, included an opera, the senior reception and ball, the commencement play, an orchestral concert, the Amards picnic, the alumni reception and banquet, and the individual class reunions and events sponsored for the alumni by the campus societies. The tone of commencement remained solemn. A stern warning from the senior class committee ("The march is to be formal. No talking, slouching, or smiling") must seem an echo from a long vanished age to those of us used to, or at least hardened to, commencements of more recent times, with their straggling lines, their bizarre defiance of academic costume, their balloons, sparklers, and the inevitable bottle passed up and down the rows while degrees are being awarded.

Collegiate sports followed close upon the establishment of the School of Physical Education. There is little to suggest their existence before 1923 - 1924, and the student publication gives scant attention to athletics until around 1930. The year before that, *Once-A-Week* had reported that

> the Ithaca Affiliated Schools for the first time in its history, will have a basketball team representing the school in major competition.

This account included school cheers and a football song.

An Ithaca football team was playing Mansfield, St. Lawrence, Cortland, Hartwick, and Colgate in 1930 (some of these only with freshmen teams); soccer began in 1931, which was also the year in which the first Ithaca baseball team to play in intercollegiate competition was organized under coach Joe Tatascore. There are some references to wrestling and track, and an athletic association was formed

in 1930. Figures like Yavits and Freeman, however, were but newly arrived on the Ithaca scene, and the big years still lay in the future.

We read little of town-and-gown relations during the 1920s and, beyond musical events, almost nothing of Conservatory-and-University. Yet the Conservatory was never quite to return to the isolationism of the pre-War years. A Men's Club, formed in 1920, debated such questions as:

> *Resolved; that the government should inaugurate a system of compulsory industrial insurance*

or:

> *that the Ithaca Conservatory of Music should have compulsory military training*

or:

> *that foreign immigration should be stopped for a period of five years.*

(They also took time out from these high deliberations to put on a minstrel show.) The Crash of 1929 left its mark on more than institutional finances: in 1931 - 1932, the students attended a "Depression Hop," for which the decorations were clotheslines hung with tattered garments.

> *There should be more clothes on this line, [the placards stated], but we are wearing them.*

The early thirties witnessed a renewed interest in international politics. Students attended an intercollegiate state conference at Kingston in 1930 - 1931, at which the principal themes were international friendship and disarmament. Disarmament petitions were circulating by that time, and the *Ithacan* ran an impassioned editorial, "Let Us Have Peace!" There was also an approving editorial comment in January 1932 when Nicholas Murray Butler won the Nobel Prize for Peace.

But the world out there was not so much Washington or Geneva as Albany — at least as far as the Conservatory administration was concerned. The period 1919 - 1932 must be concluded with an account of yet another transformation of the institutional identity — along with a number of seismic shocks in its management.

Williams would recall that for five years prior to 1931, he had been petitioning the State Board of Regents for permission to change the name of the school to Ithaca College.

Each year the State Superintendent of Public Instruction or one of his officials would inspect the Conservatory and give his approval, but when our petition came before the State Board of Regents, it was always refused. We could not ascertain why.

A visit of Harlan Hoyt Horner, assistant commissioner for higher and professional education in New York, in the fall of 1930 - 1931 clarified the nature of the opposition. Cornell's President Livingston Farrand, according to Williams, was convinced that a school in Ithaca called Ithaca College might all too easily be confused with the University. Williams immediately arranged for a meeting with Farrand, which he describes as a triumph of reason over prejudice. In retrospect, it is hard to believe that such fears could ever have existed, but whatever the behind-scenes manipulations, the fact remains that Ithaca College came into being with the Charter of March 19, 1931.

This charter empowered the College to "confer the degree of Bachelor of Science, in conformity with the rules of the Regents of the University and the regulations of the Commissioner of Education for the registration of institutions of higher education." That is to say, degree-granting powers conferred in principle by the charter had to be validated in practice by the registration of the various curricula with the State Department of Education. In itself, this was nothing new. But Albany's surveillance was proving to be far stricter in 1931 than it had been ten or fifteen years earlier. It would, in fact, destroy Williams as president.

The Regents had stipulated that new academic leadership must be secured to coordinate the educational work of the institution, and Williams had gone to the University of Ohio to interview Leonard Bliss Job for an appointment as dean. Job arrived in September 1931. There was also concern about the presence of the principal administrative officers on the Board of Trustees; they were removed and the Board reconstituted early in 1931 - 1932. And there were additional matters that needed remedial attention before curricula could be

approved — the state of the Library, the lack of scientific equipment, the shaky condition of the institutional finances, the lack of the legally mandated endowment of $500,000.

The President's annual report for 1930 - 1931 addressed itself to these problems, but the new dean, according to an unpublished memoir he would write after his retirement as president, soon made a disconcerting discovery: a critical page of the copy sent to Commissioner Horner had been deleted, at Williams's direction. When Hermann Cooper, associate in higher education, came down from Albany, his discussions with Job touched on material covered on the missing page, and Williams's action was disclosed. The president being in Florida, as was his custom during the winter months, the remaining administrative officers were summoned to Albany, and Job confirmed Commissioner Horner's suspicions. Horner's reaction was an angry refusal to have any further dealings with Williams; he would communicate only with the chairman of the Board of Trustees, Louis P. Smith.

On February 16, 1932, the Board met in emergency session to consider the ultimatum from Horner, dated February 13, 1932. The letter has not survived, but its tenor is clear enough from the minutes.

At the conclusion of the discussion, it was moved by Hickey, seconded by Stutz, that Dean Job be made Acting President of Ithaca College, pending permanent reorganization.

The Board then resolved to apprise Williams that the future of the College, as well as his own best interests, dictated his retirement. Job, present at the meeting and, we must imagine, hardly surprised by the turn of events, was ready with eleven recommendations designed to stabilize the situation, permit an orderly transfer of power, and work toward the necessary changes in the structure and operation of the College. Immediate action was taken relative to improving the Library holdings and the purchasing of laboratory equipment.

This meeting, naturally enough, prompted Williams to make a hurried return from Florida. On February 19, 1932, he appeared to read a formal statement to the Board, in which he agreed to resign as of July 1, 1932, provided that certain conditions be met. First, Horner would have to be officially assured that the Board had found "no evidence of bad faith, misrepresentation, or bad management on my part." Second, he must be relieved of his endorsements of all College notes and securities. Third, he demanded payment, with interest, on an established schedule, of a $20,000 note he held against the College. Lastly, he requested a teaching position "at a salary commensurate with my abilities and experience as a teacher" (he suggested $5,000). And, as a kind of bonus, he expressed his willingness to counsel the new management on the running of the College.

> *Should the Board of Trustees consider my thirty-five years of experience here of any value to them, it would always be a pleasure and a privilege to serve your board or the new president of the College in an advisory capacity at any time.*

The fiscal implications of Williams's demands panicked the Board, and another meeting was held on February 24th. At that time, Williams expressed a willingness to continue endorsing College notes, even through 1933 - 1934, provided that he was given a lien on all tuition receipts and the privilege of examining the College books at any time — his other demands remaining unchanged.

The deposed president returned to Florida, and the battle continued via Western Union. The trustees balked at the idea of a teaching appointment; they certainly felt that a lien on tuition moneys would severely handicap the College, by now in trouble with the Pennsylvania State Department of Education over teacher certification as well as with the authorities in Albany. Williams indicated that he was agreeable to "leaving the possibility of a teaching position open for later consideration," but he was obdurate on the matter of the lien.

> *Proposal not acceptable. Lien absolutely necessary. Cannot understand your changed attitude, doubt authority of last telegram. . . . can make no further concessions. . . . Wire reply.*

But the Board also proved capable of taking a firm, even a threatening, stand.

> *You are more concerned financially than anyone in the successful operation of the College until that is accomplished [assuming the notes endorsed by Wil-*
> *liams], and we plan to do all that is reasonably possible to protect both you and the College . . . . The pressing question is whether you wish us to publish at once the announcement of your resignation to take effect in June in a way complimentary to you or whether the Board shall take action on its initiative, which latter course we much prefer not to adopt if the other course is possible. . . . Wire your choice if you have a choice.*

Williams capitulated.

> *Announce resignation stop [am] leaving for Ithaca immediately stop Will arrive March 10 stop.*

On March 7, Job was elected president, "to succeed Mr. Williams on June 1, 1932." A "Committee on Financial Arrangements with Mr. Williams" worked out an agreement, dated March 14, 1932, by which both parties agreed to a timetable for the assumption by the College of the Williams notes and for the repayment of $20,000 still owed the ex-president ("arising from a transfer and conveyance to the Ithaca College of real estate and personal property" when the stock company was dissolved in 1926). This agreement once ratified, formal relations between Williams and the College effectively ceased. Living in Florida until his death at the age of ninety-seven on December 28, 1971, he occasionally returned to the Ithaca area (he spoke at the Rotary Club in 1951), and, during the sixties, visited President Dillingham and the South Hill Campus — "It is beyond my wildest dreams." In June 1962, the alumni presented the portrait which now hangs in Job Hall. Williams's son and daughter were present for the unveiling.

Some will insist that W. Grant Egbert was the naive idealist and George C. Williams ("Grab-Cash" Williams, as he was sometimes called), the shrewd manipulator, the "Yankee horse-trader," whose entrepreneurial talents were at least as profitable to himself as to the College. Yet careful consideration of the events of the first four decades of the institution suggests that whatever the differences in their personalities, Egbert and Williams made an effective working team. Egbert's dream of a conservatory had become a reality, however shaky and despite its legacy of problems to the new administration. Without Williams as manager, it is improbable that the Ithaca Conservatory of Music would have survived much past its first decade. The institution had survived; it had expanded; it had a new name, a new charter, a new chance. Perhaps, therefore, the plaque presented by the alumni, students, and faculty at the reunion of June 1923 (long attached to the Conservatory building on Buffalo Street) may fittingly be extended to serve as epitaph both to the first forty years and to the joint labors of both presidents:

1892   1923

AN UNFOLDING VISION
THIS TABLET IS ERECTED ON THE
THIRTY-FIRST ANNIVERSARY
OF THE ITHACA CONSERVATORY
OF MUSIC IN APPRECIATION
OF THE VISION COURAGE AND
DETERMINATION OF THE
CO-LABORERS

W. GRANT EGBERT
PRESIDENT

GEORGE C. WILLIAMS
MANAGER

THE STUDENTS ALUMNI AND
FACULTY JOIN IN THIS EXPRESSION
OF CONGRATULATION AND GOOD
WILL AND PLEDGE THEIR FAITH
TO THE UNFOLDING VISION

Plate Series I: The Presidents

W. Grant Egbert 1892-1924

Archives

The young Grant Egbert

Archives

Egbert on the steps of the Ithaca Conservatory of Music with Helen Doyle Durrett '13

George C. Williams 1924-1932

1906 Catalogue of Williams School of Expression

George C. Williams

Character Studies

A few of the many roles sucessfully portrayed by Mr. George C. Williams, President and Founder of The Williams School of Expression.

1928-29 Catalogue

As "Iago"

As "Shylock"

As "Tom Pinch"

Leonard B. Job 1932-1957

Archives

Howard I. Dillingham 1957-1970

Photo by: Fabian Bachrach

Ellis L. Phillips, Jr. 1970-1975

Photo by: Fabian Bachrach

James J. Whalen 1975-

IV.   The Job Years 1932 - 1957 (1)

Surviving: From the Great Depression through World War II

MANY years after his retirement, Leonard Bliss Job would wonder what madness has prompted him to resign a secure professorship at Ohio University in order to come to Ithaca College as dean, or what perverse fate had impelled him, after five months of direct observation of the College and its problems, to accept its presidency. He had come in large part because Frank P. Graves, New York State commissioner of education, had assured him that he was uniquely suited to take on an assignment that desperately needed doing. Once on the scene, he must have felt that the presidency would offer even greater opportunities for implementing those far-reaching changes he had perceived to be necessary. He certainly responded to the challenge of the rapidly worsening situation in 1931 - 1932. And almost a decade later, he may have been thinking of himself when he quoted some lines from Goethe to the Class of 1941: "Man supposes that he directs his life and governs his actions, when his existence is irretrievably under the control of Destiny." In any event, Chairman of the Board Louis P. Smith made the announcement to the community on March 7, 1932. Leonard B. Job, a newcomer to the campus, virtually unknown to the alumni, and acting president since February 16, would officially succeed George C. Williams as president of Ithaca College on June 1, 1932.

Job's background had peculiarly fitted him for the work that was to demand twenty-five years of his life. Born on December 23, 1891, he had spent his childhood on a small and far-from-prosperous farm in Putnam County, Indiana. There, the twelve-hour working day was normal, as he remembered in his unpublished autobiography (fittingly entitled *American Heritage*): the Job boys were lucky to get one holiday a year (the Fourth of July), and even then, they could be called back from the local swimming hole if some urgent chore required it. A gritty acceptance of what is, a determination to strike out for something better if ever the chance was offered, a fierce and bristling individualism, a horror of debt or indeed of any other form of beholdenness, an undeviating commitment to the ethic of hard work — those were the qualities essential for survival under the near-pioneer conditions of New Maysville. Those were the qualities that were to prove crucial to the survival of the Ithaca College of the 1930s and 1940s.

The young Leonard had escaped from the scrabbling existence of the family farm in characteristically American fashion — via education. He went on to the University of Indiana at Bloomington (earning his bachelor's degree in 1915 and the master's in 1919), taught in the elementary and secondary schools of that state, served as principal and superintendent, and, between 1919 and 1924, held several key positions with the Ohio State Department of Education. Author of several studies on school administration, he returned to graduate school at Columbia in 1924 and received his Ph.D. in 1926, the year he joined the faculty of the education department at Ohio University.

Out of this experience, Job had distilled a hard-headed educational realism that was, in its blunt, old-fashioned way, at the same time movingly idealistic. He could come down heavily on the side of order and discipline, decry the permissiveness of an educational system that had ceased to think of itself as acting *in loco parentis*, yet argue with equal force that education "on whatever level, must have as its major purpose the creation or promotion of change." In the 1950s, he would transform a college distinguished for its professional curricula by creating the College of Arts and Sciences, yet he could be devastating in his criticism of the grandiose and pompous slogans offered by the proponents of the liberal arts.

Some of us have already heard too much of "individual fulfillment in a creative environment." What does this mean? A thousand times I have tried to find out, yet nobody knows, nor have I found any concurrence in guesses. If educators could only know what they are doing and understand the meaning of what they say!

But even as he called for "Discarding the Deadwood of Tradition," ("Belief in the efficacy of Latin and languages, the classics, mathematics, pure science, and logic amounts almost to a fetish"), he simultaneously offered his alternatives: "men and women who are at peace with themselves and in harmony with others" or "a high degree of practical realism within the bounds of societal values."

That last phrase is vitally important for an understanding of Job's philosophy: educational institutions are created by the society in which they operate, for the purposes of that society; their ultimate justification lies in the production of useful citizens. "Education," he told the students in November 1932, "is what you have left after you have forgotten what you have learned." Sometimes, the tone was strident. In 1936, he inveighed against "the three R's: Rum, Rhythm, and Rebellion" (the last named dismissed as "a short way of expressing: 'I can't take it'".) Two years later, the *Ithacan* reporter wrote, with remarkable restraint, "Those who attended the assembly Friday, the 21st, found Doctor Job's somewhat reactionary speech very interesting.... Doctor Job rather discouraged criticism of existing standards and institu-

tions." Yet in Job's very first speech at Ithaca College, he had told the incoming students:

We are freshmen in Ithaca College together. Let us work hard together that we may find in this new adventure a richer and greater fullness of life

which is not so very different from the "individual fulfillment in a creative environment" concept that would later infuriate him.

As early as 1932, he was predicting to the members of the Adelphi society that with the decrease in the number of working hours in America, leisure would become increasingly important and its effective utilization one of the major unmet challenges of higher education. In 1944, he allowed himself an imaginative projection of an ideal collegiate program (in a speech made at the I.B.M. Corporation in Endicott, New York). In such a college, particularly qualified students would address themselves for four or five years to the arts, which Job envisioned in a sevenfold division: the communicative arts, the decorative arts, the arts of health and of homemaking, the meditative and speculative arts, the practical arts, and the fundamental arts. As in his social philosophy, Job's approach to education rejected much of the present for a dream of a future in which the virtues of nineteenth-century America might reemerge in new power.

Sometimes he despaired.

Without complete reordering of the American college campuses, without radical changes in our social systems, without almost complete change in our social structure, without complete revaluation of our ethical, social, and economic values, without radical redirection of the purposes of higher education, without unexpected changes in the operation of human chemistry, without the inculcation of a set of ethical, personal, and social values which may tend toward puritanism, American higher education will continue to retrogress in most of its human characteristics.

But mostly he doggedly persevered, in his own fashion. Defining happiness in the words of Robert Frost ("a sense of adequacy for the events of the day"), he would state, in his farewell address in 1957:

We will, I am confident, go on to higher and higher levels of attainment. . . . Greatness is a quality of those who do their work well and is a heritage which all may possess. . . . Greatness generates its own power — even in the performances of small tasks.

Perhaps he remembered being called after midnight, in the earlier years of his administration, to fire a water heater in a dormitory because a student returning from a dance demanded a hot bath.

Only rarely did he allow the underlying idealism to burn through with a note of shy lyricism. In a letter to the Class of 1936, he wrote:

To each of you I should like to give this talisman — not a trinket or charm to be worn about the neck but a positive influence working ever as a determiner of conduct, a five-star compass which shall ever burn into your consciousness. On one point will be the joyous sound of a singing heart. On another, the keenness of mind essential to rational action. A third point supports a strong body; on the fourth is the lodestone which compels generous, unselfish, and magnanimous actions toward mankind, and on the fifth point is the bright light of faith and hope for better opportunities that are to come. Take this talisman with you and your days will be joyous, your life worth while.

These phrases would be quoted to the freshmen of September 1977 by one of Job's successors, President James J. Whalen.

Job's most comprehensive personal statement was to come "eight years, seven months, twenty-seven days, and, I might add, four and one-half hours" after his departure from Ithaca in 1957. Back for the dedication of the new administration building on the South Hill campus (appropriately named Job Hall), he on October 23, 1965, focused the thoughts of a lifetime under the title "Why Administration?" Administration, he was quick to emphasize, meant the person ("And I mean it to be singular rather than plural in form") whose

responsibility it is to make sure that accomplishments mesh with means, that success results from planning based upon adequate, complete

information; from knowledgeable experiences; from competency in judging means and methods; from skill in timing; and from the finesse that only those who are aware that administration is an art are capable of using.

The administrator of a collegiate institution "must direct and control all events on campus" through his own sense of the history and philosophy of education, his intimate knowledge of the school over which he presides, and his grasp of "what he is doing and, above all, where the college is going." Job denounced governance through faculty committees: "the administrator will be well advised if he permits his teachers to earn their salaries as teachers." He waxed indignant over student disruptions at the University of California ("a few hundred beatniks and Castroites who successfully upset the educational life of 37,000 students"), to say nothing of "Easter vacation orgies at Daytona Beach and Miami." His kind of administrator must first and foremost be committed to the maintenance of order, by whatever means should prove necessary.

Moving on to the national scene, Job construed Martin Luther King's version of civil disobedience as "a valid and adequate definition of anarchy." (Curiously, in 1939 he had lauded another disciple of Thoreau: "Gandhi, in his pauperized simplicity, without any army, a balcony, or a radio, has done more for his people than have these wild men who glorify force and the show of force in international affairs.") His harsh words concerning the civil rights movement alienated many, perhaps most, of the trustees, administrators, faculty members, students, and parents in the audience. Yet he was careful to denounce *both* race riots, demonstrations, sit-ins *and* the Ku Klux Klan and police brutality. Behind his remarks lay an older America's faith in self-improvement, in *earned* status and privilege — a faith, that is to say, in the WASP way to recognition (and perhaps also, although he did not choose to make the point, the way of later immigrant waves such as the Irish and the Jews).

Decades should have been utilized by both white and non-white groups to elevate the capacities of non-whites to levels essential to successful possession and utilization of opportunities always open to the competent and the ambitious.

The wastefulness and officiousness of the federal government took their licks, especially as manifested in the control of public education, the Youth Corps, and the poverty program.

Job decried a parallel lack of firm administrative control on the international level. Under the misguided leadership of Eisenhower and Adlai Stevenson, the United Nations had passed "from a period of some potential to one of lasting and final innocuousness." Mainly he deplored

> *the admission of the new African nations, some not yet out of the stage of savagery and cannibalism, and other small splinter groups [whose] full membership in the U.N. is a tragedy of the first magnitude.*

Job unabashedly avowed his faith in colonialism and echoed James Morris's cry of "Long Live Imperialism!" Granted, the imperialists' business was profit, pure and simple. Nevertheless, from that self-interest, whether enlightened or otherwise, proceeded "roads and railroads, dams and canals, schools and colleges, telegraphs and newspapers, iron works and international trade" and whatever else was needed to bring nations out of the Dark Ages into the light of civilization.

The college administrator thus takes his place amid a distinguished company. In his admittedly smaller sphere of influence, he has but one essential function: "to establish and keep a proper balance . . . with an eye toward change." This, Job felt, is the administrator's real contribution (as surely it had been his own) to the education of youth.

Leonard Bliss Job has become a part of the Ithaca College legend. Some remember him as a hard-nosed businessman, who, by saying no to all requests that involved money, managed to keep a near-bankrupt college afloat. Others, recalling the 1965 address or the long series of baccalaureate speeches, have cast him in the role of archetypal reactionary — the denouncer of "this era of gaudy humanitarianism," of "the chattering and chirping of the reformers and world planners," who could link Hitler with Roosevelt, Stalin with "John L. Lewis, Sidney Hillman, R. J. Thomas, Philip Murray and all of their ilk who can be classed only as social highwaymen." It is true that he could reject the very concept of social security — "security and liberty of thought, enterprise, and action are as incompatible as oil and water." It is likewise true that he could applaud MacArthur's defiance of his commander-in-chief ("the testimony of a great soldier who has the integrity to place the welfare of his country above army protocol") or feel that Joseph McCarthy's activities "have earned the thanks of every American"; deplorable though his methods may at times have been, "it is doubtful that anything short of his efforts would have achieved notable beneficial results." Yet on balance, it is, I believe, nearer the truth to see him as a moralist in the American grain, a late-nineteenth-century individualist surviving uneasily amid the depersonalized welter of mid-century America.

> *If man is to be free, he must be liberated as far as can be from bodily discomforts and disease, from the drudgery and spirit-killing monotony of his employment, from want and poverty, from the demagogues and leeches which obstruct the proper functioning of his state, from the unsocial influences which thwart his efforts to rear his family in decency, from leprous dogmatism which makes his church less effective, from racial and other prejudices as may dwarf his spiritual development, and from the narrowness of life that is due to inadequate and imperfect means of communication*

or:

> *A large segment of our society has come to believe that asking is a satisfactory substitute for personal effort*

or again:

> *A democracy is that form of politically organized society in which the greatest possible measure of equality and justice is provided the members of the society, who are vouchsafed the freedom necessary to develop their own talents, initiative, and responsibility to the fullest extent.*

Cecil D. Rhodes, Andrew Carnegie, Theodore Roosevelt would have understood these words and applauded them. So too would Emerson and Carlyle. And even when the accents of conservatism came through most clearly, they sometimes proclaimed an authentic vision.

Loyalty demands that, knowing our friends, we still love them; that established institutions be supported although we may see in them great weaknesses; that laws be observed although at times they seem unfair; that obligations be met even though there is a legal and easy way to escape them; that the rights of others be respected although personal gain might be a result of violating them.

Edmund Burke, who also lived in a time of revolution and likewise sensed the terrible fragility of that veneer we call civilization, could hardly have stated the case more eloquently.

This, then, was the man who, as president, would guide the destinies of Ithaca College for exactly one quarter of a century. As "freshmen" dean, Job had set to work on September 15, 1931 — usually, he recalled, he was at his desk at 6:30 in the morning. Curricular reorganization headed the list of urgent problems. The era of affiliation had created a sprawling mass of more or less autonomous entities, with an appalling administrative overhead. Job proceeded to drop the "Preparatory Department," in which precollege music students had been receiving instruction since 1892. The departure of the Westminster Choir School as of September 1, 1932, not only pointed up the structural weakness of "affiliated" schools but also facilitated the reorganization of the remaining units. The curriculum of the Choir School continued for a while as the department of church music (under Ralph Ewing, with a Bulletin issued for 1932 - 1933), but by the middle of the decade, an essentially tripartite structure had been achieved. Albert Edmund Brown became director of a unified Department of Music; Laurence Hill and Adrian Newens held similar titles for the Department of Physical Education and the Department of Speech and Drama, respectively. Martin continued to operate his clinic and to train teachers in speech correction until in September 1936, he elected to move himself and his school to Bristol, Rhode Island. The 1936 - 1937 announcement of courses grouped a number of titles under the heading "Division of Liberal Arts and Education" (with no administrative superstructure); included were art, education (with offerings in psychology), ethics, history, sociology, economics, foreign languages, and science. A separate section was devoted to "English and Speech Arts," in which Shakespeare coexists, uneasily, with

physiotherapy, the latter apparently having developed out of Martin's clinical activities.

Compensation for administrative and faculty personnel also demanded immediate attention. With the suicide of Benjamin Johnson in July 1932, Job added the functions of treasurer-secretary to his own and thus drastically simplified the upper levels of administration. The absence of financial records make it impossible to determine just how much the senior administrative officers received during the final years of Williams's presidency. But as a survival of his Co-operative Plan, the deans enjoyed what were known as participation contracts — that is, they were expected to recruit students, were allotted 50 percent of the revenue generated by students within their departments, paid their faculties out of it, and kept the balance. The possibilities for abuse were self-evident, and one of Job's early acts as president was to cancel all the participation contracts and to put the deans on salary. Since $6,000 represented a substantial cut for them, he felt obliged to reduce his own salary to the same figure; unlike them, he was not always able to collect it.

Faculty salaries were equally chaotic. A part-time professor of history received $1,000 a year for a twenty-one hour a week teaching load; a psychology professor, hired by the hour, had created so many sections of her course that her income was as much as five times that of the history professor. Job placed all faculty members on salary; the psychology professor then discovered that all of her students could conveniently be taught in one class. But one piano instructor strenuously protested when told that she could no longer teach seventy hours a week.

Job's Board of Trustees had been reorganized just before he assumed the presidency. In 1931 - 1932, State Commissioner of Education Horner had spelled out a five-point program for the college, to be implemented "prior to the registration of degrees recently authorized." One of these stipulations was that all administrators should resign from the Board. Williams, Brown, Hill, Williamson, and Johnson accordingly had submitted their resignations as trustees as of January 18, 1932. This left a Board of five members; five more were added in March 1932. All of these were local, with the exception of Mrs. Talbott, the patroness of the Westminster Choir School (who resigned after the departure of that group for Princeton).

In the mid-thirties, there was an effort to secure trustees of

world or national renown, representative of the major interests of the College. Sergei Rachmaninoff was elected in 1934,
as was also Grantland Rice. Two years later, Brock Pember-
ton, "noted theatrical producer of New York," was added.
There is no record that these luminaries ever attended Board
meetings or benefited the College in any measurable way.
Chairing the Board from November 1933 to May 1936 was a
colorful figure, Vladimir Karapetoff. Karapetoff had been
born in Russia and had come to the United States as a
traveling fellow of the Polytechnic Institute of Leningrad.
Since 1908, he had been professor of electrical engineering at
Cornell and later became chairman of the physics department
there. Adviser to two electrical corporations as well as to the
U.S. Navy, friend of Einstein, he was elected to the Board as
"an outstanding figure in the world of electrical science whose
avocation is music." He was credited with a volume of poetry,
Rhythmical Tales of Stormy Years, and was an accomplished
pianist and cellist. In 1936, he broadcast a piano recital from
Radio City.

But for all this glitter of names and personalities, the Board
was unable to discover new sources of income for the floun-
dering college. None of the periodic reorganizations, restruc-
turings, and refinancing had ever succeeded in establishing a
sound financial basis for its work. Under the best of times, its
operations had been marginal; now, it was facing the full
impact of the Great Depression. Enrollment, for all practical
purposes the school's only source of income, plummeted. In
the fall of 1931, 559 students had registered; a year later, there
were 424, and in 1933, only 352. And not all of these were
paying full tuition: a student announcing that he had only a
hundred dollars was accepted on the principle that a hundred
dollars was certainly better than nothing. The official correspondence of the period makes for melancholy reading.

(To the president of the Ithaca Trust Company, July 22,
1933):

> *The College is experiencing some difficulty in mak-
> ing collections fast enough to meet its payroll. We
> have fallen behind somewhat in paying the salaries of
> certain administrative officers in the College. We do
> not have any additional assets to offer as security for
> an increased loan at the Trust Company. In view of
> this fact, it occurred to me that the Trust Company*

> *might be willing to advance to the College a sum of
> money on College notes endorsed by the executive
> officers individually, in the amounts due them. . . .*

(To the same bank, on May 29, 1934):

> *You are no doubt familiar with the financial position
> of Ithaca College. We should like nothing better than
> to reduce our indebtedness. It is not possible for us to
> do so now.*

In an annual report delivered to the Board in October 1933,
Job wrote:

> *It is hardly possible to overstate the magnitude of our
> financial problems. . . . As I view the year in retro-
> spect, I marvel at the fact that we were able to act at
> all.*

Yet the situation continued to deteriorate. Perhaps there was
a considerable measure of practical wisdom in the advice said
to have been given by Cornell's President Farrand to Board
Chairman Smith:

> *You have an impossible job. That college can't possi-
> bly succeed. My suggestion is that you go down the
> hill, close the college down, lock the doors, and
> throw the keys in Lake Cayuga.*

In Job's dour comment, "President Farrand seemed to know
that 'it could not be done.' I did not know, so I tried."

The Board minutes of the 1930s are a chronicle of ineffectual measures to stave off disaster. Salaries were cut and cut
again. With all of the real estate already mortgaged up to the
hilt, the College took out a "chattel" mortgage on the
remainder of its physical possessions. The infirmary was
closed in October 1933 and the health services moved to
rooms in Williams Hall. The previous February, the Board
entertained the suggestion that the College "be on the lookout
for other institutions that might consider consolidating with
Ithaca College"; one such presumably stronger institution,
the New York College of Music, was discussed at the meeting
of October 8, 1934. The expedient of issuing debentures was
explored on several occasions, inconclusively; tentative (and

unavailing) approaches were made to federal agencies such as the Reconstruction Finance Corporation, the Federal Housing Administration, and the Public Works Administration. Although the alumni organization was strengthened by the appointment of John P. E. Brown as full-time alumni secretary in 1935, little income was forthcoming from that source, even though, on March 15, 1935, the Board voted to "prosecute the drive for students to the limit" by offering a bounty of $25 a head to alumni willing to engage in recruiting activities. Current students also shared in this inducement, which was rescinded in February 1937. Every effort was made to collect from delinquent student accounts. In March 1935, the College offered a 15 percent discount to its debtors; by November of that year, student notes were assigned to the two local banks for collection (funds thus received to be applied to the interest owed by the College); in March 1936, the president was authorized to sell "certain college obligations" to a private collection agency for seventy-five cents on the dollar.

Some of the expedients considered were wild in the extreme. On October 8, 1934, after a discussion of possible approaches to foundations, it was proposed that a member of the State College of Home Economics at Cornell be utilized "as a means of contacting Mrs. Eleanor Roosevelt." On May 24, 1935, the Board debated and rejected a "baby contest scholarship" as a fund-raising gimmick, on the grounds that it could not place future Boards under such an obligation.

But nothing worked. Even the physical plant was falling into such disrepair as to be virtually uninhabitable. The banks loomed ominously in the background. The minutes of July 25, 1935, noted, with considerable understatement, "the banks are becoming rather urgent in their request that some interest may be paid." On September 3, 1935, after "a very lengthy discussion of the financial problems confronting the college," the trustees reached one firm conclusion.

The consensus of opinion seemed to be that the great need of the institution is more adequate financing. The opinion was also expressed that there has been too little action.

Help came — from the Ithaca business community.
As early as 1933 - 1934, it was rumored that a civic committee was about to be formed to consider the plight of the College. In December 1935, the Board received a communica-

tion from the Chamber of Commerce expressing its willingness to support any program "looking toward a more firmly established institution," and joint meetings of committees from the Board and from the Chamber of Commerce were clearly under way by the spring of 1936. The upshot of these efforts was a document called the "Moratorium Agreement," dated June 5, 1936. In it, the principal creditors (the local banks and merchants) recognized that the College's indebtedness amounted to $339,559 and that it was wholly unable "to meet installments of interest and principal on the said indebtedness and maintain its buildings and equipment in proper and suitable condition for carrying on its education program." They therefore wrote off all interest due before June 5, 1936, agreed to 3 percent for the next three years and to 4 percent for the two years after that, and even declared a moratorium for the entire five-year period, the interest to accrue at the rate of 6 percent on all obligations. In return, certain controls over the College's budget were set up, and a five-man "Finance Committee" was created. Three of its members were elected by the creditors, two by the Board; the representatives of the creditors were to attend all Board meetings with voice but without vote; the finance committee had power, by majority vote, to cancel the Moratorium Agreement if at any time it became convinced that the College was adopting measures or programs which drastically interfered with the interests of the creditors and mortgagees.

The Moratorium Agreement solved none of the fundamental problems of the institution; at best, it gained the College a few months' time. But it did bring to the Board, through the finance committee, a man whose assistance would prove of incalculable value — Clifford A. Allanson, an executive of Rothschilds Department Store. Allanson immediately recognized that the moratorium on interest payments was the merest of palliatives; more drastic measures were clearly indicated. In March 1937, he arranged for a meeting of about twenty-five Ithaca businessmen, united by the conviction that the College was a community asset and therefore deserving of their counsel and help. President Job bleakly summarized the situation.

Can the college pay its debts? Can it pay mortgage interest? Can it pay for the past two years of its fuel supply? Can it pay past-due insurance premiums? Can it pay $10,000 for food supplies delivered last

*year to the college dining hall? Can it pay its furnish-
ings bill at Rothschilds? Can it pay the past year's
laundry bills?*

The answer to all of these questions was of course a resound-
ing no. Job then defined the options. The College could of
course be forced into immediate bankruptcy. But

*bankruptcy will get you nothing on your accounts.
Every conceivable piece of property at the college is
mortgaged. Even the knives, forks, and spoons in the
dining room are mortgaged. The mortgage holders
will take everything and will still suffer losses.*

The other possibility was to write off the past — all outstanding unsecured obligations, principal as well as interest — in
the recognition that the College could still make vital contributions to the economy of the Ithaca area. Job recalls that all
but one of the merchants present came eventually to accept
this second position, even the grocer who had announced that
"when the bones of the college are picked, I will have my feet
under the table." A letter from another grocer, F. A. Wilcox
of Atwater's store, movingly summarizes their collective act
of faith in the future of the College.

*We are enclosing a college note of $1400 as tangible
evidence of the cancellation of this obligation. While
we can hardly say that it is a pleasure ever to write off
an obligation this comes the nearest to being a pleasure that has come within my experience.*

*For years we have all known that the College could
not carry its burden of debt and progress at all, or
even continue to operate. While that debt was not the
fault of any of us today, this refinancing does mean a
great deal to all of us. To me, it means a continuation
of the College in Ithaca and to you and the directors,
it should mean the removal of a burden which has
been tremendous.*

Thus, at one stroke, more than $100,000 in unsecured
obligations was wiped off the books. This second document,
the "Cancellation Agreement," was signed on November 17,
1937. For its part, the College formally pledged that it would
not "enter into a contract for the removal of the college from
Ithaca during the life of the said agreement." This action
rescinded an earlier Board resolution that had revealed the
College's secret weapon — the threat of leaving the Ithaca
area. On February 2, 1937, the Board had decided to seek a
firm offer for relocation in another city and then negotiate
with the Ithaca Chamber of Commerce on the strength of
that offer. Several possibilities had already been explored.
The Binghamton Chamber of Commerce had expressed an
interest in Ithaca College and had offered two unused buildings (an armory and a former Masonic temple). But Job was
not attracted by the prospect of yet another set of *old* buildings. Binghamton also possessed an abandoned racetrack,
which a wealthy widow had inherited from her husband.
Plans were drawn up for the utilization of this property, and
every effort was made to persuade the heiress to underwrite
the costs of a new campus. Nothing came of it, however.
Another nearby possibility was Endicott, New York, the site
of a growing I.B.M. plant. President Job traveled to New
York City to present his vision to Thomas J. Watson, but
again to no avail. The idea of relocation will figure prominently in the history of the College after World War II.
Meanwhile, it played some role in securing massive local
relief from the school's financial burdens.

Hence, the late thirties were unmistakably better years for
Ithaca College. Happily, the refinancing of the institution
coincided with an upturn in enrollment. After a low of 352 in
September 1933, the figures increased slowly, then improved
dramatically: 490 in 1937; 552 in 1938; 629 in 1939 and also in
1940. Raises in salaries for many members of the administration and faculty were voted in October 1937, and in February
1938, the Board heard from the president that space was being
taxed to the limit and that thought should be given to plans
for a new gymnasium with several modern classrooms. In
May, the trustees considered the acquisition of a new home
for the president at 2 Fountain Place, and in June an $18,500
mortgage was authorized to effect that purchase. Continuing
negotiation and in some cases litigation successfully reduced
the principal on some of the older mortgages.

Nonetheless, Job emphatically reminded his trustees that
the Cancellation Agreement was not the definitive answer to
the fiscal problems of the College and urged a vigorous fund-
raising program. The result was the creation, in May 1938, of
the Ithaca College council, under the direction of Adrian
Newens. The charge to the council was two-fold: "to promote

in every legitimate way the welfare and growth of the college through publicity" and "to lay and carry out plans for raising college funds from (a) alumni and friends, and (b) foundations and persons of wealth who may become interested in the work of the college." Instructed to schedule its operations over a period of three to five years, the council in effect replaced the alumni office, which had been headed by John P. E. Brown from 1935 to 1938. The announcement of this change in the May 1939 issue of the *Alumni News* must have seemed somewhat chilling to the graduates.

> *Ithaca College Alumni will probably never be able to contribute largely to funds so necessary to the growth of the College. . . . They need not fear the development of a college program that will depend basically upon Alumni to the extent that Alumni will feel any sense of imposition or embarrassment.*

A year later, this negativism yielded to a more constructive approach with the publication of a brochure entitled *A Message to the Alumni of Ithaca College from the Board of Trustees*. The accomplishments of the years were passed in review, the president was lauded as an astute and compassionate administrator, the educational achievements of the institution were extolled. Nevertheless,

> *the time has now come when definite improvements must be made in the physical aspects of the college. The out-moded buildings cannot last long without repairs which would cost more than the value of the structures would warrant. Even class rooms are at a premium. The auditorium will seat only two-thirds of the student population.*

The alumni were urged to contribute, to send more and better students, to ferret out persons of wealth within their communities, whose money might be diverted from "unimportant, even useless projects" and turned into useful channels such as Ithaca College. Somewhat defensively, the trustees pleaded for alumni confidence, "having preserved for them the institution from which they received their diplomas and degrees."

> *To build your college as it should be built, it will take more than just great concepts, more than a vigorous board of trustees, more than a superior administra-*

tor, more than a grand staff of faculty members, more than a loyal alumni, more than a large body of gifted students, more even than a great sum of money. It will take all these things and much more.

The precise nature of that additional something was not specified.

The Ithaca College council lasted from 1938 to 1942 and raised in those four years only $17,227.50, partly in cash but mostly in pledges. The president continued to remind the trustees that the institution's underlying problems remained unresolved; the 1940s would, in fact, bring another financial crisis. But the *Message to the Alumni* preferred to stress the fact that in 1942, the College would be fifty years old and hence a full-scale celebration of that anniversary was in order. John P. E. Brown was appointed chairman of the anniversary committee, which included administration, faculty, and alumni; and activities were scheduled for the entire year of 1941 - 1942. Local alumni groups held special meetings; in Ithaca, there were concerts of the College symphonic band, the College choir, the College symphony orchestra, a piano recital, and a gala performance of Verdi's *Manzoni Requiem*, with four alumni (including Margaret Daum) as guest soloists. The drama department mounted two plays, *The Kingdom of God* in March and Goethe's *Faust* in April; and Physical Education arranged a Triangle Track Meet with Cortland and Stroudsburg. The *Cayugan* published a half-century issue, and the *Ithaca Journal* gave pages of coverage to the College's "Half Century of Advancement." Tributes poured in from other institutions, from the White House, from Wendell Willkie, from Governor Herbert Lehman.

This golden year of celebration culminated on the weekend of May 1 - 3, with an impressive gathering of alumni and friends. Chairman of the Board Clifford A. Allanson presided over a banquet at the Hotel Ithaca, at which the principal address was given by Dr. George Drayton Strayer of Columbia University. A high point of that evening was the presentation of a portrait in oils of President Job, painted by Olaf M. Brauner, the artist himself being present for the occasion. The following day, the alumni met for a special memorial program in tribute to founder W. Grant Egbert. These events were described in a handsome *Commemoration Program*, which included a brief history of the College (not entirely accurate in its details) by Adrian M. Newens, which concluded:

So fifty years of the institution have passed into history. It began in the deep adversities in the early nineties; it survived the first world war and the economic reverses that followed; it came through the depression and repression of the thirties; it begins its second half century at the outset of another world conflict. What is ahead? No one knows, except that the conditions which shall face the College will be the same conditions which all educational institutions must encounter. Encouraged by the pervading spirit of the founder, W. Grant Egbert, and that early group of pioneers, enlivened by faith and hope in the newer mission of the institution, no flag of truce or surrender is raised on this present elevation as we pause to contemplate what the next great objective shall be.

Newens was entirely correct in hinting, through his reference to "another world conflict," that December 7, 1941, while not listed in the calendar events for the anniversary year, was of crucial significance for the future of the College.

President Job began his second decade in office on a note of weariness, perhaps even of exhaustion:

Some years ago I heard the president of a midwestern university say on the occasion of his inauguration that ten years is long enough for any man to serve as president of a university. . . . Throughout the past two years and more particularly during the last year your president has increasingly realized that much of the freshness and vigor which he brought to his present tasks have been expended and some of it, perhaps, wasted in trying to accomplish what now appears to have been impossible tasks and in a vain attempt to carry an imponderable burden. . . The future prospects of the college still appear obscure to me and I am beginning to wonder if the many people who have told me during these years that effort expended in preserving the college is wasted effort may not have been much wiser than I.

Even before Pearl Harbor, the shadow of war had fallen upon the College's registration figures. That September, there were only 551 students, and 504 the following year: some had been drafted, others elected to work at high salaries in defense plants rather than attend college. Job articulated these concerns early in the fall of 1941.

While the loss of students this year, unless it is much greater than is anticipated, will not seriously inconvenience us or greatly threaten the successful operation of the college, continuation of the trend over a three-year period will, in all probability be serious if not fatal to the institution unless generous financial help is obtained from sources hitherto untapped.

A year later, his evaluation of the situation was even more sombre.

The immediate prospect of the draft age being lowered to include eighteen and nineteen year old men will, if realized, take most of the men from the campus. It is difficult to anticipate any result other than the closing of the College for the duration should all able-bodied men withdraw from college.

By September 1943, his worst fears seemed virtually to be realized. In the grimmest of depression years, there had been 352 students. Now, there were only 225 — 51 men and 174 women. The figures for 1944 were only a shade better.

Ithaca College was in fact more vulnerable than most educational institutions to the strains of wartime. To be sure, it had, for the first time in its history, a substantial reserve fund (amounting to $195,000 as of July 1, 1943) — sufficient, it was estimated, to weather several bad years. But its curricular specializations precluded the establishment of programs for the on-campus training of servicemen: the College provided minimal instruction in mathematics and foreign languages and next to nothing in the sciences. The amendment of the Charter in March 1943 permitted the conferring of master's and honorary degrees as well as some additional undergraduate degrees, but these new rights were of negligible significance as long as the war continued. A major in the fine arts was announced in the hope of attracting more women, but not one student applied: there were all too obviously no facilities for such a program, no artist-in-residence, no art gallery. Instruction in nursing was slightly more successful. Sections of 2 Fountain Place were utilized for this purpose, and arrangements were worked out with the Tompkins County Hospital. But again, the lack of science and of laboratories was crippling; and, further, since the College as a whole was not accredited, the nursing program was unable to secure appropriate accreditation. Job lamented the pervasive shabbiness of the physical plant as a factor in discouraging even women students from applying.

Classrooms, lobbies, offices, and studios are, for the most part, unattractive and often definitely dirty. There are no places where students congregate in numbers that are bright, clean, cheerful, and conducive to the finer types of college life. I frequently despair of effecting any worthwhile change in this situation because there seems no place to start, none to end, and no funds with which to accomplish observable results.

Yet in his report for 1942 - 1943, he moved beyond this mood of despondency to look squarely at the challenge of the future. The primary objective for the College must be accreditation.

Its operation is handicapped; its graduates, thwarted in their attempts to procure deserved professional advancement because Ithaca College credits are not "negotiable on the big board" without strong individual action on their behalf by the president of the College and often by the State Department of Education.

Accreditation was impossible without a new plant, new programs in the liberal arts — it required, in short, a considerable amount of money beyond the present resources of the College. Job concluded this report of July 1943 by raising once again the possibility of relocation in another city. And despite his deep-seated conviction that fund-raising was the responsibility of the trustees rather than of the president, he announced his firm determination

to make a special order of business during the year the exploration of certain known possibilities out of which might conceivably come considerable money for use in Ithaca or for the relocation of the College.

There are no surviving annual reports for 1944 - 1945 or for 1945 - 1946: perhaps those years were too bleak to chronicle, or the record too dismal to preserve. But the registrar's statistics began to show improvement by 1945 (from 287 to 463 students), and then the deluge of returning G.I.s, for which the College was almost wholly unprepared — 1,192 students in 1946; 1,444 in 1947. The income generated was of course most gratifying. By 1948 - 1949, the College's indebtedness was reduced to zero, for the first time in its almost sixty years of operation. But, Job warned, "to expect that such a favorable situation will long continue, is tempting fate too far."

In fact, it soon became apparent that the College was not going to benefit significantly from public funds allotted directly to institutions for the educational advantage of returning veterans. New York State had set aside some $15 million for such purposes, but apart from some temporary housing units and a modest sum for the preparation of their site, the College's applications proved fruitless.

Requests have been made for aid in providing educational facilities but none has been forthcoming. Items which cover our greatest need have been provided other institutions in quantity — classrooms, laboratories, offices, libraries — but not one foot of such space has been awarded by the State to us.

Coping as best he could with the immediate population explosion ("the college is ill-equipped to handle effectively even half this number"), Job proceeded with his plans for relocation.

The idea was of course far from new. Egbert had been urged to move his Conservatory to a larger city and reputedly replied, "No, I won't go through life with the blot of a failure." We have discussed the possibility of a move to Binghamton or Endicott and noted the Board's commitment not to leave the Ithaca area as a corollary to the Cancellation Agreement of 1937. Despite that pledge, the College had, in 1946, begun active negotiations with the City of Utica. Job reported to the trustees that perhaps as much as $2 million might be made available and asked for a resolution that would permit public discussion of the College's interest in Utica's proposal. Chairman Allanson, by now president of Allanson-Hudson, Inc., vigorously opposed such action. Adequate facilities could be provided in Ithaca, he maintained; the College was an integral part of the Ithaca community and indeed was obligated to remain because of the Cancellation Agreement. The liveliness of the debate breaks through the drab prose of the minutes:

> *Chairman Allanson stated further that he would refuse to recognize any action of the Board to encourage the consideration of such a proposal and that he would disavow any responsibility for it. He insisted that no action be taken until a meeting could be held with absent members present and announced that he would "fight like hell" to keep the College in Ithaca.*

The motion was withdrawn.

But the Board had changed character after World War II, becoming far less local in its representation. Margaret Daum '28, star of radio and opera and long active in the alumni association, served from 1943 to 1948. John P. E. Brown provided links not only with the alumni groups but with important personages in the New York City area. George E. Stringfellow, vice-president of the Thomas Edison Company, came to give the commencement speech in 1945 and was promptly elected to the Board; in 1947, he would succeed Allanson as chairman. Conductor Gustave Haenschen began his long years of service as trustee in 1946. Major-General Frank E. Keating would be elected in 1948; his being married to Miss Daum causing some dissension on the Board, he chose to resign when she was not reelected. Captain Eddie Rickenbacker and Albert R. Hawkes (former senator from New Jersey) would arrive in 1949. It is perhaps an indication of this involvement of the world beyond Ithaca that in October 1947, the Board meeting was held, for the first time so far as I can determine, out of town — "in the offices of Mr. Stringfellow" (in West Orange, N.J.).

Hence, Allanson soon found himself in a minority. On December 13, 1946, the Board voted to express its willingness to give full and fair consideration to such proposals as may be submitted to it for the removal of the College to another locality or site, provided such proposals are made in good faith and are sufficiently substantial to warrant their consideration by the Board in the best interests of the College. But another vote would go against the proponents of relocation: the citizens of Utica rejected, by a narrow margin, a proposed bond issue that would have financed the estab-

lishment of another college in their area.

Job's interest was then directed toward the acquisition of an abandoned army camp (Madison Barracks) at Sackets Harbor on Lake Champlain. Its advantages were many: a gymnasium, a drill field suitable for collegiate sports programs, acceptable classroom space, housing that could accommodate several thousand students, sixty or seventy dwellings or apartments suitable for faculty use. It is reported that at least one faculty member actually visited the site and picked out his home in the officers' quarters. Job found it necessary to secure a cease-and-desist order to prevent Syracuse University from cannibalizing the plant and later to keep New York State from taking it over. But in the end, the obstacles proved insurmountable. Several million dollars would have been needed to adapt the property to academic uses; the area was remote from the College's established recruiting territory and the climate forbidding; the cost of moving would have been staggering. And, as war surplus property, the camp could always be reclaimed by the federal government if need arose.

So Sackets Harbor joined the growing list of unrealized possibilities, and Job began to reexamine options nearer at hand. An architect was commissioned to draw up a model of a new downtown campus, to be constructed in the area sloping up East Hill between East Buffalo Street and Cascadilla Gorge. Once again, cost proved to be an effective deterrent: at least $500,000 to acquire the land and $6 million for building. The best area for the development of a new campus in Ithaca, Job concluded, "lies on South Hill above the Coddington Road" — the approximate site on which President Williams had prematurely taken an option back in the 1920s.

The College was not ready to move in that direction, however. A new vice-president would present a case for yet another location — this time, White Plains.

There had been other additions to the administrative staff. As early as October 1934, Job's burden had been somewhat lightened by the appointment of Robert K. Devricks as College secretary. William M. Grimshaw arrived as professor of physical education in 1942, became director of Graduate Studies in the spring of 1945, and proved to be one of Job's most useful assistants. In 1948, Earl E. Clarke was called from the vice-presidency of the Polytechnic Institute in Puerto Rico to become dean of "Academic Subjects" and, shortly thereafter, dean of the newly created General College.

Joining this new administrative team of the late 1940s was

Vice-President Charles E. Haines, formerly president of Pueblo Junior College. For some time, the Board had been interested in a more professional approach to fund-raising and development. Several well-known firms were considered at the meeting of October 1947, and the John Price Jones Corporation was instructed to prepare a comprehensive study of the College. This report was considered in some detail at the May 1949 meeting, at which time it was decided not to use a professional firm but rather to engage the services of Dr. Haines.

To Job, the John Price Jones report was superficial except in those instances where it was downright wrong. His opinion of his new vice-president was somewhat less than enthusiastic, especially after the latter presented, in October 1949, his "Report of the Vice President of Ithaca College to the Board of Trustees" — the very title must have seemed an affront to the presidential office.

Haines had already made something of a splash with an elaborately printed brochure, *Ithaca College: 57 Years of Private Enterprise* — a slick promotional effort outrageously puffing the College, both in words and pictures, and unmistakably pitched toward the business establishment.

> *The feasibility of financing operating costs from current revenues derived from student tuition and fees has been proved by Ithaca College through a long record of performance. Unless a deliberate effort is made to undermine private education by hostile public policy, there is reason to expect that this record of achievement can be successfully maintained and that a well-managed private college will continue to enjoy the custom and goodwill of a satisfied clientele.*

The appeal for support was tactfully muted: the College "gladly submits the record for others to examine and appraise." If only funds for a new plant could be provided, the College could continue as the educational model of a private business, proudly operating "without benefit of endowments, taxes, or subsidies." An editorial in the *Ithacan* wistfully noted that most of the students would settle for less free enterprise and more endowment money.

This brochure alluded discreetly to the possibility of relocation; a letter to a Board member suggested that it could be followed "by a concerted effort to organize supporting senti-

ment in chambers of commerce or other civic groups." In any event, Haines zeroed in on the target of relocation in his report to the Board of Trustees.

Reviewing earlier efforts "in such areas as Binghamton, Utica, Glens Falls, Sackets Harbor, Middletown, Auburn, and Westchester," he came down hard for the last mentioned, that is, White Plains. It had, he maintained, a population of 600,000, including 40,000 youth of college age, and one of the highest concentrations of wealth of any area in the United States.

> *By no stretch of the imagination is it conceivable that a multi-million-dollar sum could be raised in Ithaca. In Westchester, on the other hand, a single individual may offer a sum of $5,000,000 to a college in which he is interested. The "glamor" character of some of Ithaca College's specializations, such as music, drama, radio, and sports, could conceivably attract the patronage of well-to-do persons residing in an area where these specializations were practiced. A fine symphony orchestra performance in the County Center at White Plains, or a dramatic production with a Broadway celebrity as guest star, might conceivably receive favorable attention from patrons of the arts, whereas a comparable performance in Ithaca would fall on barren ground as far as substantial financial aid was concerned. Good bait catches big fish only where big fish are swimming.*

A University of Westchester, he concluded,

> *can be expected to take its place among the great universities of the country, and [its] founders who had the courage of their convictions will be honored in the same way that Ezra Cornell and Andrew D. White are honored today.*

Haines's report was discussed at length at the Board meeting of May 1949, the president's reaction being predictably negative. In fact, he would himself visit White Plains in the early 1950s to inspect a mansion and its surrounding acres as a possible home for the College. But by the time Haines resigned in November 1949, the Board had already authorized the purchase of the acreage on South Hill. Haines had rather naturally become somewhat impatient, Job observed tartly, when Ithaca College had "failed to provide adequate outlets for [his] capacities."

By choice or necessity, then, Ithaca College would remain true to the geographic implications of its name. The good news was announced, and both alumni and community breathed a sigh of relief. In the words of Claude L. Kulp, president of the Chamber of Commerce,

> *It is gratifying to know that this institution of which we are very proud will continue to be known as Ithaca College and will always be a cherished local institution.*

No problems had been solved, and surely no one knew just how to proceed. But a turning point had been reached, and passed, in College planning.

Nevertheless, buying acreage was one thing; building something on those acres was to prove far more difficult. The College's efforts at fund-raising had never proved conspicuously successful. As we have seen, the Ithaca College council (1938 - 1942) had produced no significant new resources. A fresh impetus came from an alumna at the 1948 reunion: Florence Sidur '33 expressed the desire "to do something to encourage greater alumni participation," and by the following year, she and her husband, Herman Muller, formally proposed the establishment of a "Loyalty Fund," which they were prepared to inaugurate with an anonymous gift of $1,000. Job announced the formation of the appropriate committee in February 1949 (it included Mrs. Muller, Lillian Vail, Robert Boothroyd, Joseph Short, and Ben Light, among others), and the drive was under way. But before the year was over, Vice-President Haines had resigned, and the Loyalty Fund was left without adequate administrative support. Its volunteer alumni "trustees" attempted valiantly to cope with an impossible assignment; their work was made even more difficult by College alumni releases that stressed recruiting rather than giving.

> *Sending I.C. student prospects is one of the ways that alumni can assist the college without spending much time, effort, or money*

or:

> *One good student is the equivalent of a $500 gift.*

This assessment was no doubt realistic, but hardly a stimulus to the writing of checks of any size. By 1950, with little collected beyond the Muller contributions, the Loyalty Fund board declared that they were unable to continue with their work and that they considered their assignment terminated.

The College then turned temporarily from the dreary work of fund-raising to a far more enjoyable activity — a grandiose celebration of the indisputable fact that the twentieth century had just passed its mid-point.

On May 11 and 12, 1951, after months of well-organized planning, some 2,400 persons converged upon Ithaca for the "Mid-Century Peace Convocation." Invitations had been mailed to 15,000 alumni and friends; over four hundred leading citizens of the city of Ithaca and its surrounding area had agreed to serve as a sponsoring committee. The theme of the convocation was proclaimed as one of deep and abiding concern to every American — how to "Reach the Minds and Hearts of Men throughout the World to Promote International Understanding and World Peace." Two days of speeches and panel discussions were scheduled — at Foster Hall in the Senior High School, at the Strand Theater, at Ide's Drome. George V. Denny, Jr., founder and moderator of American's Town Meeting of the Air ("the man who brought the town meeting back to America") beamed from the front page of the announcement flyer. Joining Denny was a battery of distinguished guests: James A. Farley, former postmaster general (known, it was stated, for "his amazing memory for names and faces" but who confused the name of the Metropolitan star who preceded him on the program); Benjamin A. Cohen, assistant secretary general of the United Nations; Gene Tunney, billed not only as former heavyweight champion of the world but also as businessman and author of *A Man Must Fight* and *Arms for Living*; Judge Justin Miller, chairman of the board and general counsel of the National Association of Radio and Television Broadcasters; Dorothy Kirsten and Eleanor Steber; conductor Gustave Haenschen; Michael R. Hanna, general manager of WHCU, with a distinguished record in promoting public service broadcasting; Mark Woods, of the American Broadcasting Company; George E. Stringfellow, of the Edison Corporation; Carroll V. Newsom, associate commissioner for higher education in New York; Leon C. Stowell, president of the Underwood Corporation, and President Job.

The speeches, read after more than a quarter of a century, are enthusiastic restatements of the hopes (and the fears) of the era.

Behind all of our relations with our fellow beings there must be a common faith — faith in the fundamental integrity of man, in his constant effort to realize his highest ideals and his essential nearness to God. . . .

I sometimes think that Thomas Jefferson meant by "the pursuit of happiness" the winning of friends. . . .

Today our democratic way of life is challenged by a sinister philosophy that requires all men to be tools of the state. . . . We must recognize also that there are persistent efforts on the part of communist agents to create dissension upon the campuses of our institutions. Recently a friend of mine provided me with a photostatic copy of an article that appeared in a Communist publication. . . .

Perhaps the Olympic games may prove a more potent factor in establishing world peace than the threat of the atomic bomb!...

The most common ground of understanding between men from the beginning of all human relationships has been business. . . .

Of the ability and power of radio, and more particularly of television, to reach and to influence the minds and hearts of men there can be no question. . . .

The College Choir sang; the band and symphony orchestra performed creditably; athletic events filled up the busy weekend. Perhaps the liveliest gathering of all was the alumni luncheon at which some eighteen distinguished graduates were honored with appropriate citations. Included among them were M. Ethel Nichols '97, surviving member of the first graduating class of two; Lt. Col. George S. Howard '24, chief of bands and music for the U.S. Air Force; Robert M. deLany '30, of the American Red Cross; Mrs. Carl Vail '21, whose citation paid tribute to her untiring work in alumni relations;

Margaret Daum '28; and Eddie Sawyer '35, manager of the Philadelphia Phillies.

The mid-century convocation was, in short, an all-out effort in public relations. It certainly succeeded in its immediate objective: to assemble the largest and most prestigious throng of guests in the sixty years of the College's history. The Board recorded its satisfaction, though noting the high cost of public relations to date (some $25,000). An outside consultant agreed that the College had received exemplary coverage in the newspapers of upstate New York. Several of the distinguished guests would become members of the Board of Trustees.

But the key question remained unanswered. Would there be more dollars to meet the essential needs of the institution? And so, after all the glitter and the speech making and the music, the hard realities of development had to be faced anew.

In June 1950, Marts and Lundy had been engaged to do a survey of the College, and Earle Snelgrove had been appointed assistant to the president with the specific assignment of working with that outside firm. Snelgrove served from February to October 1951, at which time Howard I. Dillingham was appointed to replace him, arriving in December of that year.

In a report to Job and the trustees, dated February 29, 1952, Marts and Lundy commented on the progress of the Development Fund program. Their initial survey had determined that perhaps $150,000 could be raised from the local community and another $100,000 from the alumni — this over a ten-year period, with competent direction, preferably someone trained by themselves; it had also tactfully been suggested that strengthening the Board of Trustees was very much in order. The mid-century convocation had provided good initial publicity, and between September and December 1951, the local campaign had realized approximately $160,000 in cash and (again, mostly) pledges. The alumni campaign launched early in January 1952 under the enthusiastic leadership of Joseph Short '35 was already showing promise: leadership meetings were being organized in New York City and elsewhere. Finding the big givers remained a problem, the consultants concluded, but the resignations of Stringfellow and Rickenbacker had opened up vacancies on the Board that could perhaps be filled by men with access to persons of substantial wealth.

But despite this sanguine report, Job pointed out to the

trustees on the very next day that, so far, disbursements to Marts and Lundy had amounted to twice the amount of money received. Their connection with the College was declared terminated at the May 1952 meeting of the Board, and Dillingham was assigned the task of continuing the fund-raising effort.

An immediate result of Dillingham's involvement was the most attractive brochure the College had yet issued, *After Sixty Years A Campus.* This appeal zeroed in on a target certain to appeal to a sports-minded community. "The First Step in the New Campus Development Program for Ithaca College is a New Physical Education Plant."

"Let us look at the problem together" went the invitation. A map indicated in red the facilities used by some three hundred Physical Education majors — the two gyms, the Masonic Temple, the rented dance studio on West State Street, and the distant outdoor areas: Percy Field, Stewart Park, the New-man Municipal Golf Course, and the area at the intersection of Meadow and Wood Streets.

At least one hour, three times a day, is wasted because of the necessity of going back and forth between the present gymnasiums and the athletic fields which are located at the north and south ends of town.

It is necessary for students to dress in one building and go several blocks to classrooms in another build-ing during all kinds of weather. The young women who are enrolled in the Physical Education Depart-ment dress in the Masonic Temple and then must go outside to one of the two gymnasiums or to the athletic fields.

Four pictures pointed up the limitations of the present plant. Then, moving from "these inadequate quarters," a sketch unveiled the proposed new gymnasium and field house on South Hill — capable of seating 3,000 people for athletic events, splendidly equipped not only for instruction but also for alumni reunions and homecomings or indeed for any meeting of the entire campus community. The accomplish-ments of the other divisions of the institution were then paraded, both in text and in illustration, and a centerfold dramatically depicted the entire South Hill campus as it might someday look. (All of the buildings shown are on the west side

of the Danby Road; the playing fields are across from them, where in fact the College now stands.) The various activity areas (stadium, track, baseball diamonds, archery range, ten-nis courts) were, it might be noted, laid out by Job himself, in his characteristic fashion.

To me, an interesting aspect of this development was an offer from a local engineer to do essential survey-ing on the site for $15,000. We needed the work done, but we did not have the $15,000. I purchased a used transit for $100 and did the work myself. The layout wasn't difficult. It was time-consuming when cou-pled with the supervision of the two bulldozer opera-tors. I found it possible, since the operators went to work at 7:00 A.M., to spend an hour with them before going to the office. Again at noon, because lunch was not important to me, I spent much of the hour with the machine operators and in planning. Late in the afternoon I could leave the office for additional necessary presence on the developing site.

After Sixty Years concluded with the expected appeal: anyone purchasing at least one share ($150 over thirty months) would have his or her name inscribed on a bronze tablet, to be placed in an appropriate spot in the new gymna-sium. Job and Short wrote eloquent endorsements; a chart itemized the tax savings for donors; the back cover tantaliz-ingly revealed a pastoral scene looking down over South Hill toward the lake — without a single building yet to be seen.

This brochure was followed by yet another — *Twenty-Four Pages Complete the Story.* Some pages were reprinted from the earlier effort, but now the newer pictures were chosen for their crude shock value: the cramped rooms in the downtown gyms; battered, decrepit lockers; murky staircases with exposed plumbing; a grimy shower; open toilets and urinals. The prose addressed itself primarily to the interests of the business community: "Giving Builds Bulwarks of Free Enter-prise!" the caption ran.

American prosperity depends in no small measure upon a proper degree of free enterprise. Today the most perfect demonstration of American free enter-prise is that vast network of schools and independent colleges supported by the voluntary gifts of men and women who care about the moral and educational fibre of the American people.

The centerfold offered a glimmer of hope, for the South Hill landscape now unmistakably bore the marks of Job's transit and bulldozers. The brochure concluded by invoking a patron saint of free enterprise, John D. Rockefeller; several pages summarized *his* advice on determining which of many worthy causes may most deserve the attention of a prospective donor.

There is the complete story. . . . The rest is up to you!

There was however an addendum, a smaller pamphlet entitled *A Community Asset.* This was designed for strictly local consumption.

It is a fact that Ithaca College annually expends in the City of Ithaca just under $2,500,000 (the actual figure is $2,490,000).

As the city's fifth largest enterprise, the College could appeal to the self-interest of the citizenry for some tangible demonstration of support.

The Development Fund aimed at raising $300,000. It did not. The Board was informed in October 1952 that $195,000 had been pledged, $70,000 received, and $91,000 consumed by expenses. In August 1953, it was apprised that $110,000 was on hand in cash and securities. One must wonder whether "securities" included "pledges," for in November 1953, Job announced to the advisory council that while $186,000 had been pledged, only $81,000 had been received. By February 1955, he was forced to report to the Board that the Development Fund campaign had produced "no tangible results" and could only urge the trustees to assume a greater responsibility for fund-raising. The minutes note that "the discussion . . . was inconclusive."

As in earlier periods of the College's history, there was much casting about for untapped sources of revenue. New members were added to the Board — Herman Muller in 1950 (becoming chairman in 1951); Harold Allen and S. S. Venitt in 1952; George C. Textor and Roland G. Fowler in 1953; Edward R. Eastman in 1956. Honorary degrees were awarded in profusion: to Katherine Cornell, Gertrude Lawrence, James A. Farley, Dorothy Kirsten, Eleanor Steber, James J. ("Gene") Tunney, Jeanette MacDonald, Mary G. Roebling,

among many others. Feelers were sent out to still other persons of wealth and presumed generosity. At one point, Trustee Hall Griffith, who had made a strong plea "for the creation of an institution that would appeal to big business on the basis of fostering free enterprise," dangled the hope of securing up to $150 million from a donor in Fort Worth, Texas, and persuaded the Board to retain a New York City attorney for the purpose of making the necessary (though fruitless) contacts. Harold Allen volunteered the services of the underwriting firm of which he was a partner for the sale of "mutual shares as a means of increasing the revenue of Ithaca College." Job offered part of the College's land west of the Danby Road to the Westinghouse Corporation for the construction of an electronics tube factory (Westinghouse had been turned down in its request for land from Cornell).

Although land is important to the college in its development plans, the community interests are of prime importance.

But the lack of an adequate rail connection wrecked this scheme, and the land was sold in 1953 to National Cash Register for $60,000. This money helped to buy additional land on the other side of the highway and to pay for the new Library building downtown. In 1956, a grant of $327,000 from the Ford Foundation — comparable grants were made to all private colleges — was gratefully received even though the income from this money for ten years was exclusively designated for the improvement of faculty salaries.

By the mid-fifties, Job was frankly conceding that it would be impossible to build the projected gymnasium on South Hill while the rest of the College remained downtown. More and more, he hinted darkly that the only option open to him was to continue to buy property "piecemeal" in the DeWitt Park area. "I have no intention of starting any project on the hill unless we can see it through." This sentence both epitomized President Job's personal philosophy and defined the stalemate in which the College seemed to be caught. It owned a magnificent site on South Hill and a collection of disintegrating buildings several miles from that site. It seemed impossible to move, and equally undesirable to remain.

As Job's presidency drew toward its quarter-century mark, there was little he could do except shore up the physical plant, buy additional property as opportunity offered, work for accreditation, and leave the rest to time.

V. The Job Years 1932 - 1957 (2)

Old Ways and New Directions: The Professional Schools and the Humanities

WE have watched President Job and his trustees wrestling with the larger questions of the College's survival and — if in fact it were to survive — of the location most appropriate to its future. One by one, the out-of-town offers faded, then disappeared; perhaps they had never been so very real in the first place. Ithaca College, it was clear, was to remain in Ithaca. But where in Ithaca? In its decrepit downtown plant? In the projected East Hill campus? On the west shore of Lake Cayuga, in a recently vacated state tuberculosis sanitarium? On South Hill? In the fall of 1955, David A. Saperstone, of the Board of Public Works, even suggested a three-way switch in the DeWitt Park area: the old City Hall on North Tioga Street would be demolished and its location turned into a parking lot; the city offices would be moved into the College property; and Ithaca College would occupy the former High School (now the DeWitt Building). And at least one other option would be considered, after Job's resignation, before the decision was finally reached to break ground on South Hill.

But during all this high-level planning and dreaming, the College lived and worked not as it might desire but as it could.

In the early thirties, the Boardman mansion continued to dominate the DeWitt Park "campus" and to figure prominently in College publicity. The newly acquired Music building offered an eminently photographable colonial facade throughout these years. There was, moreover, something endearing about the entrance to the Little Theatre, abutting on the park itself — it was a favored location for pictures of graduating classes and other campus groups. And, after 1938, the president lived, in some considerable elegance, at 2 Fountain Place.

But apart from these showpieces, the College was critically lacking in space for its essential activities. The administration (including the president, the registrar, and the business officers) was crowded into an annex at the north end of the Theatre. Job recalls that when he first came to Ithaca for his interview:

I returned to President Williams's office, which was a small room about 10' by 14' on the first floor of the "band" building in the dark, back corner. Miss Van Dyne's desk was also in the room. To approach President Williams's desk, it was impossible to pass Miss Van Dyne without disturbing her and interrupting her work.

Job's reference to the "band" building points to the other uses of the administrative annex. A press visitor reported, with some astonishment, that a strenuous rehearsal of "The Ride of the Valkyries" provided background music for his interview with President Job, who had moved to the annex from the second-floor office over the College kitchen which he had occupied as dean. In the early forties, Job and Newens escaped to the comparative quiet of rented space in the Seneca Building; the presidential office was established on the second floor of the Boardman mansion from 1943 on. Academic deans and directors were located in their respective buildings; other administrators were wedged into whatever space could be found for them.

Although some of the private music studios were comfortably appointed, classrooms were always a scarce commodity in the downtown campus. Job lists some fifteen locations used in the early years of his administration — the first and third floors of the Boardman building (the latter an extreme fire hazard), the Music building, the Theatre, the Green Room, 123 East Buffalo Street, the Seneca gymnasium, and some others — not one of them satisfactory for classroom instruction. As early as 1935, Job had applied for funds from the Federal Emergency Administration of Public Works for the construction of a four-story classroom structure, to replace the Music building, with residences for women on the top two floors. But nothing came of this, and when the bumper enrollment of 1937 - 1938 taxed available space to the limit, Job asked his Board to engage a fund-raising organization to provide the means to construct a new gymnasium, with several modern classrooms. The trustees merely recommended caution in such ventures, however, and instruction was relegated to whatever space could be rented — in the Y.M.C.A., in the Masonic Temple, in the First Baptist Church.

The Catalog of 1936 - 1937 lists four residence halls for women (Williams, Griffis, Newman, Westminster), two fraternity houses (Phi Epsilon Kappa and Phi Mu Alpha), and three sorority houses (Mu Phi Epsilon, Phi Delta Pi, and Sigma Alpha Iota). Chadwick Hall was acquired by 1939, and Hilliard and Thomas Halls were opened by 1940 to accommodate additional women. Despite the promise, in 1936, of a dormitory for freshman men, male students were left to their own devices — those not living in fraternity houses or in the Y.M.C.A. found quarters in private homes.

The return of the veterans set off a mad scramble for space. "Large Incoming Class Swells Ranks of College" ran the *Ithacan* headline in January 1946: where to put them? There were frantic appeals to the community to find additional rooms to rent; by September, students were engaged in a house-to-house canvass in a desperate attempt to find lodgings. The College's Camp Danaca, in Danby, could serve until the cold weather came, and Cornell University made a former

C.C.C. camp east of Ithaca available to fifty Ithaca College students (who had to be bused into town for their meals). Others slept in rented space over the Jamieson-McKinney store on South Cayuga Street.

Some additional real estate was purchased or rented. The nurses' home at 115 Valentine Place was used in 1946 - 1947; also acquired at that time were 204 Stewart Avenue (Stewart House), 717 East Buffalo, 415 North Cayuga. Cascadilla House was bought in 1947, as was 412 North Tioga. Lyon Hall (at 608 East Buffalo) dated from 1953.

But the most obvious solution to the influx of students was temporary housing made available from the federal government. In January 1946, the press reported that Ithaca College was slated to receive a structure from the Federal Housing Administration large enough for thirty-four returning servicemen, to be located at 402 East Buffalo Street, on a tennis court adjacent to the Phi Delta Pi sorority (then occupying Egbert Hall). When this "dormitory" was found to be too large for the site, property was acquired for its erection at the northeast corner of Hancock and Third Streets: sixty-five single men would live there.

Married veterans presented a more complex problem. In June 1946, it was announced that 102 family units were expected for their use, but by the following January, that number had been reduced to 37, and the completion even of these was delayed by an acute shortage of plumbers and plumbing materials. Nevertheless, the 37 apartments at Titus Flats in southwest Ithaca were ready for occupancy in April — just in time for an unusually severe spring flood. The students and their families were evacuated from "The Meadows"; the American Red Cross provided emergency relief; there were angry words about building such a housing project on barely reclaimed lake-bottom. But the College cleaned up the mess and moved to reactivate its FHA contract for 37 additional units. By March 1948, 74 families were in residence. Some of these "temporary" structures were eventually moved to the Coddington Road, where, considerably remodeled, they are still in use as private homes near the present access road to the College.

Some desperately needed classroom space was also obtained through war surplus. In December 1946, the community was apprised that three buildings suitable for instructional purposes were on their way from Rome Air Base (the ones that eventually arrived came in fact from an army hospital in Brentwood, Long Island). Two of these buildings were placed behind the Music building — one with twenty-one rooms for the use of the School of Music, the other for the newly created radio department. A third — a former laboratory transported in sections and reassembled at 402 East Buffalo Street on the grounds of Egbert Hall — became the headquarters of another recent addition to the College scene, the Division of Physiotherapy. Job, in his annual report of 1946 - 1947, noted with satisfaction that

> *all three are excellent buildings and constitute the three best buildings on campus. They cost the college about $3,000.*

Also in 1946, the College purchased the Crescent Theatre on North Aurora Street and converted it into a second gymnasium, with a hall usable for large classes. More space was released for instruction when the Library moved from 123 East Buffalo Street to the top floor of the Ezra Cornell Public Library on North Tioga Street. The infirmary left Williams Hall for a remodeled carriage house at 3 Willets Place. But for the most part, teaching went on as best it might in the nooks and crannies of downtown Ithaca — in "The Sprague" (rented space on State Street over Woolworth's and the Home Dairy), in the Colonial Building (over Atwater's grocery), on the upper floors of the Tompkins County Trust Company, over Miller's stationery store. Professor Emerita Marguerite Rowland recalled the extreme inconvenience of such arrangements.

> *For weeks we did not have enough chairs. Finally some uncomfortable benches were found. Although they had neither backs nor provisions for writing, they were better than the floor.*

One instructor, noting that Woolworth's was erecting a new and bigger sign over its store, is said to have remarked, "Ah, beautifying the campus!"

In the later forties, there was some remodeling of existing facilities: a refurbished accounting room, new equipment for Professor Roberta Barnett's speech laboratory, a music listening room. The Little Theatre was redecorated and the Green Room equipped with a stage. Student lounges were demanded and set up (with strict segregation of the sexes).

The inadequacies inherent in a dilapidated plant were exacerbated by a series of disastrous fires — some of them almost certainly the work of an arsonist. In May 1937, fire ravaged the third floor of the administrative annex, destroying invaluable music, including the Conway collection of band arrangements. In September 1951, the *Ithacan* informed the returning students that during the summer, Williams Hall had been damaged and the Theatre gutted (the latter, ironically, when firemen from all over upstate New York were parading through the streets of Ithaca). That November, just after intruders ransacked the administrative offices, there were two more fires — one in the Graduate School building (123 East Buffalo Street) and the other in a music studio over the women's dining hall. And in February 1955, a blaze in the Music building damaged or destroyed, among other things, invaluable library and archival materials stored there in the basement.

By 1950, the urgent need for adequate classroom facilities promoted the construction of a new downtown building — the "Annex," an L-shaped structure in what had been a parking lot between the administration building and the dining hall, with a connection to the Little Theatre. The Annex, a severely functional cinder-block affair, offered no frills of any sort, yet instructors joining the faculty in the 1950s from Cornell observed that it provided classrooms superior to those in which they had taught on the hill. Some of this space was soon diverted to noninstructional purposes, however. Townspeople objected to the hordes of Ithaca College students using the Public Library building, and by 1951, the floor where the College collection was housed was declared unsafe. The Library perforce was then jammed into three former classrooms in the Annex, with no direct access to one another. Another classroom held desks for a dozen or more professors; the arrival of the director of the School of Business (and later of Dean Hickman) preempted more space for offices; insistent student pressure required the creation of a lounge within the Annex. So even with classes running from 8:00 A.M. until well into the evening (and also on Saturdays till noon), the strains were close to unendurable.

By 1953, there was no alternative (given the failure of the first bid for accreditation) but to move the Library out of the Annex to another new building erected in the courtyard (128 East Buffalo Street, now used for county offices). This decision was not without its risks. The community had enthusiastically accepted the idea of a South Hill campus and had been watching with interest as athletic fields on that location were developed and ground broken for a field house. Much excitement had been generated in 1950 with the prospect of a new gymnasium on South Hill, the primary target for the Development Fund campaign inaugurated in the fall of 1951. Local citizens who had pledged sums for the proposed gymnasium registered some sense of outrage when the College undertook to build the new Library building downtown (which would later acquire a second floor for the TV-radio studios). The College was accused of acting in bad faith: was it really serious about its high-sounding talk of a new campus on the hill? The alumni also needed reassuring that the contributed funds were not being diverted to downtown building projects.

Perhaps these fears and some cancelled pledges were not wholly without justification. As late as February 1956, the Board resolved to hold on to the South Hill land but to continue buying downtown property — "quietly" - just in case.

What was happening, educationally, on this makeshift campus?

On April 25, 1932, Hermann Cooper, associate in higher education for the New York State Department of Education, issued a "Report on the Registration of Courses Leading to Degrees at Ithaca College, Ithaca, New York." From this document there emerges a reasonably comprehensive picture of the administrative and curricular structures with which President Job was initially confronted.

Cooper began by noting that the Charter of 1926, which had transformed the school from a proprietary corporation to an "educational institution," had contained an important proviso.

> *. . . that the power to grant degrees should depend upon the presentation of evidence satisfying the President of the University [of the State of New York] that property in an amount sufficient to come within the provision of Section 61 of the Education Law was to be transferred to the new corporation.*

Section 61 stated, unequivocally, that

> *no institution shall be given power to confer degrees in this state unless it shall have resources of at least*

> *$500,000; and no institution for higher education shall be incorporated without suitable provision approved by the Regents for educational equipment and proper maintenance.*

The Regents had determined that a "college" must have "a minimum productive endowment beyond all indebtedness of $500,000." It was self-evident that Ithaca College, with no endowment at all and considerable indebtedness, could not meet that requirement; furthermore, there were grave doubts about the adequacy of its equipment and maintenance. Hence the crisis of 1931 - 1932.

Cooper's report made every effort to salvage the degree-conferring status of the College. He had obviously been impressed by the dramatic changes in administration — Williams's forced resignation, Job's election to the presidency, changes in the composition of the Board of Trustees. It is likewise clear that the president-elect had succeeded in conveying something of his own optimism, or at least determination, to the examiner from Albany. In any event, Cooper, while alert to manifest inadequacies, was willing to gamble on the future of the institution and would even devise a convenient equivocation to cover the letter of the law. Ithaca College, he suggested, might continue to confer degrees upon its students "if it be considered a technical and professional school rather than a college." Only colleges needed that half-million dollars of endowment; technical and professional schools, while answerable to the Regents for "educational equipment and proper maintenance," might squeak by with a firm promise of amendment of their delinquencies.

Cooper juggled the six existing divisions of the College to fit his saving formula. The Conservatory of Music and the Westminster Choir School were to be classified as "technical" schools, while the remaining four — the School of Public School Music, the School of Expression and Dramatic Art, the Martin School of Speech Correction, and the School of Physical Education — were to be considered "professional schools of education." Ithaca College might thus have forfeited its claim to be called a college, but at least it would be permitted to function like one.

The specifics of Cooper's report throw some light on the educational operation of the institution in the early 1930s. Admission standards, spelled out, were deemed satisfactory, and most of the several curricula (again analyzed in some detail) seemed adequate. The question of the Westminster Choir School was deferred for a separate study. Cooper recommended the abolition of only one program, the major in health education, which he found indistinguishable, for all practical purposes, from the Physical Education major. He made a plea for greater flexibility in the academic programs and strongly recommended that in an institution noted for its work in physical education, all students should be required to complete "a minimum of four hours of floor work" in that area. The faculty impressed him as well compensated and not overworked, although 50 percent of the instructors in the professional areas were undercredentialed.

> *It is recommended that all staff members assigned to the faculties of the professional schools be required, by September 1, 1937, to have completed training equivalent to that presupposed by the master of Arts degree.*

The deficiencies of the Library (it had far fewer than the required minimum of 8,000 volumes) loomed large, but Cooper was willing to extend full credit to the good faith of a Board resolution authorizing the expansion of Library facilities and the hiring of a competent librarian. Further, he noted, "the executive head of the college had already made arrangements to set aside one entire building for the school library" (a promise that would not be fulfilled until almost twenty-five years later). Dependence on the facilities of the Ithaca High School for science laboratories was deplorable, but here again:

> *On February 16, 1932, the Board of Trustees of Ithaca College voted the sum of one thousand dollars or such part thereof as may be necessary for the purchase of laboratory materials and equipment essential in the anatomy and biological courses required in the physical educational curriculum.*

Cooper accepted a skeletal statement of the financial picture:

Income	163,755.92
Expenses	161,564.27
Net Profit	2,191.65
Buildings & Grounds	567,745.14
Debt	330,146.50

That left a "net worth" of about $235,000. The school was marginally solvent, on paper anyway, and with its new leadership, it would almost certainly work toward a sounder financial basis. All things considered, Cooper could therefore recommend that provisional registration of most of the existing programs leading to degrees be granted.

Thanks to Cooper's manifest good will, some emergency decisions by the Board, and Job's convincing presentation, the crisis had been passed. Ithaca "College" could continue.

The academic restructuring of the College was facilitated, as noted previously, by the removal of the Westminster Choir School in 1932 and of the Martin Speech Institute in 1936. The era of "affiliated schools" was over, and the familiar tripartite model — Music, Speech-Drama, Physical Education — reemerged.

Curiously, Music seems to have lost something of its historic preeminence. To be sure, its performances continued to make impressive contributions to the cultural life of the local community and beyond. Early in 1935, Mrs. Roosevelt invited the a cappella choir to the White House to sing at a garden party; in 1949, three ten-inch shellac records were made of the orchestra and band; on December 20, 1950, the choir broadcast a program of Christmas carols over the CBS radio network. In Ithaca, the tradition of spectacular choral presentations continued under Bert Lyon, Victor Rebmann, Jackson Ehlert, Donald Bubé — parts of the *Messiah* as a fairly regular Christmas offering, to say nothing of *The Creation* (1938), *Elijah* (1940), the Verdi *Requiem* with Margaret Daum as soloist (1942), *Judas Maccabeus* (1949), the Mozart *Requiem* (1950), the Dvorak *Stabat Mater* (1955), the Bach *Magnificat* (1956), plus some Buxtehude and Stravinsky. There had been a *Student Prince* in 1937 and a performance of DeKoven's *Robin Hood* the following year; indeed, opera would come into its own in the 1950s. A highly successful "American Folk Evening" in 1950 included Weill's *Down in the Valley;* Beatrice MacLeod of the drama department collaborated with Craig McHenry in a production of Britten's *Let's Make an Opera* in 1951; *The Telephone* and *The Devil and Daniel Webster* appeared in December 1951; there was another double billing in March 1953 — *The Secret of Suzanne* and *The Lowland Sea;* and in 1957, Mozart's *Bastien and Bastienne.*

College groups went on tour and were regularly featured at professional meetings. The College band achieved new distinction under Walter Beeler. The local press continued to report its satisfaction with the endless round of recitals, concerto programs (from 1946 on), Christmas presentations, and the like. There is little evidence of visiting celebrities being brought to the College (perhaps because of the lack of funds). The young Morton Gould had dazzled the students with his own compositions and his improvisations in May 1931; Mrs. Edward MacDowell played her husband's compositions in a concert sponsored by S.A.I. in 1936. Those of us who have savored the recordings of Madame Jenkins's "concerts" may be amused by this apparently straight-faced social note in the *Ithacan* of November 16, 1934:

> *Through the good offices of Vladimir Karapetoff, Chairman of the Board of Trustees of Ithaca College, Mrs. Florence Foster Jenkins, a leader in music circles, founder and President of the Verdi Club of New York, will be guest of honor at a reception to be given at Griffis Hall.*

But perhaps sufficient lustre was provided by the resident faculty. Some of the important names have already appeared in this chronicle — Lyon, Beeler, Bubé, McHenry, Sampaix. Lynn Bogart had come in 1922 to study violin with Egbert and would remain until his retirement in 1967, recipient of the first Warren Benson Distinguished Award for his contributions as performer, as teacher of music theory, and as head of the violin department. Benson, who joined the faculty in 1953, established an enviable reputation as a composer; among other things, he wrote the music for the second College Alma Mater song, still in use today. Pianist George King Driscoll '32 was appointed in the spring of 1939; also in the piano department, Joseph Tague and Frank Burton Page arrived in 1945 and were regularly featured in two-piano recitals for some years thereafter. Celia Slocum supervised music pedagogy from 1935 to 1967. Her activities during those many years of devoted service included the operation of a highly effective system of teacher placement, the conduct of summer workshops on music and the humanities, and, with Helene Wickstrom, the chairing of the New York State School Music Association festivals held in Ithaca each May. The Wickstroms — Carl and Helene — joined the staff in 1946.

Nevertheless, sagging enrollments in Music caused concern even in the mid-thirties. The problem was exacerbated by the war years, and after 1946, most of the new directions in which the College was moving lay in other areas. Changes in the administrative framework in which the Music students and faculty worked further the impression that the role of the School of Music was becoming slightly less central to the College than had been the case before 1932.

Adrian M. Newens had come to Ithaca as "Dean of the School of Expression and Administrative Head of the Conservatory of Music" in 1931. Although he had operated his own School of Music in Lincoln, Nebraska (which he sold to the University of Nebraska), Newens's interests lay mainly in the arts of elocution. The *Ithacan*, in a story on his arrival, reported that he had given some four thousand "monodrama" presentations, including two thousand repetitions of his best-known offering, "A Message from Mars." Newens soon moved entirely into the area of Speech-Drama (one of the three "divisions" of the College from 1932 to 1943). He headed this administrative entity under various titles, except for his four years in public relations as chairman of the Ithaca College council (1938 - 1942), from May 1932 until his retirement on September 1, 1943.

As Newens dissociated himself from the Conservatory, Albert Edward Brown, dean of the School of Public School Music since 1924, became, by 1932, chairman of a gradually consolidated division (or department) of Music (the terms fluctuated, without apparent reason, from Catalog to Catalog). He was succeeded in September 1936 by Victor L. F. Rebmann, who could boast of degrees in law and philosophy from the University of Freiburg, a Ph.D. in music from the University of Heidelberg, with further studies in violin at Leipzig. Coming to the United States "on a vacation" in 1907, he had remained to study and teach at Columbia, New York University, Boston University, and the University of Pennsylvania, and, most recently, had been director of music for the public schools of Westchester County. Before the time of his retirement in June 1950 (with an honorary degree), his title had been changed, in yet another restructuring of the College, to that of dean of the School of Fine Arts.

On November 5, 1942, the Board of Trustees, after taking "a discouraging look" at prospects for future enrollments, especially of male students, resolved that there would be three schools, each with its own dean: the School of Health and Physical Education, the School of Liberal Arts, and the School of Fine Arts. Physical Education was already substantially in place, and, lacking Regents' approval, it would prove impossible to proceed with the School of Liberal Arts until the mid-fifties. The School of Fine Arts could be set up immediately, with curricula in art, music, speech, drama, and radio. Limitations of resources prevented the establishment of a curriculum in art, but the School of Fine Arts (under Jackson Ehlert after Rebmann's retirement) remained in existence from 1943 to 1952.

Ehlert's resignation set off a new effort at reorganization in the fall of 1952, at which time the trustees dissolved the School of Fine Arts, transferred speech, radio, and drama to a "General College," and restored the School of Music, with Conrad Rawski as director. Rawski had joined the Music faculty in August 1940. In an interview, he explained his reasons for relinquishing his appointment at the University of Vienna: "I didn't like to be told what my research must prove, and besides I have no predilection for marching tunes." An authority on medieval music (his dissertation was on the work of the fourteenth-century composer Roman de Fauvel), a visiting fellow at Cornell (1952), recipient of a faculty fellowship from the Fund for the Advancement of Education (1952), member of the Royal Music Association (1954), Rawski brought much of the profound and pervasive humanism of the European intellectual tradition to Ithaca College. President Job would remember him as "probably our most intelligent and well informed professor." As the College began seriously to move toward liberal education in the mid-fifties, Rawski became one of the most eloquent spokesmen for the humanities — sufficiently so to generate considerable tension with those members of the Music faculty for whom music constituted the totality of a conservatory curriculum. His sudden departure (because of a personal involvement) in February 1957 was a major loss to the institution.

Where the Music curricula should be placed within the larger framework of the College may have been problematic, but there can be no doubt that for Physical Education, Dean Laurence Hill was firmly in control. Hill had come to Ithaca in 1929 and would remain almost to the end of the Job era; he was incapacitated by a heart attack in 1957 but retained the title of dean until his death on July 25 of that year.

In 1930, another educator from the Albany school system would join the staff — Isadore ("Doe") Yavits, whose record, *The Ithaca College of My Time,* has already been cited in this history. In it he recalls that almost immediately after his

arrival, the need for a man to coach both football and baseball became critical, and so James A. ("Bucky") Freeman was invited to fill that position beginning in 1931. Since Freeman had been teaching at the Albany High School, the "Albany Trio" was now complete.

Yavits describes the Physical Education program around the time of his arrival.

> *Gymnastic classes were held in the Seneca Street Building, formerly the Star Theatre, mostly in the larger of the two rooms. An asbestos curtain divided the rear room, or stage, from the former seating hall. Elsie Hugger, who had been in the department from its inception, supervised the girls' activities. Mr. Yavits taught the men. . . .*

> *Much of the equipment used at I.S.P.E. was of the formal type, including chest weights, Indian clubs, dumbbells, wands, and even a Swedish boom for the girls' activities. There were ladders for pyramids, a side horse, a set of parallel bars, a buck, stall bars, and a minimum number of mats. A Swedish box and a springboard were also among the muscle-building apparatus. Two baskets mounted on rickety backboards had been installed at each side of the larger room. . . . Athletics for girls were conducted Tuesdays and Thursdays; the boys were coached the other days of the week. The athletic activities for men included football, soccer, basketball, wrestling, baseball, and track, and there was an intercollegiate schedule of competition for each one. The girls participated in soccer, field hockey, basketball, softball, and track activities for women.*

Summer programs were conducted at Dean Hill's summer camp in Vermont (Singing Cedars) and, later, at Camp Danaca (the name of which telescoped that of its Danby location and Ithaca). Yavits was in charge of Camp Danaca, and activities there included, among other things, a course in bow making taught by President Job.

Additions to the faculty led inevitably to changes in curricular emphases — away from the rigid formalities of the German or Swedish schools. The "Albany Trio" were firmly committed to the tenets of the New York State director of physical education, Frederick Rand Rogers: these were, in Yavits's summary, physical fitness and its measurement, competition between evenly matched teams, and "player control" or "giving the game back to the boys."

In order to develop student leadership in athletics, the captain of the team was responsible for all changes during the contest. The coaches sat together and supervised the action. All future physical educators were instructed to use these techniques.

Steady progress in the performance of the intercollegiate teams can be noted throughout the thirties, even though financial limitations and the inadequacies of plant and playing areas were severe handicaps. Yavits reports a confrontation between a hard-pressed president and the basketball team.

Dr. Job, economizing, curtailed the expense of warm-up jackets for the players. Most college teams wore colorful jackets and trousers. So this Ithaca gang of "Outlaws" made up an act. While Dr. Job witnessed the Ithaca team take the floor for practice, he was amazed to see them wearing outlandish, discolored and torn garments. The boys won their case. With no further protest, neat, colorful warm-up jackets were provided for the squad members.

A rousing football victory over Middlebury was attributed in part to the decision to cut on expenses by putting the team up, on a particularly cold night, in the largely unheated lodge at Camp Singing Cedars: tempers ran so high that anger proved a stimulant to success on the following day. Players were transported in a variety of ways — in an inadequate bus that took twelve hours to reach New York City, in seven-passenger taxis, in a rented bus. As late as 1952, four of Yavits's soccer players could get to a soccer forum in Sarasota only by thirty-two hours of nonstop driving in the College station wagon — two up front, two sleeping in the back, in shifts. In the same year, the *Ithacan* found it necessary to take up its editorial cudgels to secure funds for training tables in the College dining hall.

Despite such difficulties, the *Ithacan* and the upstate newspapers chronicled a steadily growing number of triumphs. In 1933, Yavits was hailed as "Coach of Victories" after eight

straight wins in basketball: in a touching gesture of camaraderie between the schools, the department of drama dedicated a performance of *The Importance of Being Earnest* to the coach. There were headlines for Bucky Freeman's baseball team, and 1934 was "an almost perfect year" for I.C. football. In 1940, the track team emerged as conference winner.

The year 1937 saw Ithaca College elected to membership in the National Intercollegiate Athletic Association. The *Ithacan* elaborated upon the significance of this recognition.

The "Cayugans" can now engage in athletic contests with schools of higher rating in intercollegiate circles than the normal schools and teachers' colleges to which they have been limited up to this time.

The reference to the "Cayugans" points to a question of some concern at the time — what name should be given to the College's athletic teams? In 1936, the *Ithacan* had announced a contest for an appropriate designation; many suggestions were received, and by January 1937, the students had determined that the "Cayugans" was the most felicitous choice. The will of the majority was not to prevail over the power of the press, however, for by 1940, the name "Bombers" had surfaced in the sports releases and soon drove out its official competition. John Mason Potter credits Harold Jansen with effecting this change: Jansen, a member of the publicity staff and sports writer for several newspapers, apparently coined the name and by using it repeatedly in his own stories, assured its ultimate acceptance. So "Bombers" they are, to this day.

World War II hit Physical Education especially hard as the College was virtually drained of able-bodied males. In the mid-thirties, the press had had fun with Coach Freeman's perplexity when a woman ball-player (Yolenda Klaskin) turned up; now the situation was all too serious. Yavits was put in charge of a physical education program for a dominantly female enrollment, and even pitted his all-women soccer team against the boys of the Newfield High School. And when the postwar expansion created all those problems of housing and facilities that we have considered elsewhere, the situation was particularly acute for the School of Health and Physical Education. Even the construction of playing fields on South Hill did not resolve all the difficulties — their solution had to wait for the eventual removal of the entire Physical Education operation to the new campus.

Staff members added in the forties and early fifties included Robert Bigley, Herbert Broadwell, William Grimshaw, Joseph Hamilton, Carl Schrader, Cecil West, Arnold Wilhelm, Carlton Wood, and Christopher Wuest. Ben Light's special contributions to the College will be considered later in this history.

The major curricular development in the Physical Education area was the emergence of the Division of Physiotherapy. As early as 1936 - 1937, a course in physiotherapy had been listed in the Catalog as an adjunct to the offerings of the Martin School of Speech Correction. In May 1945, the Board of Trustees directed President Job to organize a School of Physiotherapy with a four-year curriculum (said to be the first in the United States) — two years to be spent in Ithaca, two in New York City. This mandate apparently legalized a move already under way, for in May 1946, the *Ithacan* reported that Physiotherapy students, presumably finishing their sophomore year at the time, were about to start their work in New York City. One would infer that since the first-year courses of Physical Education and Physiotherapy students were virtually the same, some Physical Education students entering in 1944 - 1945 had been moved into the Physiotherapy program formally established in the spring of that year for the following September. A director for the program was soon found in the person of A. Garman Dingwall (September 1947), with K. Gösta Hansson, M.D., serving as medical director. Ithaca College, it was announced, was "the first to win approval from the state department of education to train students for licensing examinations as physiotherapists" — for some twenty years, no school within the state had succeeded in meeting the Regents' requirements. There were about sixty students when "Ding" arrived; an upgrading of standards had already been effected since we read the curious boast that "not a student who began the course in the fall of 1944 is now enrolled."

Expanded offerings in Ithaca made it possible to reduce the period of clinical training in New York City to just the senior year by 1947 - 1948. Instruction in orthopedics, abnormal psychology, medicine, neurology, surgery, and so forth was given, first at the New York Hospital and the Hospital for Special Surgery, later at the Kings County Hospital in Brooklyn and elsewhere. There were local affiliations, including Packer Hospital in Sayre, Pennsylvania, the Auburn Hospi-

tal, and of course the Tompkins County Memorial Hospital.

Nevertheless, there were nagging problems of full accreditation, particularly by the American Medical Association. Job attributed this failure to secure national recognition to "concerted opposition from the New York State [Physiotherapy] Society." Further:

We were, for a while, frowned upon by the National Foundation for Infantile Paralysis through its refusal to award scholarships to students wishing to attend our college.

National approval would be withheld until the early sixties, despite the efforts of Dr. Jack Applebaum, a liaison between the state professional organization and the N.Y. State Department of Education (who visited the campus in October 1949 and became the recipient of an honorary degree). But even though its graduates could be licensed only in New York, the program flourished, and in 1950, the first post-graduate courses in the country for physiotherapy practitioners were instituted by the College in New York City.

Thus from such small beginnings in a speech correction program, Physiotherapy had become a full-scale division within the School of Health and Physical Education (the Catalogs between 1948 - 1949 and 1953 - 1954 suggest this process in the awkward heading "School of Health and Physical Education and Physiotherapy"). A comparable response to the opportunities offered by the educational marketplace can be seen in yet another development — this time in TV-radio.

In February 1931, the *Ithacan* announced that a professor in the Williams School of Expression and Dramatic Art, Dr. Sydney Landon, would inaugurate a course in radio. Landon, well known on the Chautauqua circuit, could claim six years of practical experience in radio, and his course would stress program making, announcing, timing, and the use of the microphone — all this for only $10. In 1933, Ithaca College programs were being carried each Monday, Wednesday, and Friday, from 3:00 to 4:00 in the afternoon, over Station WESG in Elmira. By the mid-thirties, the Board became seriously interested in expanding the College's involvement in the communications media. The drama department was instructed to develop courses both in radio and in motion-picture making — perhaps a twelve-month course — and

$600 was appropriated for advertising purposes. This pioneer effort was to get under way by the fall of 1937 - 1938. But apart from some College broadcasts of music and drama over local stations and the institution of a course, Speech for Radio, by 1939 - 1940, little would come of the Board's initiative until the beginning of the new decade.

In his annual report for 1940 - 1941, President Job pointed out to the trustees that

it appears now that the major outlet for persons trained in speech is radio. More of our graduates have found satisfactory employment in radio than in other fields. Some of them have been very successful. In view of these facts, it has seemed wise to introduce a limited number of definite courses in radio. Mr. Michael R. Hanna, Manager of Station WHCU, has been retained to initiate this work by offering a general introductory course in radio during the fall of 1941. This will be followed by special courses the second semester and the following year as the need requires and opportunity offers.

Hanna, who would become a member of the Board of Trustees in 1956, thus began his long and fruitful association with the College. An illustrated brochure described the new curriculum and its director. The lack of facilities was neatly bypassed.

While the station is owned and operated by Cornell University (with which Ithaca College is in no way connected) the courtesies of the station, as a place for actual broadcasting when opportunity presents itself, are granted to those students who pursue the Speech and Drama courses in Ithaca College.

Hanna's credentials were impressive — he was eastern representative of the educational department of the Columbia Broadcasting System and radio adviser to the New York State Council of School Superintendents. He would be assisted by Joseph Short, an Ithaca College graduate, then program director and production manager at Station WHCU.

The success of the pilot program led to more ambitious plans. In the annual report for 1941 - 1942, it appeared "that we shall have to set up a definite radio curriculum if we are to accomplish more than a mere beginning in radio training." In addition to the general introduction, the Catalog of 1942 - 1943 had added a course called Radio Production, Writing, and Microphone Technique, taught jointly by Hanna and Short. There was no Catalog for 1943 - 1944 (a lean year), but the "Supplement to the Catalogue" detailed the new curricular option — a four-year program, with thirty-four hours specifically in radio. The Regents obliged with their blessing for both undergraduate and graduate courses, and by the fall of 1951 - 1952, their number had risen to fifteen, including Public Service Broadcasting, Radio Advertising, Current Broadcasting Developments, and Station Administration.

As an administrative entity, radio gradually outgrew its original home in the speech-drama department; the Catalog of 1948 - 1949 is the first to list it as a separate department, with John Groller as its chairman. Groller had come to the College in September 1946 after extensive experience with radio stations in Nevada and California. As chairman, he enlisted the cooperation of some fourteen stations throughout the country in providing opportunities for senior field training for Ithaca College students. And under his direction, the College programming entered into a period of some considerable distinction. The Ithaca Radio Workshop players were producing a half-hour weekly program over WHCU in the spring of 1947, and by 1948 - 1949, the "Campus Radio Theatre" was being heard not only locally but, through the Rural Radio Network, in New York, Pennsylvania, New Jersey, and Connecticut. Combining the talents of the drama students and the radio majors, it specialized in "comedy, mystery, romance, fantasy, classics, westerns"; Cornell's distinguished folklorist, Harold W. Thompson, held forth on "Folk Tales of Our State"; and of course Shakespeare was well represented, with adaptations of his major plays and a festival honoring his birthday in 1950. In 1949, Station WGHF in New York City was requesting transcripts of some of these programs.

Another Groller project involved College participation in the Empire State FM School of the Air: in 1949 - 1950, four fifteen-minute programs on conservation were carried over eighteen stations, followed by a second series, "Land of Make Believe," designed for students in kindergarten and the earlier grades. Local events received their share of coverage — the alumni luncheon at the Hotel Ithaca in May 1950, for example. Also in 1950, the Radio Workshop produced an eight-part series on the theme of racial discrimination entitled "Of One Blood," under the sponsorship of Ithaca ministerial groups. Station WITJ would begin to cover all home basketball games in 1953 - 1954, and football beginning in the fall of 1956.

Groller left in 1951 to accept the position of Secretary for Religious Broadcasting with the Presbyterian Board of National Missions. He was succeeded by Fred A. Brewer, who had been appointed to the faculty the previous year. Brewer continued the energetic work of his predecessor, and WITJ joined the Rural Radio Network, becoming, according to the *Ithacan*, "the first non-commercial station in U.S. to belong to a network." Robert Earle, from WKTV in Utica and Hanna's brother-in-law, became chairman in 1953.

In the earliest days, the technological aspects of the radio curriculum were primitive in the extreme — beyond the occasional use of the facilities of the Cornell-owned WHCU. A window was cut between two actors' dressing rooms; one thus became the "control room," the other the "studio." In December 1943, the press announced that Ithaca College now had its own "broadcasting station," assembled in a corner of the Little Theatre building by Professor George Hoerner of the drama department. But, alas, this was only simulated broadcasting: the studio was wired for amplification in the Theatre itself, for any audience that might choose to assemble there. Even so, it was possible to put together a full day's entertainment over "WHIC" — with some fleshing out from regular network programs. WHIC became WICR, still closed-circuit, though with a wire direct to WHCU for recording. By 1947 - 1948, the arrival of the surplus army buildings provided radio with a new home on West Court Street, complete with three studios and control room, a shop, a library, and office space. In November 1948, the College applied for an FM permit, and WICR-FM became a reality the following autumn, with a forty-five-foot antenna on the top of the Music building and a range of some three to five miles. Unfortunately, its signal interfered with that of a Rochester TV transmitter, and operations were almost immediately suspended until the difficulty could be obviated by a change of frequency.

A course in the Catalog of 1948 - 1949 entitled Radio Stagecraft necessarily looked beyond radio to television. But even earlier, an enthusiastic alumnus, Paul Mowrey '39, had taken the first steps in that direction. Mowrey's academic status as an undergraduate had sometimes been in question since his energies were channeled almost exclusively into stage lighting; he would recall that at his graduation, President Job whispered, "I didn't think you'd make it." But make it he did — to Hollywood with a contract for a movie that was never produced, next to TV as lighting consultant for CBS, and then communications manager for television with that network. Later, he would hold a similar position with ABC. In the fall of 1946, Mowrey organized a series of lectures, seminars, and field trips in TV at his alma mater — possibly the first such program in an American college or university. Mowrey himself led several seminars: there were visiting executives from the three major networks (including the director of the "Superman" series) and from important TV agencies, plus visits to TV studios in Schenectady — all this with considerable press coverage and detailed summaries of the contents of the lecture series in the *Ithacan*.

From this time on, more and more courses took on a double emphasis — Radio and TV Newswriting, Radio and TV Acting, Radio and TV Field Work, until, by the Catalog of 1955 - 1957, the department had officially become radio—TV; by the fall of 1958, the order would be reversed to TV-radio. Yet for all this intense interest, the College could not at first afford the equipment to move beyond a largely theoretical approach to television. The Middle States Association examiner in 1953 noted that

> *television instruction is handled with visual aids drawn on a blackboard rather than with equipment students can use.*

He went on to recommend the purchase of at least a 16mm silent camera.

> *The camera, plus some editing equipment and a few lights, would allow students to produce their own TV shows with sound either dubbed in or on tape. Much of TV programming is now done with film, so the instruction could be entirely realistic.*

College dramatic productions were seen on television screens — *The Trojan Women* in 1955, *Ivanoff* in 1956 — but this was possible only by transporting the cast to the studios of WHEN in Syracuse. The full development of TV at Ithaca College would come after 1957.

It is startling to discover that the radio department at first fell within the jurisdiction of the School of Fine Arts. Later, it would be absorbed into the General College and then become part of the College of Arts and Sciences. But its original home in the School of Fine Arts rather wistfully attests to the hope that at least on a college campus, radio and later TV might serve a civilizing as well as a commercial function — a point that would later be powerfully enunciated before College audiences by Jay Kennedy and Rod Serling. Nonetheless, of the fourteen or fifteen courses that constituted the radio curriculum, only one addressed itself to "the application of the basic principles of Imaginative Writing" to script preparation. Originally, two degrees were offered — the B.S. for those interested in the more "practical" aspects of radio and the B.F.A. for those to whom its creative possibilities were important. The B.F.A. option was abandoned by 1957. Indeed, four years earlier, the Middle States Report of 1953 had observed that the radio curriculum

> *is too highly specialized for a baccalaureate degree, but the commercial broadcaster would find the graduates extremely well trained in the field of radio.*

There would be important contributions to culture and to public education made by Ithaca College television in the late fifties and early sixties, and the Middle States examiner was only one of a swelling chorus of voices extolling the possibilities of creative interplay between radio and the related disciplines of drama and music. Yet ultimately, the unreality and eventual frustration of that vision must be a part of this history.

Graduate studies at Ithaca College came into their own in the post - World War II years. For many decades before that time, summer programs had leaned heavily upon teachers seeking additional credits for certification or increments: as early as 1925, the Martin Institute had announced a "normal training course" for supervisors of speech improvement. By the summer of 1930, the College would issue an attractively illustrated brochure describing courses in a number of areas — the Conservatory, the School of Public School Music, the Band School, Physical Education, the Liberal Arts, and the Martin Institute. Comparable efforts were continued throughout the thirties, and the Catalog of 1937 - 1938 went even further, hinting at the possibility of formal programs leading

to an advanced degree: "No definite promise of a Master's degree can be made at this time." In February 1937, President Job reminded the alumni, so many of whom were teachers interested in advanced degrees, of expanding opportunities for graduate studies at the College.

Progress was slow, however. The trustees discussed once again "the great desirability of the College's offering graduate degrees" at their meeting on February 10, 1942, and the following petition was approved:

> *WHEREAS, Ithaca College during the last ten years has made remarkable strides in improving its curricula and the excellence of the training given its students and*
>
> *WHEREAS, the present regulations of the Board of Regents of the University of the State of New York governing the permanent certification of teachers require a minimum of thirty semester hours of graduate work and*
>
> *WHEREAS, there are great numbers of Ithaca College graduates and others who desire to do their graduate work at Ithaca College now therefore*
>
> *BE IT RESOLVED: That the Board of Trustees of Ithaca College through its president petition the Board of Regents of the University of the State of New York to grant the amendments to the college charter necessary to grant master's degrees. . . .*

Albany was not immediately responsive, however, as Job reported in October 1942.

> *Upon finding the Associate Commissioner unwilling to ask the approval of the Regents for the graduate degrees, I asked him to delay presenting the matter pending a clarification of some of the Regents' policies relating to higher education. I cannot at this time predict the final decision of the Board of Regents on this important request.*

The amendment to the Charter was eventually granted (as of February 19, 1943): along with new bachelor's degrees and honorary degrees,* the College was authorized to confer the Master of Science (programs were contemplated in physical education, in health, and in nursing education); the Master of Fine Arts (for music, speech, drama and the fine arts); and the Master of Music. There were thus three possibilities for a graduate degree in music: the M.S. for music education; the M.F.A., "with a major in music"; and the M.Mus., in applied music. The "Supplement to the Catalogue" in 1943 made the long-expected announcement.

A Graduate study program will be inaugurated at the opening of the summer session on Monday, June 28, 1943.

The turnout for that first summer was something less than spectacular — fewer than twenty students registered, fourteen of them in music. But Job was optimistic: "The program will improve from year to year." In fact, aggressive leadership had already arrived from Springfield, Massachusetts, by September 1942 in the person of William M. Grimshaw. Grimshaw is said to have offered the first officially graduate-level course at the College — Health Education, to a total of three students. But this was only the beginning. As vice-chairman of the graduate committee (chaired by the president and including the deans, the registrar, and three faculty members), Grimshaw produced a Bulletin for Graduate Study in April 1944. His hard-headed administrative philosophy was apparent in this publication: graduate study at Ithaca College was to be a no-nonsense affair, designed for teachers and specifically addressed to their "practical" needs. Unprofitable areas soon disappeared (or never proceeded beyond the talking stage) — nursing education, art, the grandiose program in English with its heavy emphasis on Anglo-Saxon and medieval language and literature. What remained comprised a substantial section of the Catalogs from 1944 - 1945 on; separate graduate bulletins were regularly issued from 1952 - 1953.

The first master's degrees were conferred in May 1946, and by the following September, graduate study had become a year-round activity at Ithaca College — initially in Physical Education, later in Music. Enrollment grew: October 1948, Grimshaw reported, 106 degrees had been conferred and some six hundred students had been enrolled, some commuting for more than a hundred miles. His own role in the institution took on new lustre. In February 1945, he was named director of Graduate Studies; by May 1949, the title was upgraded to director of the Graduate School. Grimshaw would leave the College at the end of the fall semester of 1951 - 1952 to accept an appointment as professor of physical education at the University of Massachusetts. But after two years (during which interim Dean Rawski attended to graduate matters), he was back in Ithaca as professor of education and director of the summer session. By May 1954, he had regained much of his former position, with the title chairman of Graduate Studies.

After 1950, additional areas were explored. The first graduate courses in radio were offered in the summer of 1950, and a Master of Science progam in speech was announced for the summer of 1951. And upon his return from Massachusetts, Grimshaw began a massive movement into in-service education for teachers. Even before his departure, the Catalog of 1947 - 1948 had stressed in-service opportunities in Ithaca during the evening hours and on Saturdays, and as early as 1947, he had set up an outpost in Rochester under the sponsorship of the local board of education. In 1954, advertisements began to appear with an extended list of night-school courses, and the press regularly reported on the openings of scattered off-campus locations. The latter generated considerable revenue for the College and were amazingly simple to administer. Grimshaw depended largely on the instructor who was anxious to teach a graduate course, whether a member of the Ithaca faculty or some coach, teacher, or principal in the field. The instructor not only organized his course but often recruited his students (sometimes from the personnel he supervised); the College's role was mainly to legitimize the operation. Qualitative controls were minimal or nonexistent, and by the 1960s, this far-flung operation, covering much of upstate New York, would prove an embarrassment to the College and even a threat to its accreditation. But President Job has recorded another view.

As a result of Doctor Grimshaw's indefatigable efforts . . . the Division of Graduate Studies became

---

*The College's first honorary degrees were conferred in 1943 upon Ralph Lyman Baldwin, music educator and composer, and Professor Bert Rogers Lyon.

one of our most respected and widely acclaimed efforts. The program proved to be of inestimable value, not only because it set us up as an institution doing effective graduate work, but also, to our great advantage, a valued source of college income.

By October 1942, Job was discussing yet another possibility for expansion with his Board.

Throughout its history, the College has justly taken pride in the fact that its activities have been of a highly specialized character. For the most part, this specialization has been justified in terms of particular educational or social needs. In more recent years, we have taken pride in the fact that our efforts were concentrated on three fields. Should it be found wise to enlarge the scope of our efforts by including Fine Arts in the curriculum, I should like also to propose that we add to our offerings, specialization in the secretarial sciences. This might be done by including; first, short-term courses of approximately one year, leading to prompt employment in offices and shops; second, longer courses, perhaps two years in length, which would give command of the secretarial sciences with considerable liberal cultural background for those who wish to take limited advantage of some college training; and third, four or five year courses leading to appropriate degrees and certification to teach in the public schools. There has been a scarcity of trained teachers of secretarial sciences for a number of years.

Implementation of such a program must necessarily wait until World War II was over, for now "it would be impossible to secure an adequate number of typewriters and other office machines with which to equip the laboratory." Job sensed some resistance to so mundane a program.

There are those who would object to the addition of secretarial science to our curriculum because the College has come to be known as an institution devoted to the cultural arts. This objection can hardly prevail, however, if it is remembered that physical education is probably no more in line with the cultural arts than

the secretarial sciences. Furthermore, it may be seriously debated if the College, if it is to survive the war and the period following when we shall probably suffer from post-war adjustments, should not take full advantage of the opportunities which may be presented to contribute to meeting the social and educational needs as they emerge.

Job opted for a realistic accommodation to changing market conditions.

Principally, we should be concerned here with the question as to whether or not our best interests lie in limiting our activities as we have done in the past, or if in the nature of things, we should undertake new ventures, partly to absorb the shocks of war and readjustment, but more importantly, [to] remain ever alert to demands of the society in which we live.

No action was taken until the spring of 1945. In May of that year, Miss Louise Williams announced her readiness to sell the Williams Practical Business School, which she operated in Ithaca, on North Tioga Street, "over the Corner Bookstore." On July 25, 1945, the Board formally accepted her offer (for $3,100), although the press had announced the sale as consummated a month earlier. The proprietary school thus acquired went back to 1876 and to the first days of the typewriter; its story — a fascinating chapter of local history — is recounted in the fall 1978 issue of *Ithaca Horizon*.

The Ithaca College "School of Business" commenced operations in September 1945, still over the Corner Bookstore until it was moved to the newly built Annex in 1950 - 1951. Miss Marcelite Wallace, secretary to President Job, was named acting director; when the State Department of Education insisted on a certified public accountant, Charles K. McGurk, a Harvard M.B.A., was appointed director (August 1946). John Hardy, formerly principal of the Williams Practical Business School, continued for a while as instructor.

The curriculum, that first year of 1945 - 1946, was a one-year program in secretarial sciences — typing and shorthand, business English, business arithmetic, business letter writing, business machines, and accounting. The following year, the offerings were expanded: there was now a choice of either a one-year or a two-year program. By 1947 - 1948, the stress was on a four-year curriculum, with concentrations in business management, in accounting, and in business education (that is, training teachers of commercial science for secondary schools); the first students, transfers, were graduated as "commercial teachers" in June 1948 — Jane Peters and Everett Knobloch.

The School of Business had from the start established close ties with local businesses and industries: many executives, lawyers, bankers served as part-time faculty members. Relations with the National Cash Register Company were especially close, through the good offices of Roland ("Red") Fowler, who would become a Board member in 1953. Field work opportunities, lectures and seminars, and career conferences were set up, and the curriculum moved more and more toward business management and accounting rather than the secretarial sciences (which were phased out in the mid-fifties). In October 1954, the trustees even directed one of their members to investigate the possibility of establishing a School of Economics.

Nothing came of that idea, however, and the falling off of the postwar peak enrollments caused some serious difficulties. McGurk left in 1952; business, reduced to the status of a department in the General College, floundered without a chairman until the arrival of James Winter in 1953. The accreditation team of that year found much to deplore: programs not recognized by Albany, inadequacies in liberal arts background courses as well as the absence of a general orientation to business, an unwarranted claim in the Catalog that the accounting curriculum prepared students for the C.P.A examination.

This jolting criticism elicited appropriate remedial responses, so that the four-year accounting program was in fact approved by the State Education Department by the end of 1954 - 1955 and Ithaca College graduates became eligible to take the C.P.A. examination. A new era began in 1954 with the arrival of Frank Kolmin, and business would emerge, in the Dillingham years, as one of the strongest departments in the newly created College of Arts and Sciences.

Now we are ready to consider what was certainly the most radical shift of emphasis in the history of Ithaca College — from General College to College of Arts and Sciences (and eventually School of Humanities and Sciences).

The General College (even its name has a defeatist ring to it) began to emerge in 1947 - 1948 as a far-from-adequate attempt to resolve the question of where the humanities fitted into the Ithaca College picture. In the earliest days of the institution, courses in literature, history, languages, and sometimes ethics could be more or less successfully accommodated within the Williams School of Expression, but increasingly the Catalogs reflected some uncertainty as to just where such "academic" courses should be placed. Leonard B. Job had come to Ithaca College in September 1931 as, among other things, director of the Division of Liberal Arts and Education, and after his elevation to the presidency, the division continued in name, but without an administrative head.

Even in the mid-thirties, the College had begun to think of the humanities as something more than background courses for students in the professional curricula. In May 1935, the *Ithacan* announced that a program for the training of English teachers had been approved. Now, by the simple investment of some eighteen hours, "everyone may qualify himself for a teaching field outside his major." The Catalog of 1940 - 1941 attempted to give a larger philosophic context to the minor, without neglecting its "distinct material advantages."

> To balance our highly specialized programs the College offers a group of strictly academic courses administered on a college level calculated to enable the student both to strengthen and broaden his specialized training in the several fields. . . . He is introduced to the aesthetic principles and the ethical possibilities of human development, the intangible forces of human intellect, and the fine distinctions possible in the polite use of the English language.

Throughout the 1940s, the annual presidential reports reflected the growing perception that the future of the College lay with the humanities, or at least with some fruitful coexistence of professional and liberal education.

> Ithaca College has always been a specialized institution. In the last decade there has been an increasing emphasis on the academic portion of our curricula but we have not as yet considered it wise to expand our background of academic courses to the degree necessary to ask for the right to give the Bachelor of

Arts degree in the academic fields. I have always believed that offering curricula upon which such degrees could be granted would contribute to the growing health of the College and at the same time enrich the training of those students who have specialized majors. [1941 - 1942]

The place of our college in this scene may well lie in the direction of expanding its curricular offerings to meet the general rather than the specialized needs of post-high-school youth. Our facilities, such as they are, can accommodate 1500 students. The registration in physical education, our largest department, should be reduced, probably drastically. Music should be reduced within a year or two. . . . It appears, therefore, that by 1950 we should have no more than 1,000 students in our present departments. If facilities are needed if all who wish to go to college are to be accommodated, there are good reasons for planning a general college program for 500 students. [1946 - 1947]

The report of 1947 - 1948 disclosed an additional reason for developing the liberal arts majors: to facilitate the accreditation of the existing professional curricula, which could not be accomplished until the College as a whole was fully accredited.

Annually there is increasing evidence of the high regard in which our graduates are held. This recognition offsets, in part, our repeated embarrassment because of non-membership in regional or national accrediting associations. . . . [The Middle States Association of Colleges and Secondary Schools] has no membership for which we can apply. . . . So far as I can discern, the best chance lies in the direction of offering at least one liberal arts major and thus qualify for inspection as a Middle States Association member.

Job was not optimistic of success in the attempt to amend the charter to permit the conferring of the A.B. degree. Nevertheless, he decided to try. In the winter of 1947 - 1948, the Grimshaws visited Puerto Rico as guests of Dr. Earl Clarke,

vice-president of the Polytechnic Institute and former U.S.O. director there. Clarke left Puerto Rico for Ithaca as of July 1, 1948. The newspapers, announcing his arrival, referred to him as "Dean of Academics."

Clarke's first year proved eminently successful. In Job's words:

The addition to the staff of Dean Earl Clarke has done much to strengthen the work of the General College. He is a competent educator and highly skilled in handling academic and personnel problems. The integration of the work of the General College going on under Dean Clarke's direction should enable us to apply successfully for an amendment to our charter, permitting the offering of degrees in the "academic" majors as well as in specialized subject majors.

The phrase "General College" had thus come into use by 1947 - 1948 and made its appearance as an official division of the College in the Catalog for 1949 - 1950.

But for some years, the administrative boundaries were even more loosely drawn than usual at Ithaca College. The School of Fine Arts continued as before, comprising music, drama, and radio (even though the last mentioned was far more a "practical" than a "fine" art). Speech and English had for some time been moved, more or less at random, from one division to another; now, along with education, social science, and science, they found a home in the General College. By 1953 - 1954, history was separated from the other social sciences, and mathematics was added.

Nonetheless, the General College would not remain uniquely devoted to liberal education. The dissolution of the School of Fine Arts in the fall of 1952 restored Music to its original independence, and both drama and radio were incorporated into the General College. Then, the School of Business ceased to exist as a separate entity, and its curriculum, including the courses in shorthand, typing, and business arithmetic, were transferred to Dean Clarke's jurisdiction. In sum, the General College soon became something of a catchall — not only for assorted "academic" subjects but also for those professional curricula for which no other home could conveniently be found. Once again, the College had modified its structure, not through any educationally coherent plan but pragmatically, with a sharp eye fixed on economic advantage.

As President Job had apprised his Board, the General College, to be meaningful, must be empowered to confer A.B. degrees, and for that, yet another amendment of the Charter was required. The Regents acted on September 14 - 15, 1950, authorizing the College "to provide, in addition to the instruction already authorized, instruction in the liberal arts and to grant the additional degrees of Bachelor of Arts (A.B.) and Associate in Applied Science (A.A.S.) in course, and the honorary degree of Doctor of Laws (LL.D.)."

By 1955 - 1956, the General College would be the largest unit in Ithaca College, and even before that status was attained, there had been an important change in its leadership. After the first bid for accreditation had been rebuffed, Clarke was given the new title of "Dean of Students" (September 1954), and was succeeded as dean of the General College by Warren L. Hickman. An historian with a specialty in international relations, Hickman held degrees from Colgate, Columbia, and the University of Geneva (Docteur ès Sciences Politiques); he had joined the faculty at Ohio Northern University in 1949, becoming dean of the university in 1951. A young man with boundless energy and enthusiasm, the new dean addressed himself to the task of transforming the General College into a fully accredited College of Arts and Sciences. This program would be substantially accomplished by the end of the Job administration, and Hickman's pervasive influence on the educational life of the institution would be felt long past 1957. On May 9, 1956, the Board renamed the General College: the College of Arts and Sciences began its official existence.

Let us turn back to the rejection of the College's petition for accreditation by the Middle States Association in 1953.

A team of evaluators, headed by Harry V. Masters, president of Albright College, had visited the campus from March 9 to March 11, 1953, and had subjected the institution to a penetrating scrutiny. Their report pinpointed the major areas of weakness:

1.) Although the College professed its dedication to such noble objectives as equipping its students with "broad general and professional knowledge as well as professional skills," developing "character, varied interests, and an inquiring mind," guiding them toward "more effective citizenship in our evolving democratic society," and inculcating "an under-standing of fundamental values encompassing all humanity in an atmosphere unhampered by prejudice and intolerance," the examiners found little evidence that such triumphs of the critical intelligence were in fact occurring.

> *Apart from the courses in American and European History, there is practically no opportunity for students to come to grips with present-day political, economic, social, philosophical or religious problems.*

2.) The organizational structure of the College lacked coherence. Further, too many people reported directly to the president. There was no tenure system and little communication between the faculties of the various divisions. The faculty pay-scale and student personnel services were woefully inadequate.

3.) The Library budget was only half the recognized minimum; its physical plant was intolerable even on a temporary basis (those nonconnecting converted classrooms in the Annex). And there was distressingly little evidence that what books there were were being used either by the students or by the faculty.

4.) Offerings in the General College were deficient, especially in philosophy, political science, sociology, and languages.

5.) While some departments (notably drama and physical education) were doing outstanding work under difficult conditions, and while speech and Music seemed adequate, other departments presented problems, some of them serious problems. The Physiotherapy curriculum came in for a devastating critique, both in its courses and in its practical work: the examiners were shocked to discover that at the Tompkins County Memorial Hospital, Ithaca College students were carrying out treatments of patients, as part of their training, without any supervision whatsoever.

> *This is a rather irregular and dangerous servicing of patients and exposes both the trainee, the hospital, and Ithaca College to liability if any accident or injury is sustained by a patient while under treatment.*

The graduate program in Physiotherapy was beyond salvage, and its immediate discontinuance forcefully urged. Indeed, most of the College's graduate programs were suspect.

The music faculty is adequate in numbers and training, but it is doubtful if any of the other faculties have sufficient training and experience to support a graduate program. The head of the department of physiotherapy does not even have a college degree, and it is believed that the number of men with doctor's degrees are too few to support a graduate program.

6.) The financial picture disturbed the accreditation team since even the official request of its chairman failed to produce certain necessary records. It was clear, to the examiner at least, that statements of net worth which included accounts receivable for student tuition going back more than a decade and which assigned new and inflated values to college properties could hardly be taken seriously.

7.) Although there was abundant evidence that Ithaca College graduates were finding jobs, no data was available that would make possible a comparison of their work and that of students in similar programs in other institutions.

These are merely the highlights of the 1953 accreditation report — sufficient, perhaps, to indicate why approval had to be withheld at that time. Immediate and drastic action was in order.

Hickman's appointment as dean provided the stimulus for a concerted effort to ready the College for a fresh evaluation, just as Clarke's reassignment was designed to meet the criticism relating to student services. The results of frenzied activity in 1953 - 1954 and 1954 - 1955 can be seen in a second evaluation report, this time by a new team headed by John J. Theobald, president of Queens College, which visited Ithaca from February 28 to March 2, 1955.

It would be difficult to find two documents more different in tone. The recently instituted core curriculum (English composition, Western civilization, social science, literature, science, and speech) was deemed to be in full conformity "with the normal practice of other institutions." Programs leading to the A.B. degree were now available in English, history, economics, and American civilization, with a two-year foreign language requirement. The controversial graduate programs in speech and in the Division of Physiotherapy had been abolished.

The offering of graduate work is now limited in time to the summer sessions, and in subject matter to

courses of value to teachers in the fields of music and physical education who are seeking to advance their professional status. This is a service designed mainly for graduates of the College, in relation to teaching certification.

The "leave-it-to-President Job" syndrome was less pronounced, and there was some evidence of greater faculty participation in policy determination, notably through expanded committee work.

In general, the report radiated satisfaction — even enthusiasm:

That which impressed the evaluator . . . most about Ithaca College, aside from the almost superhuman job which was done in getting the institution out of the red and on a sound financial basis, was the evidence of progress in the educational sense. There are strong indications that much of the attention in the last three to five years has been directed toward better curriculum, improved library facilities, and increased participation by the faculty in the development of educational policy. Similarly, the development of the general areas which would normally go into the making of a student personnel program is a marked sign of consciousness of student needs. The students themselves, as they move around the campus, their performance in the dining halls, and the like are excellent evidence that fine things are happening and that good attitudes are present.

Not everything had been set to rights, of course, and further progress reports would be required, with a reevaluation in ten years. Nevertheless, in May 1955, Ithaca College joined the ranks of those institutions fully accepted by the Middle States Association.

And so the Job quarter-century drew to its close. President Williams, in his autobiography, was pleased to recall his departure from Ithaca with evident satisfaction, if not self-congratulation (and some inflated statistics).

Personally assuming all financial burdens, I continued and, overcoming the bitter opposition of Cor-

nell University, the Conservatory of Music was now "Ithaca College," with a student body of over one thousand, a faculty of one hundred teachers, many of whom were a recognized authority in their particular field, and the college was now the proud owner of sixteen buildings. I was content.

Job, ever the realist, was far more cautious in *his* summation.

The vision so long entertained has become a reality. It remains for us to see if what we saw was a vision or only a garish nightmare.

Those of us who are the beneficiaries of that vision need not doubt its fundamental soundness; Job's commanding place in the history of Ithaca College becomes clearer with each passing year.

Over tremendous odds, he had taken on a near-bankrupt institution and brought it to solvency; he had willed that it endure, despite depression, despite global conflict, despite the shifting and treacherous tides of American higher education. More than that, he had guided it to new opportunities for growth, in excellence as well as in mere size. The dean who had been called to a tiny institution threatened with the loss of its degree-conferring powers would leave behind him a fully recognized college of more than 1,550 students.

Perhaps the accreditation of Ithaca College was the greatest accomplishment of his administration. Without that, the professional curricula would probably have languished, the hordes of post-World War II liberal arts students would have turned elsewhere, the South Hill campus could never have been built. President Job had accurately identified the only "door" to the future, and, whatever his personal reservations, had resolutely taken his College through.

Plate Series II: Downtown Buildings

Photo by: J. P. Harcourt

"The four rented rooms" on East Seneca Street

Archives

The Wilgus Building on the corner of State and Tioga Streets

Photo by: Marion Wesp

The Conservatory Building at DeWitt Park
(later the administration building)

Photo by: C. Hadley Sm

The Concert Hall (later, The Little Theatre) and the Administrative
Annex (band room)

The Seneca Gym

Photo by: C. Hadley Smith

Photo by: The Ithaca Journal

The Music Building on North Cayuga Street

Photo by: C. Hadley Smith

The Aurora Gym

Aerial view of the Downtown Campus showing Annex and Library

Williams Hall corner of Buffalo and Tioga Streets

Photo by: C. Hadley Smith

The "new" Radio-TV Building

Photo by: C. Hadley Smith

The Annex

Photo by: Curt Foerster

The Physiotherapy Building at East Buffalo Street

Phi Delta Pi (formerly Parke Hall) Dormitory,
111 Osmun Place

Westminster Hall Dormitory, 323 North Tioga Street

Plate Series III: Downtown Activities

The Twelfth Night Revels (Lillian Speakman Vail as queen)

Grecian dancers: De Witt Park

Performance in The Little Theatre

Dancing Class in The Little Theatre (seats removed)

Gym class in Seneca Gym (formerly Star Theater)

Commencement, De Witt Park

Archives

Walter Beeler's Band in De Witt Park

Float parade 1964 on State Street

Downtown dormitory life

Dining in Williams Hall

Downtown TV: The Frank Kolmin Show

Photo by: C. Hadley Smith

The new downtown Library, 1954

VI.   The Dillingham Years 1957 - 1970 (1)

"A Time to Build . . ."

IN his final annual report (December 31, 1956), President Job undertook to define "the present problems of the College" — problems which, he was candid to say, were "monumental in scope and difficulty," calling for nothing short of heroic action by the Board and of course by his successor. Accreditation was a fact, but only barely so. The Middle States Association had made it clear that notable progress must be achieved in three main areas before February 1958 if recognition were not to be withdrawn. The Board would have to start functioning like a Board; the president must surrender some of his powers to the Board and some to other administrators and to the faculty; the plant must be improved and the finances of the College strengthened.

Job also recorded his discovery that the absence of a deficit had in fact been a disadvantage in fund raising.

> . . . a man of wealth will much more readily give his check for a million dollars to erase a college deficit than give to a college that has no deficit. Strange as this conclusion may appear to be, it might well suggest that the College would be well advised to undertake a comprehensive program of development on borrowed money on which it could not even hope to pay amortization charges.

The outgoing president was surely being ironic; he would never become reconciled to the fact that the College would take precisely that course of action within a few years of his departure (though with more sanguine expectations of repayments). In 1968, he would even disclose that once

> I was able to get the promise of a loan from the federal government adequate to construct a complete campus "on the hill." I saw no prospect of ever being able to repay the loan of some $8,000,000 when I had tried hard for nearly twenty years just to pull ourselves out of bankruptcy. Consequently, I did not mention the loan possibilities to the college trustees.

In the 1956 report, he adverted, more characteristically and with evident distaste, to the rumors of state assistance in scholarships and loans to private colleges: "Most of us have seen equally strange and un-American projects become realities even in our own time, both on the state and national levels."

There were references to the South Hill acreage but in tones that lacked conviction: Job mused over how useful a gift of $150 million would be to create a campus for 15,000 students. More realistically, he summarized the needed renovations and additions to the downtown campus — some $4.5 million worth. And even at the end of his administration, he was reluctant to relinquish the notion that Ithaca

College might be relocated in some other, more generous, community. As a "last final resort," the Board, he pointed out, could always elect "to give the College with its assets to Cornell University and cease operation." His fears for the future were undisguised: "some future administration, made, perhaps, of less stern stuff, may falter, even crack, under the pressure and eventually fail." Yet he could end with a warm tribute of confidence in his successor.

> *Under Dr. Dillingham's administration, you may be assured of leadership on the campus that will be of high order. His ability is superior, his integrity above question or corruption, his general philosophy of life and of education is sound and highly ethical, his knowledge of the College is comprehensive, and his devotion to its purposes is unassumed and unassuming.*

This fourth president of Ithaca College, Howard I. Dillingham (he would later drop the middle initial), was born in Elba, New York, on October 11, 1904, of Quaker parents — a religious tradition that would be pervasive throughout his life. Like that of his three predecessors, his background was essentially small-town, rural America; he fondly remembers the district school he attended near Auburn, where all eight grades were taught in one room. Later came the Wharton School of Finance and Commerce at the University of Pennsylvania; then a master's degree and, in 1938, a Ph.D. in education from Syracuse University. After six years with the Gorham Company in Providence, Dillingham became director of the Auburn Collegiate Center of Syracuse University (1933 - 1937), then dean of Rider College, headmaster of the Manlius School (1944 - 1950), headmaster of the Riverside Military Academy in Florida, and, at Ithaca College from December 1951, at first assistant to the president and later vice-president (as of May 1953).

President since February 16, 1957, Dillingham was formally invested in the office at a general convocation, held in the Presbyterian Church on October 12 of that year. The inaugural ceremonies set up curious resonances when reviewed in the light of the events of the late sixties. The guest speaker, George K. Anderson, chairman of the English department at Brown University, deplored the fact that those in academic life "must expend their energies in resisting pressures of one sort or another."

> *Should we desist from teaching* Huckleberry Finn *or* The Merchant of Venice . . . *simply because they may produce emotional stresses and strains among certain minority groups who do not understand a different age and a different set of mores?*

The key word in the new president's address was "community." Recalling that the medieval universities were in some instances actually controlled and governed by their students and that the concept of academic freedom originally applied to students rather than to faculty members, he came down hard for increased student involvement in college governance.

> *The degree to which a college community permits students academic freedom is a measure of its success in meeting one of the chief obligations of higher education, that of developing the capacity for self-government.*

True to his Quaker heritage, he decried the institutionalization of the American college; the task is "to uncover the community made up of scholars and students that we may discover those forces which release the individual from conformity and make it possible for him to attain self-realization." A college community must be a free community, in which "democracy may work its reasonable triumphs of accommodation, its vital process of union." As we shall see in the next chapter, some quite unreasonable triumphs of confrontation lay ahead, but in October 1957, these were still decently veiled by the mists of futurity. Whatever conclusions he might later reach in the troubled spring of 1969 - 1970, Dillingham was convinced, at the time of his inauguration, that even when the exuberance of students gets out of hand, that "zest for life, though sometimes expressed in socially questionable actions, springs from an awakening of inner forces which can be channeled to further social progress." Even the clergyman succumbed to the prevailing spirit of egalitarian optimism in his prayer that "education of the people, by the people, and for the people may not perish from the earth." Restated some dozen years later as "Power to the People," the connotations, perhaps even the denotations, would be different; the impact of slogans painted on walls with spray cans would prove more disturbing than those ministerial sonorities.

The era of democratic consensus did not become immediately apparent. Job had expressed the fear that through the malign influence of the Middle States Association, the president would become merely the "hired man," whose function was only to carry out the directions of the faculty on the one hand and the trustees on the other. Dillingham and his Board would work together with remarkable effectiveness, but in the crucial decisions that had to be made in the late fifties, there would be only a limited faculty involvement, and the students would not be heard from for quite some time.

Within a few days of Dillingham's assuming office, the press carried the announcement that "in all probability, Ithaca College will not develop a campus on its Danby Road property." In the May - June newsletter, the alumni were apprised that money that had been contributed to the Development Fund was in fact being used on South Hill — for additional athletic facilities since Percy Field would soon become unavailable with the construction of the new Ithaca High School. But the interest of the administration was now focused on the Tompkins County Memorial Hospital properties, to be vacated as its facilities were transferred to the former state tuberculosis sanitorium on the west shore of Lake Cayuga. Here were buildings immediately convertible to dormitories and laboratories; if the purchase could be effected, they might even become the nucleus for a complete campus within city limits.

Job had also been investigating the hospital site after the College's bid for the Biggs sanitorium itself had been rebuffed. But being unable to foresee how the existing structures could be renovated with the funds available, he had not acted. Dillingham, at his first Board meeting as president, suggested a way. Early in 1956, Ithaca College, along with most other American private colleges, had been awarded a grant from the Ford Foundation — $297,500, the income from which, for ten years, was to be used to augment faculty salaries. Some $20,000 of this sum had already been expended for the purchase of an additional house downtown to serve as an income-producing dormitory. Of the remainder, the College could use $152,000 for its purchase bid and the remainder for furnishing and remodeling. It was the discussion of this proposal that had led to the announcement that the College was abandoning the idea of moving to South Hill. In May, it became official: the College would place a bid for the hospital

plant; failing in that, it would continue its expansion in the downtown area.

The year 1957 - 1958 was one of preparation, planning, and anxious waiting. Wanting the hospital site rather badly, the College made strenuous efforts to enlist local support. In February 1958, Dillingham gave additional reassurances that the College would not abandon Ithaca and alluded to scientific equipment already on order, to be used, it was to be hoped, in the new laboratories that would be set up in the hospital utility building. He also hinted at far more elaborate developments at the Quarry Street location: "at some distant time, the property might be developed into a compact campus." The alumni were urged to contribute in support of the desperately needed biology laboratories.

The tension mounted. As background to the College's planning, the city was in the throes of an extended discussion on urban renewal; there was keen interest in just how the College and its downtown properties would fit into the projections being made by the City Planning Board. The College was the lone bidder on July 7, 1958, but of course the bid did not have to be accepted. An urgent press release listed the many reasons in support of the acquisition and rather pointedly reminded the citizenry that in the past year, the College and its employees had pumped some $2,140,650 into the local economy. The *Ithaca Journal* saw fit to lend its editorial support. The days lengthened to a week. Then, on July 14, 1958, it was announced that the County Supervisors had accepted the bid, with only one dissenting vote.

Ithaca College now owned eleven acres halfway up State Street hill, on the rim of a gorge, with three buildings — the hospital itself (to become the Quarry dormitory), the former nurses' home (to be Valentine Place), and the utility building, the second and third floors of which would be converted for the biology and chemistry departments. The Physiotherapy operation would be moved into the old hospital laboratories. Eventually, a physics laboratory would be set up in the basement of Quarry, an auditorium would be designated as Alumni Hall, and there was even an apartment available for use by guests of the College.

Occupation of the new dormitories involved elements of high drama. John Mason Potter reports that two days before the students were scheduled to arrive, it was noticed that one rather critical item was missing — the beds. Frantic phone calls to the manufacturer elicited the information that they had been duly shipped by rail; a railroad president was awakened by a call in the middle of the night, and it was discovered that the missing furnishings were waiting on a siding somewhere in the Midwest. An urgent order got them moving, at least as far as Buffalo, where the College arranged for them to be picked up by chartered trucks. But they ended up on yet another siding, one inaccessible to motor vehicles. More calls to railroad officials, more orders, and eventually the beds were on their way to Ithaca. Progress was closely monitored; a work force recruited from the administrative staff stood ready from midnight on and worked throughout the night as the trucks rolled in. The work, it is said, was completed minutes before arrival of the first students, who must have been startled on being assigned to rooms still labeled Morgue, Labor Room, Delivery Room.

But for the first time in its history, the College was able to provide housing for all of its male freshmen.

The hospital site opened up dazzling new vistas. Below, Six Mile Creek flowed through a wooded gorge, the far rim of which was relatively unused; upstream, the creek flowed out of a large tract of park land. We can sense something of the feeling of escape from a congested downtown area in the Catalog of 1959 - 1960: "freshmen men live in dorms which are located in a wooded area overlooking one of the scenic gorges with which Ithaca is blessed." Why should this area not be the future home of Ithaca College? Clearly, Dillingham was fascinated by the prospect. Job reports that he had passed up an opportunity to buy the the hospital property for $50,000 partly because he found his vice-president's interest in a complete Quarry campus alarming in the extreme — the "Dillingham nightmare," he would call it.

In any event, even as hints of such a possible development were being conveyed to the public in the spring of 1957, feasibility studies were being made and architects were working at their drawing boards. A detailed promotional brochure was made ready by April 1957, complete with Tallman and Tallman's preliminary estimate of the costs of each of ten buildings — to a total of $6,020,000. While the details changed as hopes for funding rose and fell, the plan seems to have been for buildings to be constructed on both rims of the gorge, with two suspension bridges connecting them. And, down at creek level, elaborate recreational facilities — tennis courts, football fields, softball fields, and so forth — to be made available to the community at large during the summer

months. There were other hitches besides money, however; much of the needed acreage had been deeded to the city for use as a public park and transfer of title would be difficult — another round of public bidding was mandated by law. But the College elected to move in that direction. The faculty minutes for May 8, 1958, record that "a blueprint of the Quarry Street hospital property was circulated with proposed buildings to be erected thereon, provided the College is the successful bidder on the tract." The following October, the project seemed real enough to prompt Mr. and Mrs. Allan H. Treman to deed additional land off Valentine Place to the College, the very first donation of property to be received by the College, the *Ithacan* noted. In May 1959, the Board examined plans for a new Science building, for which, it was said, Dean Hickman confidently expected a gift of one million dollars.

But by fall of 1959, the dream began to fade. A Quarry campus would forever limit development to about 1,500 students, and even with that number, there were virtually insurmountable problems of access roads and parking facilities. For many, fears about spring flooding had not been dispelled by the feasibility studies, and there was a nagging concern over a location a few miles downstream from the dams that impounded the Ithaca water supply.

And so, on August 11, 1959, Dillingham dispatched a memorandum to his trustees acknowledging the inadequacies of the Quarry site and urging the reactivation of plans for South Hill.

South Hill, with its 180-odd acres, its beautiful location, its flat terrain, and its lack of construction obstacles, offers an unparalleled opportunity for the establishment of a campus of consequence, ideal to meet the needs of an expanded educational economy.

Tallman and Tallman were ready with a new preliminary budget and timetable. To begin with, there would be an Arts building, a Science building, the Student Union, and four dormitories for six hundred students in all — at a cost of $5,099,000. Phase II would include a gymnasium, a field house, the Library, an administration building, the "Music Department," four more dormitories for another six hundred students, "Additional Space for the Drama Department," and a house for the president — totaling another $4,569,000. If work were to begin on September 1, 1959, the first grouping could be ready for occupancy just two years later.

The executive committee responded favorably, although cautiously, at its meeting of August 13, and its resolutions were communicated to the other trustees. The president's annual report of October 1959 provides an interesting context to this drastic change of plans. Even then, Dillingham registered some reluctance in abandoning the idea of "a relatively inexpensive and, hence, early attainable campus." Yet he recognized that vastly improved facilities were, if anything, even more urgent, since widespread recognition of a new curricular development, "The Ithaca College Plan," necessitated a building program appropriate to its full implementation. And part of the altered mood was attributable to international politics.

Sputnik touched off a surge of public interest and critical appraisal of American education. The State Department and the Department of Health, Education and Welfare reflected the reaction of the public. Representatives of these departments visited Russia to appraise its educational system and reported to Washington that education was the Communists' secret weapon and that, while our educational personnel, facilities, and methods lagged and were retrogressive, tremendous progress had been made in Russia and China.

Hence, the word from Washington suggested the imminent availability of federal money for the support of private colleges.

In such a climate, reappraisal of the future of Ithaca College by its administration was called for, particularly in view of the expectation of federal funds and increased interest of foundations in providing support for new college facilities.

The recent appointment of Ben Light as secretary of the College (July 1, 1959) would free the president to pursue these enticing possibilities of financial assistance (although in fact it was Light who would do much of the legwork). In conclusion, Dillingham urged his trustees to seize the felicitous moment.

The unprecedented interest now being evidenced in education, coupled with the birth rate since the early 1940's, have conspired to create a peculiarly advantageous climate in which colleges such as ours may acquire new facilities. We should and intend to take full advantage of it.

On October 16, 1959, after viewing a model prepared by Tallman and Tallman, the Board of Trustees formally opted for South Hill.

Now that the decision had been reached, where was the money coming from?

From the earliest days of the planning of the South Hill campus, considerations of budget loomed large, as always in the history of Ithaca College. But while in New York City, President Dillingham had noticed an older building in the process of being demolished in order that a replacement, no larger, might be built. The reason, he ascertained, was that a more modern construction would be cheaper to operate. This argument carried considerable weight with the trustees and in fact turned out to be valid. In his report for 1962 - 1963, Dillingham would note that operational and maintenance costs per student on the new campus were only half those for the downtown buildings; in fact, "savings in maintenance and operation of the new buildings more than paid for the interest and amortization of the construction loans."

But whatever the budgetary constrictions, the new campus could not be conceived in any niggardly, scrimping way: the sheer beauty of the hilltop location offered irresistible challenges to the imagination. Dillingham would always maintain that the esthetic impact of the College on prospective students and their parents was of the utmost importance. In his homely idiom, "people, in buying a car, look for more than that which is under the hood." The College had the enormous advantage of planning an entire campus at one time — at first as a ten-year project, then with a considerable acceleration of the timetable and with the addition of a number of major items. Plans were changed repeatedly as the work proceeded, but, at every stage, the campus was viewed as an organic whole and in relationship to defined educational objectives. Its architects, Tallman and Tallman, and its chief designer, Thomas Canfield, would see the task through to completion.

For the details of the financing, let us go back to August 11, 1959, when Dillingham sent that confidential memorandum to the trustees. The executive committee of the Board would be convened two days later, he told them, to consider a proposal for a $5,100,000 building project on South Hill. He anticipated that $3,100,000 could be borrowed from the federal government (from the Community Facilities Administration) at 2.7 percent over forty years; he emphasized the presence, in such agreements, of a "forgiveness clause." The other $2 million were to be sought from other branches of the federal government, from foundations, and from "various other private philanthropies."

The executive committee met on August 13, and its actions were summarized in a memorandum sent to the trustees on August 20. The administration was granted permission to file a preliminary application for a $498,000 grant for the Ithaca College Plan and another for a $3 million loan from the Community Facilities Administration for the construction of dormitories and the Student Union. An outside consulting firm, Harris, Kerr & Foster, would be asked to provide a cost study of the project, and, if this evaluation proved favorable, the executive committee would recommend to the Board that the South Hill site be developed as the new campus. The question of establishing an R.O.T.C. unit at Ithaca College would be investigated, "with a view to getting a drill hall and gymnasium built with federal money." And, apparently in response to fears of the Music lobby that the historical preeminence of that school might be threatened by the rising fortunes of Arts and Sciences, a subcommittee was formed and directed to work with Dean McHenry to study and implement ways of securing funds for the construction of a new Music building at the earliest possible date. But Dillingham pointed out that while the Student Union might temporarily be used for the Library and for administrative offices, an Arts building and a Science building were urgently needed — and within two years' time — if there was to be any hope of securing federal subsidies for the "new experiment in curriculum economy and effectiveness" known as the Ithaca College Plan. He concluded by pledging all concerned to secrecy: "no public announcement is to be made of the new building plans as funds must be in hand or assured before the Board commits itself."

The omens continued propitious, and on September 1, 1959, a preliminary application was made to the Housing and Home Finance Agency (of which the Community Facilities Administration was a part). The momentous news was announced to the faculty on October 8. By the middle of that month, Tallman and Tallman (still not officially commissioned by the College) had completed a second cost study, now considerably expanded. An Arts building, a Science building, five dormitories, and the Union would be built in the first round; Phase II would include six additional dormitories, a theatre, an infirmary, the Library, a maintenance building, a gymnasium, field house, and stadium, an administration building, and a chapel. The grand total now reached $13,686,700 — or, including furnishings and removable equipment, $14,624,700.

On October 16, the Board met in Ithaca. The model they viewed was not quite current, so fast did the plans shift: it shows only eight standard dormitories and one high-rise (not on the hillside, where the Towers now stand). The model, in fact, was almost totally unlike what was even then on the drawing boards, but, the trustees were impressed. They authorized the architects to proceed with the drawings and the administration to look to the funding: the Harris, Kerr & Foster projections were so encouraging that it was voted to inaugurate a $15 million fund-raising campaign. President Dillingham was directed to purchase the remainder of the Miller property — the twenty-three acres, with house, cottage, and two barns, at the intersection of the Coddington and Danby Roads, which Job had not included in his 1949 acquisition.

The following day, the College held its fall convocation, at which President Dillingham made the official announcement. The headlines in the *Ithaca Journal* that evening proclaimed that the "$15 Million Campus" would be in operation by 1966; the pictures juxtaposed the architects' model with a panoramic view of a bulldozed field, with Lake Cayuga in the far distance. Senator Jacob K. Javits was on hand as convocation speaker, his plea for a free-world partnership clearly upstaged by more local developments; his very presence was suggestive of the College's new relationship to government and its agencies.

After this gala weekend, the president left directly for New York to confer with Ralph Cornell, regional director of the Housing and Home Finance Agency, and to submit a revision of the preliminary application of September 1, 1959. The meeting was eminently successful and the good news was telephoned back to Ithaca — the College might expect to borrow, perhaps within ten days, the sum of $2,878,000 (which would subsequently be increased to just under $3 million). Since the Housing Agency could finance only income-producing projects, the College was obliged to commit itself to the extent of $372,000 (for site preparation and utilities, extra features in the Union, and so on).

But the period of anxious waiting was to be considerably longer than ten days. On December 9, the press noted that the College's proposals did not appear on the listing announced by the Community Facilities Administration: it would seem that the College had not established a sufficiently high credit rating with the Housing Agency. At this critical juncture, the assistance of a Board member, George C. Textor, proved invaluable. Textor had been a trustee since 1953 and would chair the Board from 1965 until his death in 1968; he was also at that time President of the Marine Midland Trust Company. A line of credit for $300,000 was forthcoming, and then another $250,000 from the Tompkins County Trust Company. With this firm backing from the banking community, the picture brightened considerably.

In mid-January 1960, Ralph Cornell met with the Board and gave his unofficial assurance that the funds would be forthcoming. Tallman and Tallman proceeded with their drafting; the faculty, meeting in small groups throughout the academic year, forwarded suggestions; the interfraternity council was reassured that there would be a place for such organizations on South Hill; the Town of Ithaca was petitioned for a new sewer district. On May 13, 1960, it could at last be announced that the loan had been granted. The bids went out and were opened on June 29 and July 7, and the William E. Bouley Company of Auburn set to work soon after.

Before very long, the time was at hand for the laying of the Union cornerstone — October 22, 1960. President Job returned for the ceremony and to attest that "those who came after me have displayed courage and wisdom," and the principal address was given, in the auditorium of the National Cash Register Company just across the Danby Road, by Homer D. Babbidge, assistant commissioner and director of the U.S. Division of Higher Education, HEW. Babbidge gracefully compared the work that was beginning on South Hill with the founding, some one hundred fifty years earlier, of Union College — "the first planned campus in the nation, or indeed in the world."

Let us hope that by our symbolic act in laying the cornerstone of Ithaca College's new campus this afternoon, we bestow upon this monument to a fresh conception of education that element of harmony and beauty which will prove an inspiration to all who enter here, and a reminder to all who come after us that this campus represents the aspirations, the ideals, and the vigor of purpose of an institution, and of the people who were able to conceive it and willing to build it. In a very real sense, what we put in place today — in a cornerstone and in the large edifice it signifies — constitutes a memorandum to posterity.

At the site itself, members of the College community stepped forward, one by one, to deposit in the capsule to be placed in the foundations of the Student Union copies of the *Cayugan,* the *Ithacan,* the Student Directory, an alumni record, a list of Friends, brochures from the various divisions of the College and from the student organizations, the current Catalog, and finally, a Bible. The returning alumni inspected the work in progress during their April 1961 reunion.

And so, beginning in September 1961, the College would be operating three campuses — downtown, Quarry, and South Hill. The complexities of the busing arrangements were staggering — and expensive. Fortunately, the local transit company went out of existence at just the opportune moment, and the College was able to acquire a fleet of five busses (especially geared to cope with the Ithaca hills) plus their garage. By November 1961, 586 of the institution's 1,539 students were living on South Hill. These were students from the School of Arts and Sciences. There had been some dissension as to which segment of the College would be moved up first: some felt that Music should lead the way because of its historical primacy; others stressed the grossly inadequate downtown facilities which Physical Education had had to endure for so long. But the decision was for Arts and Sciences — partly to give its relatively new programs greater publicity and wider recognition, but mostly for logistical reasons. Although the President could rightly claim that "on the back lots of an abandoned farm, a new community has been built, boasting its own water district, sewer system, paved roads, street lights and sidewalks" the fact remained that there were only five dormitories and a partly finished Union building actually there. In effect, the humanities were being invited to rough it.

And rough it they did — in a sea of mud, amid armies of workmen. The borrowed money could be used for dormitories, a cafeteria, the Union, but not for classrooms, faculty offices, or the Library. Having moved almost six hundred students up the hill, the College had then to improvise some kind of instruction for them. A room on the second floor of the Union (now the Pub) became a "branch" library, equipped to cope with only the most urgent needs — reserve books and a few reference works. The faculty teaching on South Hill were herded into a large recreation room in the basement of Dormitory 3 (now Rowland Hall), where their "offices" were cubicles separated by six-foot bookcases. Classes were held in any available location — in the recreation room on the third floor of the Union, in the Union listening rooms, in dormitory lounges, in basement trunk-rooms. This was of course an unauthorized use of government-funded space (with the possible exception of the Union, for which some College funds had also been used). Faculty members were warned that if inspectors appeared on campus, they and their classes might have to effect a discreet but speedy disappearance. The Arts and Sciences faculty even moved that "it is the sentiment of the faculty that the administration not feel the pressure to provide offices for the faculty on the new campus, if in doing so, steps will be involved which will be likely to jeopardize the standing of the college in the Federal Aid program." Oddly, there was, within a year, a fine outdoor swimming pool, which prompted an indignant letter to the *Ithacan* charging that the College had "subordinated a library to a swimming pool." (Actually, the pool was constructed for Camp Music Land, which leased the campus during the summer months on terms highly advantageous to the College.)

Questions of legality apart, instruction during those first years posed some unusual problems, to say the least. The *Ithacan* ran a good-humored editorial, "Men Working," which described lectures accompanied by "the crashing bulldozers, the noise of cranes, and the thud of steamrollers." A history professor found that during one of her classes, tile cement had been put down in the hallway outside so that she and her students were forced to remain until the tiles were in place and completely set. Teaching in dormitory lounges could be distracting as hairy figures, clad only in towels,

lumbered by in full view. When, slightly later, the Textor Lecture Halls were being built, an instructor teaching *Hamlet* while the heating system was being installed, mentioned the critical view that Ophelia committed suicide because she was pregnant. At the end of the class, one of the workmen approached the podium and remarked, "You know, professor, I never thought of Ophelia in that light before."

However makeshift the instructional arrangement may have been, the South Hill campus was formally dedicated on October 21, 1961. The convocation was held in the Union Recreation Room (which occupied the entire east side of the third floor). Metropolitan tenor Jan Peerce was on hand to add lustre to the occasion and to make a spirited plea for greater attention to the cultural dimensions of American life.

But what was immediately needed was more buildings. More than a year earlier, the Board had begun to move on Phase II, which turned out to be five additional dormitories and an infirmary, later to be known as the Health Center. Application was made for $2,310,000 from the Department of Housing and Urban Development, College Housing Division, in September 1960. But in February 1961, the College found it prudent to request that the government delay action on its application; there was good reason to believe that approval would not be granted for additional dormitories on a campus that could not point to so much as a single classroom or other academic facility.

"Who is to bail us out?" Dillingham had asked his Board, some years earlier. The question had been largely rhetorical then; now it was desperately real. The South Hill construction had been begun, but how could it be continued? Or, alternatively, how could the College stop at this juncture?

Enter the Friends of Ithaca College.

Fund raising had moved once again into the foreground as soon as the College opted for South Hill. Despite Harris, Kerr & Foster's optimistic estimate of the institution's potential resources and the campaign for $15 million launched on the premise of their report, not much cash was coming in. The earlier Development Fund had produced relatively little, and that money had been expended for the playing fields and the field house; some $47,574.32 in unpaid pledges were finally written off in January 1960. William Silag, assistant to the president since the fall of 1958, had organized a many-pronged appeal — to foundations, to the alumni, to the faculty and administration, to the local community. The alumni succeeded in raising $79,000 to help furnish the Union by October 1962, but little was forthcoming from the other sources — with one notable exception.

The breakthrough came from the citizens of Ithaca. Back in 1957, Roland G. ("Red") Fowler, manager at National Cash and a College trustee since 1953, had begun to organize a small group of persons sensitive to the needs of the College and willing to contribute at least one hundred dollars a year. If, Fowler reasoned, a sufficient number of "Friends" could be found — say, a hundred or more — their annual gifts would become equivalent to the income from a substantial endowment. The idea caught on with the State Street merchants and others; meetings, small at first, were held in the Red Room of the Hotel Ithaca. Early in 1958, the original nucleus — including David Saperstone, William Burns, Arthur Stallman, Harold Carlyon — expanded into a full-fledged organization with Fowler as president and Cecil Shulman as vice-president. At the College end, alumni secretary Lillian Vail managed the bookkeeping and the paperwork.

Thus the first academic building on the South Hill campus was made possible by using the Friends of Ithaca College as a base for a fund-raising campaign: PROJECT ITHACA COLLEGE. Under the chairmanship of Raymond McElwee, a group of Friends appraised and rated the giving ability of every potential giver in Tompkins County as well as persons of known interest elsewhere. In the spring of 1961 they set out to raise $250,000.

IF $250,000 IN LOCAL SUPPORT IS FORTH-COMING, it will be matched to the extent of $750,000 from other sources, providing in total the $1,000,000 required for the construction costs.

A list of "Memorial Opportunities" in the campaign brochure makes it clear that the building was at first conceived of as a Science building, manifestly one of the institution's most urgent needs if the curricula of the College of Arts and Sciences were to become functional on South Hill.

The Friends' campaign went over the mark: at the Chamber of Commerce annual dinner in March 1962, the proud announcement was made that $250,852.66 had been contributed or pledged ($240,024.93 was actually received). This was

magnificent, but what of the remaining three-quarters of a million? No foundation appeared willing to pick up the tab; hopes that federal money would be made available for the construction of classroom buildings dwindled. Something had to be built, yet clearly it could not be a Science building. And so it was decided to do what could be done with the money in hand. A simple shell of what, at this stage in the planning, was thought of as an eventual administration building, was begun in the summer of 1962 and was in use by the following January. This structure, later to be substantially expanded and twice remodeled — now elegantly refinished both inside and out — still carries the name that recalls its origins: Friends Hall.

Thus with a building that could serve temporarily both for classroom space and for the Library, the College could reactivate its request for the funding of Phase II. The application made in 1961 - 1962 for $3 million was approved, construction on the five dormitories and the infirmary was begun in the spring of 1962, and the newest buildings were ready for use, more or less, by the opening of the academic year 1963 - 1964.

The "Lower Quad," with some 1,261 students, was now complete.

But this was little more than a toehold on South Hill. The shuttle-busing of students between three campuses continued to be a vexatious problem. Although most of the College of Arts and Sciences was functioning, after a fashion, on the hill, the activities of the speech-drama and TV-radio departments continued of necessity on the downtown campus; service courses to the professional students in Music and Physical Education also had to be offered in the old locations. The sciences were at the Quarry campus, so that students both from downtown and from South Hill had to be transported there. Operating two libraries, with a collection of books that was minimally adequate at best, was a serious obstacle to effective instruction. Clearly, it was imperative that all operations be moved to the new campus at the earliest possible moment.

As Dillingham pointed out to the trustees in October 1962, there was no way to go except forward.

With six and one-half million dollars already invested in non-academic facilities on the new campus, the die is cast.

But money continued in short supply. The Development Fund of the fifties became history when, in 1961, the names of the donors were inscribed upon a plaque (now in Job Hall). The drive for $15 million so enthusiastically announced in 1959, faltered, then ground to a halt. The presidential annual reports, which from September 1963 become elaborately printed promotional brochures rather than confidential reports to the trustees, are remarkably silent on the subject; indeed, there are few references to it after the initial announcement. Despite much scurrying about from foundation to foundation, from philanthropist to philanthropist, no significant sums were forthcoming, and the persistent dream of a single benefactor of enormous wealth was never to be fulfilled. Beyond PROJECT ITHACA COLLEGE and the alumni effort to equip the Union, there were only modest gifts: the parents of students, organized into a Parents Association by the fall of 1963, provided a flagpole and contributed to the decoration of the main entrance of the campus. Throughout the sixties, the principal source of private capital was the gradual liquidation of downtown real estate (a plan to demolish some of the buildings and erect income-producing apartment complexes was abandoned as impractical).

The South Hill campus would continue to be built largely with public money, however. The earlier proud boast that the College was a luminous example of private enterprise at work soon gave way to a celebration of the harmonious working relationship between government and the private sector, with a new emphasis on the College's social role: "Society has helped Ithaca College so that Ithaca College can continue to help society." Convocation and commencement speakers, so often from government, state or national, powerfully underscored this theme.

In 1960 - 1961, there had been hope that a federal aid to education bill would provide the answer, but by August, it had become clear that the College would have to finance the Science building so desperately needed for the implementation of the Ithaca College Plan in some other way. Since no funds materialized to match the quarter million raised locally, Friends Hall had been hastily scaled down and redesigned for general classroom uses. Then, a new possibility loomed into view — the State of New York. In October 1962, the trustees were apprised that

since the defeat of the federal academic facilities

legislation, projected interest and amortization costs have been keyed to the provisions relating to academic facilities of the New York State Dormitory Authority. Preliminary negotiations have been entered into with this agency for the financing of a science building to be started in the spring of 1963.

By December, the Board learned that the Dormitory Authority would probably provide funds for three buildings — a Music building and a gymnasium as well. "Series A" bonds to a total of $6,295,000 were issued for this purpose.

The ground-breaking for a radically redesigned Science building (now costing almost $1,900,000 and never given a distinctive name) was held on May 4, 1963, just before the annual dinner of the Friends of Ithaca College, with Chairman of the Board Herman Muller turning the first shovelful. The formal dedication occurred on October 17, 1964. That occasion was marked by a day-long conference on "Science Education in the Liberal Arts College," under the sponsorship of the College Center of the Finger Lakes, with Professor Robert Pasternack, principal architect of the College's science programs, serving as chairman. Donald Coates, of the National Science Foundation, was the luncheon speaker; Cornell's Dean W. D. Cooke spoke at dinner on "Some Views of Science Education in the Next Decade." Much of the day was given over to small discussion groups led by faculty members from the various colleges in the Finger Lakes consortium. President Dillingham paid tribute to science as "a special kind of philosophy," which, in fact, constituted "the essence of our culture," and dedicated the building "to the spirit of adventure, to the enrichment of our intellects, and to the glorious age of science."

The dedication of the new gymnasium on December 5, 1964, was also planned as part of a professionally significant program — this time, the Eastern regional meeting of the American College of Sports Medicine. Some two hundred leaders in physical education and in student health problems gathered to read and hear papers on the physical effects of exercise and on the role of women in sports. The dinner speaker was Arthur Steinhaus, dean emeritus of the George Williams College in Chicago. At the dedication ceremony, Director of Physical Education Arnold Wilhelm presiding, Trustee Michael Hanna spoke for the president, with a special tribute to the "fathers of the Department" — "Doe" Yavits, A.

Garman Dingwall, and "Bucky" Freeman. The building would later become the Laurence S. Hill Physical Education Center; hence, it was entirely fitting that the widow of the former dean (who served from 1919 to 1957) should be present. After a standing ovation, Mrs. Hill pressed a button, the paneled partitions slid open, and "a gymnasium came to life." The building was used for the first time for an intercollegiate basketball game on December 8, 1964.

John Mason Potter gives an interesting bit of information concerning the construction of the gymnasium.

One day, while riding in the country, President Dillingham came upon a brickyard which was not operating and apparently was abandoned. There were a large number of red bricks which had been aged by time and mellowed in hue by exposure to the elements. He decided that they would be ideal as facings on some of the new College buildings. The College purchased the brickyard and its bricks, and the exterior of the Physical Education Center is of these bricks.

Some of them were also to be used for interior facing when it came time to erect the four-building complex now anchored at the western end by Job Hall.

That was not all — the year 1964 - 1965 was a year of dedications. The Music building, occupied by late fall 1964, was dedicated at the seventieth baccalaureate service on June 4, 1965. A brass ensemble played "tower music" as a medieval background to the academic procession that took its way across the campus and into the new building. Present was the man who would give it its name — Walter Burton Ford, mathematician and benefactor of the College, then in his early nineties, stood on stage in patriarchal dignity as the plaque was uncovered and his statement of appreciation read.

The new building, with facilities for five hundred students and a concert hall that could seat seven hundred fifty people, was a joy to behold — and appropriately central in its location on the campus. Yet more than a few former students and faculty members would feel a pang when, in July, the *Ithaca Journal* ran a picture of the bulldozers and cranes ruthlessly demolishing the proud old columned Music building downtown.

A year of dedications, yes, but 1964 - 1965 was also a year of other "firsts." Perhaps the *Ithacan* was anticipating slightly in its editorial of October 2, 1964, but it keynoted the new academic year.

For the first time in a few years, we greet a college functioning primarily on one campus.

The Music building and the gymnasium would not really be occupied until well into the first semester: substantial units of the College were still active on the two other campuses; one hundred or more Physical Education students would have to be housed in the Clinton House, all the floors of which above street level were taken over as a makeshift dormitory. But in February, it was possible once again for the entire student body to be assembled at one time and in one place — in the gymnasium for a convocation at which the president and his principal architectural advisers outlined plans for further building. And, as spring approached, the campus was opened to the community for an "Ithaca Day": students, faculty members, and staff welcomed the townspeople with guided tours, art and photographic exhibits, a performance by a gym team, a piano recital, plus a freshman baseball game and intercollegiate tennis matches. For the first time in decades, it was possible to hold commencement on College property instead of in a downtown theater or church. On the previous evening, the academic procession marched to the baccalaureate service, again to the accompaniment of tower music played from the roof of the Music building.

The president's annual report of 1964 - 1965 proudly narrated the intense intellectual and cultural activity on the unified campus. Ford Hall and the Hill Physical Education Center provided, for the very first time ever, really adequate facilities for the College's musical and athletic events. A concert series presented the Syracuse Woodwind Quintet, the Rochester Philharmonic, and Carlos Montoya, the flamenco guitarist. The art collection was growing at an impressive rate, with important acquisitions in African, Mexican, and Oceanic primitive art including works from New Guinea given by Cedric Marks. There were on-campus exhibitions, and a Creative Workshop had been started. The Distinguished Visitor Series of lectures brought eight prominent Americans — among them Max Lerner — to speak on various aspects of the creative arts. The Forum series featured local talent — members of the faculty and administration addressing themselves to significant educational and cultural topics. Perhaps most important of all, the C. P. Snow lectures began. Dr. Robert Pasternack, later to become the College's first Charles A. Dana Professor, had conceived the idea of a series of lectures bridging the gap between the sciences and the humanities — a gap definitively explored by Snow in his concept of "the two worlds." Approached by Pasternack, Lord Snow graciously consented to lend his name to the series. That first year, seven scientists, including Nobel prizewinner Peter DeBye, were brought to the campus. Not without reason, therefore, could Dillingham claim that

> *the student at Ithaca College now can enjoy the advantages of a creative collegiate environment — a sound and diversified academic program, supplemented by an exceptionally wide range of cultural and recreational activities, housed in modern facilities and situated in a spacious, rural setting.*

Our next chapter will consider the intellectual life of the campus in further detail — back now to the building of the South Hill campus. The most recent facilities had only slightly alleviated the classroom shortage: classes were no longer being taught in the cafeteria during meal hours, but dormitory lounges and other improvised areas were still in use. Most Arts and Sciences faculty members had been moved out of the trunk rooms and into the Science building, but humanists were uneasy in offices equipped with laboratory sinks and gas jets. And it was more than time for the central administration (still on East Buffalo Street) to join the South Hill family.

So, prior plans for several separate structures west of the Science building were scrapped, and substituted for them was an integrated unit with a long connecting arcade, referred to at the time as "the academic complex" or "the General Studies complex." It would include, using some names subsequently bestowed, the Muller Faculty Center (to be home of the College of Arts and Sciences), the Textor Lecture Halls, a remodeled and expanded Friends Hall, and the administration building, Job Hall. The New York State Dormitory Authority had authorized $4,980,000 in "Series B" bonds, so that it was possible to proceed, not only with the academic complex but also with the Library and a performing arts building. The last mentioned would require an additional $1,125,000 in "Series C" bonds, and, when finally passed in 1963, the Higher Education Facilities Act provided construction grants for these projects to a total of $2,118,360.

The performing arts building lay somewhat in the future, but the Library soon became a reality. Only the first three of a projected five stories would be completed at this time. Nevertheless, for the first time in the history of the College, there would be a Library spacious enough to house the still less than wholly adequate collection and geared to the changing curricular patterns of the institution. Few buildings were more satisfying to plan — the result of unusually harmonious teamwork between librarians, faculty members, and architects, with expert counsel generously supplied by Dr. Stephen McCarthy, head of the Cornell University library system. And, although staff members still grumble about unutilized space, few edifices give greater delight to the esthetic sense — "the most elegant building of all," the president declared.

With the exception of the performing arts building, these new facilities would come into use early in the academic year 1965 - 1966. Simultaneously, the College was moving toward expanded student housing. In 1964 - 1965, there had been more than 2,300 students (compared with the 1,100 of ten years before). In that same decade the budget had increased by 644 percent (from $806,838 to $6 million): mounting expenses necessitated not only higher tuition (up 181 percent) but also increased numbers of students. The planners were contemplating a total enrollment of 3,000 by the end of the sixties (it would in fact reach almost 3,700). Already, some of the local politicos were conjuring up the spectre of a "South Hill Collegetown," complete with motels, restaurants, and possibly a shopping plaza, somewhere on the periphery of the campus.

More living space had to be provided. In May 1963, the Board had authorized the construction of a fourteen-story high-rise dormitory. By the following October, since the Department of Housing and Urban Development seemed almost eager to lend $4,250,000, it was decided to build two of them, with a connecting dining hall. At this time, the College still forcefully proclaimed its adherence to the *in loco parentis* concept; hence, the East Tower would house the women, its western counterpart the men. Even so, Robert Mueller, assistant to the president for construction, would publicize them as being designed for "fun living." Work was under way in 1964 - 1965 — monster cranes dominating the southern skyline (one of them once toppling ingloriously into the mud, but without injury to anyone). The students moved in in September 1965. In October, the Towers beaconed the letters U.F. to the community in the valley below to mark the beginning of the United Fund drive; they would dramatically signal the changing digits of the year at midnight on December 31. (There had been a few angry protests about a cross outlined in the lighted windows for the Christmas season.)

Beyond the high-rises, the Board was thinking of yet another cluster of dormitories perched on the hills south of the Music building and the gymnasium. These, rather prematurely billed as the "Final Phase" of South Hill construction, would later be known as the Terrace dormitories, or, in the less reverent terminology of the students, as "Instant Hong Kong." At first, they were referred to as the "duplex" area.

It represents an unusual, perhaps unique, concept of campus living. Twenty-five houses will accommodate small groups of upper-classmen. In the junior and senior years, students may elect to live with others of their choice in an intimate, home-like atmosphere. It is with this concept we hope to counteract the impersonal I.D. card frustrations of today's students.

This development, with its own dining hall, required yet another loan of $7,430,000 from HUD.

A religious center or chapel had long been projected; more immediately realizable was the College farm. A country road wound its way up from the Coddington Road through woodlands and past a pond — part of this area had been a farm and would now be restored.

During the past year [1964 - 1965], the farm was stocked with domestic animals, and a stable of riding horses. The woodlot is being preserved in its natural state. Especially for students from metropolitan areas, the campus farm not only attracts interest, but provides enlightenment for a way of life that seems virtually to have disappeared in many places.

So firmly did President Dillingham cherish this bucolic vision that at one point, he considered using the farm road as the main entrance to the campus — a graceful transition from the bustle of city life to the serenity of academia. The farm, unfortunately, did not long outlast his administration, and the woodlot has been sadly hacked into for utility buildings and all their ugly appendages. In October 1965, the farm population had numbered six horses, one pig, thirty-five chickens, two goats, one donkey, one lamb, three peacocks, and two head of Hereford cattle. One faculty member recalls his young son returning in horror from watching the safety personnel shooting the last survivors.

Not all of the proposals for the South Hill campus were brought to fruition. In January 1961, President Dillingham had startled his faculty by announcing that a "faculty dormitory" was about to be constructed and would be ready for occupancy by August of that year; registration forms could be picked up at the end of the faculty meeting. The press reported that some professors "showed verbal disapproval while others greeted the plan with a standing ovation." The nays soon won out, however ("My children aren't going to be happy about it!"), and the project was quickly and quietly dropped. Architects' drawings for the "Ithaca College Primate Laboratory" (an adjunct to the Science building) also came to nothing, although monkeys played a prominent part in biology instruction and were kept as pets at 2 Fountain Place.

Activity was not confined to South Hill, of course. The College continued to use the Valentine and Quarry dormitories — they were expensive to operate, yet indispensable as, in the later sixties, we hear more and more about a shortage of space. The Union, constructed for a student population of about 1,250, was becoming less adequate each year as the enrollment shot upward toward 4,000; the removal of the administrative offices and eventually the classrooms of the College of Arts and Sciences and the remodeling in 1965 - 1966 helped only a little. By the fall of 1969, as the *Ithacan* bemoaned triple occupancy in some of the rooms on campus, a downtown motel had to be leased for the overflow population.

One remaining piece of downtown property was imaginatively transformed as the old administration building (the Boardman House) became the Ithaca College Museum of Art. Since Dorothy Hoyt Dillingham, the president's second wife, was herself a well-known painter, she had contributed notably both to the esthetic dimensions of campus planning and to the use of art objects about and within the newly constructed buildings. The Union had featured an exhibit of paintings from the Rockefeller collection in the winter of 1964 - 1965 (the only painting ever to be stolen from that collection was taken from the Union and never recovered), and there were periodic art shows by students and by faculty members. Objects collected by the Dillinghams in their travels through Mexico, South America, and Africa could be seen in virtually all the lobbies; Cedric Marks, as previously mentioned, had contributed examples of primitive art from New Guinea; there were exhibits of Eskimo art, of Matthew Brady photographs. In his report of 1964 - 1965, Dillingham wrote:

> . . . *painting, sculpture, and artifacts are displayed in nearly all the campus buildings, enhancing their interior beauty as a complement to the natural beauty of the campus, and serving as a reminder that creativity and aesthetic appreciation are an important part of the educational process.*

The New York State Crafts Fair was one of the many organized groups attracted to the campus during the summer months. And surely the most visible *objet d'art* was the aluminum sculpture *Disc*, by Ithaca artist Jack Squier, given to the College by David Mandeville (who would become a trustee in the seventies) in memory of his grandfather, Hubert Mandeville. Described as a creation "of polyester resin over fiberglass over styrene foam placed on a steel frame" and covered with aluminum leaf, *Disc* had been commissioned by the Dillinghams after they had seen its prototype in a New York City gallery. Campus reaction ranged from serious interest to amused disdain to active hostility ("Why spend money on this when so much else is needed?") to acts of vandalism and defacement. But *Disc* (whatever the nicknames invented by the undergraduates) was gradually assimilated and has become a landmark, dominating the campus from the top of the Textor Lecture Halls — though still lacking the reflecting pool of black glass integral to Squier's original design. Another piece by the same artist, *Machine-Beast,* was placed at the foot of the stairwell in Job Hall.

But of course it was the Museum that was Dorothy Hoyt Dillingham's especial pride. Opening on May 4, 1966, with Gretel Leed in charge and with its own board of directors, the Museum used the refurbished Boardman House to splendid advantage — modern paintings on the ground floor, African and South American art upstairs, two rooms for the works of Ithaca College students, and a collection of drawings and lithographs. There was an impressive sequence of more than seventy-five visiting shows (even though the Picasso graphics and ceramics were misplaced in transit and didn't make it for the grand opening): included were works by Paul Klee and Andy Warhol. The Museum issued handsome programs and published two important contributions to local history: *New York Crafts 1700 - 1875* and *Henry Walton, 19th Century American Artist.* Mrs. Dillingham — or, to use her professional name, Dorothy Hoyt — and Professor Salvatore Grippi exhibited their work at the Museum, and there was a training program for undergraduates interested in a career in museology. The Museum would close in 1971 - 1972, axed by an "austerity" budget — the building sold, the collections eventually stored in the basement of 2 Fountain Place, where they remain. The last show briefly recreated the Boardman House as it must have been in its prime — an elegant Victorian town house. When it was over, the downtown Ithaca College also vanished into history.

After the mid-point of the sixties, the pace of construction slowed. Now that a self-contained community had come into being, the amenities were added one by one — a post office, a tailor shop, a barber shop. In November 1965, student leaders were conferring with their counterparts at Hamilton as to the proper procedures for operating a pub; the Pub, then located in the dining area between the Towers, opened shortly thereafter. As the academic facilities became available for use, the students were able to claim space originally designed for them — the listening rooms, the game room and the billiards room in the Union, the dating lounge on the fourteenth floor of West Tower (that area would be disputed territory until, with changing mores, dating lounges became obsolete). The fourteenth floor of the opposing Tower was given over to a handsomely appointed restaurant — nominally, the Tower Faculty Club, although generally, faculty members constituted a minority of its users. Many will remember the elegance of its first days — the decorative motifs, the well-designed china and flatware, the impressive menu (even if one item was listed as being served "with au jus"). Outside the Union, the Venitt Memorial Terrace was added in the fall of 1969, just in time for the rallies and demonstrations of that era.

By 1967 - 1968, with the performing arts building under construction and the Garden Apartments not yet dreamed of, the College was ready for a celebration of all that had been achieved. And what more felicitous occasion than the marking of its seventy-fifth birthday — 1892 - 1967? The anniversary was conceived of as a year of festivity. The Board had received the "Preliminary Plans" in October 1965; a year later, the faculty "Celebration Committee" was appointed, with Professor Raymond Kaaret as chairman and Colonel Richard H. Comstock as executive director and administrative aide. A year of intense planning followed, with innumerable subcommittees and endless meetings (only faculty members were involved — the *Ithacan* would protest the exclusion of student members, but this was only 1967 and no one worried too much).

The principal event was to be the fall convocation, for which the most grandiose of plans were formulated. No less than President Lyndon B. Johnson would be invited to be the speaker; failing him, the follow-ups were U Thant, secretary-general of the United Nations, or Vice-President Hubert Humphrey — with Senator Robert Kennedy described as a "fourth and perhaps more realistic choice." Other possibilities considered were the U.S. ambassador to the United Nations, the secretary of defense, the secretary of state, the chief justice of the U.S. Supreme Court, and the governor of New York. For the after-dinner speaker, C. P. Snow was the first choice if indeed he could be persuaded to cross an ocean to visit an institution which boasted a lecture series named in his honor. Other suggestions were McGeorge Bundy, Robert Hutchins, Margaret Mead, Buckminster Fuller, and the president of Mexico. The theme of the anniversary year was to be "Towards Personal Fulfillment in a Creative Environment."

Inevitably, there was some scaling-down of these ambitious aspirations. But even so, the convocation on October 6, 1967, was a memorable occasion (with a budget of more than $18,000). The Snows arrived from England; delegates from other colleges and universities converged on Ithaca. A colorful academic procession made its way across the campus to the gymnasium, where, in the absence of Lyndon Johnson or U Thant, Lord Snow gave the address. Ruminating on the mysteries of gifted children, particularly those with extraordinary abilities in music and in mathematics, he wondered what startling things might be achieved if young people in these two categories could be brought together in an intensive educational experience. Ithaca College, he felt, with its tradition of musical excellence, and Cornell University, with its reputation in the scientific disciplines, were uniquely suited to launch such a program.

I want to leave you with a problem which I think is solvable. It is a problem which has a real meaning for all of us and the next generation. And I believe that this community with its remarkable academic institutions is one of the best places to begin to do some serious thinking about it.

At the close of the convocation, President Dillingham introduced the chairman of the Board, George C. Textor, who proceeded to dedicate the campus as a whole to the ideals enunciated for the anniversary year. The plaque he uncovered reads:

Commemorating the 75th Anniversary of the founding of Ithaca College, this campus was dedicated on October 6, 1967, to serve those who teach and learn by providing opportunities for personal fulfillment in a creative environment.

Lord Snow's challenge was respectfully received but of course would not be acted upon. The day moved to less solemn observances — the dedication of *Disc,* the presentation of an illuminated citation from the trustees to Dorothy Hoyt Dillingham commending the deployment of her considerable artistic talents in the planning, furnishing, and decorating of the campus, a cocktail party for a group of invited guests, and then a banquet, for them and for the College community. Almost eight hundred persons dined together and drank wine from souvenir glasses inscribed with the seal of the College.

Speakers that evening were hardly world famous — the chairman of the Board, two members of the faculty, and the president of the student body. Lynn Bogart, professor emeritus of Music, brought the past of the College to life with his deeply felt reminiscences of W. Grant Egbert. Mr. Textor surveyed more recent history under the title "How Did We Do It?" The writer of this history, invited to look to the future, predicted that the era of student docility would soon be over, that "the student is about to come into his own on the American campus, as a contributing member of the academic community, and as a responsible voice in the determination of institutional policy." He urged both administrators and faculty members to look forward, with authentic openness, to a future that was problematic, but certain not to be dull: "Nothing can be taken for granted. We can proceed to a truly impressive realization of achieved excellence. We can also slip into some chronic state of amiable mediocrity." That very uncertainty, he maintained, provided an almost unique condition for creativity. Lastly, Peter Burrill '68 acknowledged some of the frustrations of adjustment to the new College scene but confidently asserted that "with patience we will grow into the campus we have created."

The anniversary celebration was planned not merely for that one Saturday in October but for the entire year. Each school and division had its own series of events. Arts and Sciences planned a year-long program of symposia, lectures, and conferences: President James A. Perkins of Cornell appeared to analyze the problems of higher education; Arthur Schlesinger spoke on "Illusion and Reality in Foreign Affairs"; other speakers tackled African unity, private enterprise in the public interest, public education in American cities. More specialized symposia focused on the verbal and mental effects of stuttering; Visiting Professor Rod Serling presented a discussion of the impact of the mass media.

Health and Physical Education brought some five hundred scientists and physicians to the College for a conference on bioelectricity; a two-day special study institute considered "Newer Concepts in Physical Education for the Mentally Retarded." More technical presentations were arranged on cardiovascular disease prevention and rehabilitation and on proprioceptive neuromuscular facilitation. With a bow to the anniversary theme, the year also included a seminar on "Personal Fulfillment through the Physical."

Musical activities were especially impressive. They included a flamenco dance recital and a two-piano concert; workshops conducted by Shinichi Suzuki in methods of teaching violin to toddlers; and Jeanne-Marie Darré, "France's first lady of the piano." A major event was the installation and dedication of the baroque concert organ, made possible in part by a gift from Walter B. Ford: it had taken two years to assemble its four divisions, eighty ranks, sixty stops, and 4,316 pipes. A series of concerts by visiting organists signalized its completion. And for those of less exalted musical tastes, the Jefferson Airplane group came to the campus.

In October 1967, a full-page advertisement in *The New York Times* announced that the American Symphony Orchestra under Leopold Stokowski would open its season in Carnegie Hall with a guest appearance of the Ithaca College Choir. The choir, under its director, Gregg Smith, had recorded music by Ives in 1966. Now, at two concerts paying tribute jointly to the United Nations and to the College's anniversary, they would earn a standing ovation for their rendering of Ives's "Four Songs for Chorus and Orchestra." Stokowski was moved to cry out "Bravo Ithaca!" This music was made permanent on recordings issued by Columbia Records and the Voice of America.

The culminating musical event was surely the Stravinsky festival, held from December 8 to 10, 1967. The two choral groups, the Ithaca College Concert Choir and the College Chorus, had moved into international significance under Smith. The connection with Stravinsky went back to December 1965, when Stravinsky's associate, Robert Craft, had come to Ithaca to conduct the first performance in the United States of the master's *Les Noces* in the original Russian. The work was recorded under the composer's supervision. Stravinsky then invited the choir to perform his *Persephone* at the Los Angeles Music Festival in May 1966; this work was also recorded. After a European tour, the choir participated in a Stravinsky festival held at Princeton in October 1966, and plans were initiated to have the composer himself as visitor on the Ithaca campus during the anniversary year. Unfortunately, illness prevented him from coming, but Craft was on hand. Four concerts presented a variety of works including two one-act operas, the *Requiem Canticles*, and the *Symphony of Psalms*. The choir and chorus were joined in these endeavors by the Opera Workshop, the Jazz Lab Band, the Wind Ensemble, the College orchestra under Don Wells, and by faculty soloists.

The retrospective mood of the anniversary year prompted a flurry of building-naming activity. Some of this work had of course been done earlier. In October 1961, the Board had resolved that the two rooms opening off the Union cafeteria should be designated the Merle Patrick Job Room (in honor of President Job's first wife) and the Earle W. DeMotte Room (in tribute to the former owner of the Corner Bookstore and a longtime friend of the College). Furnishings for these rooms were provided by the Alumni Association. In the fall of 1962, the Board accepted a gift from Trustee Harold Allen for the development of an athletic field to which his name was given. We have discussed Friends Hall (1962 - 1963); in the spring of 1964, at the tenth annual Physiotherapy Institute, the Cecil David West Memorial Laboratory was dedicated in memory of a beloved faculty member. The Music building was from the start Ford Hall, and the Union became Egbert Union on June 5, 1965.

That spring, one of the College's most distinguished faculty members, James A. ("Bucky") Freeman, retired at the age of seventy and was feted at a testimonial dinner on May 30, 1965. At its meeting on June 4, Board moved that the baseball field adjacent to the football stadium be henceforth known as Freeman Field — a fitting tribute to the man who, between 1931 and 1965 (omitting the war years), had coached thirty winning seasons in thirty-one years.

A convocation to dedicate the still unfinished administration building had been convened on October 23, 1965. President Job returned from Florida to inspect the building named in his honor and to give that ill-fated address excerpted in a previous chapter. It was a weekend shattered by tragedy. Two members of the Board — Herman E. Muller, chairman, and Weldon Powell, just recently elected a trustee — and their wives were killed in an automobile crash on their way back to New York City. And, within the week, a disastrous fire struck the Delta Sigma Pi house (in downtown Ithaca): two students died, and several others were injured.

April 1966 saw the naming of the Paderewski Room, to be used for piano seminars and instruction in theory and recalling the master's visits in the second year of the Conservatory's existence and again in 1922. Another link with England, along with the C. P. Snow lectures, was forged when the College's already well-known speech clinic was named the Sir Alexander Ewing Speech Clinic. Its founder and director, Dr. T. Walter Carlin, had done graduate study at the University of Manchester, where Ewing headed a world-famous program in speech pathology. Sir Alexander and Lady Ewing were present for the dedication, and at the convocation (on October 22, 1966), Ewing spoke eloquently on behalf of greater attention to the needs of handicapped children and to the study of child development in more general terms: "Quite simply, it is at this point that we make our chiefest contribution to the future of the race."

The naming ritual climaxed in 1967 - 1968. As far back as June 1961, the Board had discussed the question of the designation of the dormitories; the initial system of a simple numerical sequence was hardly satisfactory. At first, the matter had been closely tied into fund raising; prospective donors might the more easily be persuaded to write generous checks if there was the possibility that buildings might be named after them. But by October 1966, the trustees were willing to settle for benefactions for even parts of a dormitory; these hopes too yielded to the gradual realization that

no one was really interested in giving money when the building was already standing.

In October 1967, the need to reach a decision of some sort was pointed up when the Board received a student petition asking that "Dorm 8" be named in honor of the dean of students, Earl E. Clarke. A committee made up of three faculty members, two administrators, and two students (with a junior, Joseph Bogardus, as chairman) began to meet early in December; in February, the trustees indicated their willingness to receive some fifteen names from that group, out of which they would choose ten for the dormitories in the lower quad. The "Dorm Naming Committee" considered many options: prospective donors; famous scholars, authors, musicians, and so forth; classical names in keeping with the towns and cities of central New York. But almost from the beginning, the preference was for faculty members and administrators who had made a distinguished contribution to Ithaca College. At first, the committee was willing to christen all the dormitories on the campus, but it soon divided its work into two stages, beginning with the first ten (the others have not as of this writing been named). About thirty names were considered; eventually, all but thirteen prime candidates and two others were eliminated. Relations between the campus committee and the chairman of the Board committee, John P. E. Brown, were amicable, and on February 7, 1968, the Board accepted eight of the proposed names and added two of its own. Letters of invitation went out to those honored or their representatives, plaques were commissioned, and appropriate dedicatory ceremonies arranged for the Friday before commencement — May 17, 1968. The list comprised Lynn B. Bogart (professor of music, 1924 - 1967), Earl E. Clarke (dean of the General College, 1948 - 1954; dean of students, 1954 - 1967), Edward R. Eastman (trustee, 1956 - 1970; counselor to students, 1961 - 1968), Herbert B. Hilliard (professor of music, 1904 - 1905; 1907 - 1916; vice-president, Board of Directors, 1909 - 1916), R. Mae Holmes (professor of music, 1904 - 1947), Helen Hood (professor of biology and zoology, 1946 - 1960; dean of women, 1960 - 1968), Sydney W. Landon (professor of English, 1930 - 1953), Bert Rogers Lyon (professor of music, 1922 - 1959), Marguerite Rowland (professor of history, 1930 - 1965), and Jennie W. Tallcott (professor of education, 1925 - 1952).

Some worthy candidates (like Cecil West and "Bucky" Freeman) had already been honored in comparable ways, and at the same February meeting, the Board decided that the gymnasium would be the Laurence S. Hill Physical Education Center, containing the Ben Light gym. In June, it named a dance studio in honor of Elsie Hugger Erwin, professor of physical education from 1920 to 1954. In February 1969, the Board named Yavits Field in honor of Isadore ("Doe") Yavits, who until his retirement in 1963 had served for thirty-three years as exemplary teacher and coach. At the 1969 commencement, two components of the "academic complex" became the Muller Faculty Center and the George C. Textor Lecture Halls.

Returning to our anniversary year, commencement 1968 was a gala occasion, a fitting climax to an *annus mirabilis*. For many years, the dead time on commencement eve had been filled in with a perfunctory bow to religion in the form of a baccalaureate service (one Lutheran preacher had startled both President Dillingham and the audience by declaring that such ritual gestures were a stench in the nostrils of the Lord). But in May 1968, tradition yielded to innovation: the graduates and their families, the faculty, administration, and friends gathered for a nostalgia trip as Trustee Gustave Haenschen recreated the well-known radio program he had conducted for so many years — "The American Album of Familiar Music." Metropolitan soprano Roberta Peters (who before long would herself become a member of the Board) starred; the narration was provided by Milton Cross, of Saturday Metropolitan Opera broadcasts fame, in the first of his several appearances for such an occasion. Another distinguished singer, Marian Anderson, gave the commencement address, and with Miss Peters, received an honorary degree of Doctor of Music.

The party was at last over. President Dillingham, summing it up, would write, "In all respects, the 1967 - 1968 academic year was less a celebration of our past than a demonstration of our capabilities for the future." And indeed, although the "final phase" had been announced, the last years of Dillingham's presidency would see yet another grouping of dormitories under construction. The College had admired the simple organic functionalism of the lower quad units, then the dramatic statement of the twin towers, later the zany-wonderful Terrace dorms clinging so precariously to their hillside that students would swear that the buildings swayed when the winds blew up from the lake valley. And now the Garden Apartments, reflecting the changing image of the student that had emerged out of the turmoil of the late sixties — living

areas planned for a freer lifestyle, with individuality and space, and with kitchens that provided at least for some students a blessed emancipation from regimented college dining à la Saga. Authorized in February 1969, the Garden Apartments were begun by the following December. But President Dillingham would have retired before they were actually occupied in September 1971.

The last major dedication and naming ceremonies were for the building that would become the Dillingham Center for the Performing Arts. Constructed between 1966 and 1968 at a cost of $3,800,000 and dedicated at impressive ceremonies on April 12, 1969, the performing arts building at long last brought all the essential functions of the College together on the South Hill campus. The pictorial brochure, "Previewing the Performing Arts," reviewed the past achievements of drama, dance, TV-radio, and instructional resources, which now would share — and compete for — space within the new building. The drama department, which had been operating on the hill throughout the year while construction was still in progress (staging its fall productions in the Union) looked forward to the luxury of not one, but two, theatres — the Main Theatre and the Arena Theatre, designed for more experimental ventures. The first play to be produced in I.C. drama's new home was Pirandello's *Enrico IV*, on January 22 - 25, 1969.

A few years later, in October 1973, after the annual dinner of the Friends of Ithaca College, the performing arts buildings would be named for the man who by then had become president emeritus. The Board resolution caught the essential rightness of attaching the name of Dillingham to a structure which, in a special way, embodied "the creative spirit which he brought to campus planning" as a whole. A videotape, played through the color television given to the Dillinghams on this occasion, reviewed the achievement of the South Hill miracle.

The chapel was yet to be begun; the Library would later receive its two top floors and become the Gannett Center; the dream of a Fine Arts building would remain unfulfilled. Yet the South Hill campus was virtually complete by the end of 1969 - 1970 — the decade of building was over. Before we turn, in the next chapter, to the uses to which this $36 million plant was being put, it is fitting to pay tribute to one of its builders — Ben Light.

A member of the Class of '36, Light had distinguished

himself in football, basketball, and baseball; at the beginning of his senior year, he had been named football coach when "Bucky" Freeman was incapacitated by a serious illness. Even before his graduation, he had been invited to join the faculty of the School of Physical Education. Except for the World War II years, he would remain with the College until his death on January 19, 1971. After many years of successful coaching, and with a national reputation as college basketball and football official, he became the College's first director of admissions and placement in 1952. In 1959, he was given the title of secretary of the College: once the decision to move to South Hill had been taken, both Board and president recognized in Light the man who could expedite that vast undertaking.

The following nine years were the most exciting and productive ones of my adult life. . . . My assigned responsibilities included: purchasing for the whole college, supervision of transportation (7 busses and 15 cars), food service management for the college, management of vending operations, real estate transactions, and, most important during this period, complete and sole responsibility for the financing; liaison between college, architects, and contractors, expediting of the building program and all the many activities pertaining thereto.

The trustees and President Dillingham would certainly wish to qualify "complete and sole responsibility for the financing," but Light's description of his many assignments is substantially accurate. In 1968, when apparently at the point of death, he was named vice-president for development; recovering, he tackled the duties of his new office with customary energy. Just a year before he died, he was casting about for further opportunities to use all that he had learned at Ithaca College.

I do not feel that I am anywhere near the end of my productive life. The thrill and stimulation of planning, doing, building, and the sense of fulfillment acquired therefrom continue to present a challenge I am eager to accept.

Many of us remember Ben Light — his driving ambition, his fierce loyalties to his College, to his family, and to his friends, that urbane and generous courtesy that coexisted with the instincts of a hard fighter. At first bitterly opposed to the creation of the College of Arts and Sciences, he was able gracefully to accept the changing directions of the institution — he would spend a decade facilitating the development which he had initially deplored. The Ben Light Gymnasium pays only partial tribute to the work he did at and for Ithaca College. Professor John Ogden, at the memorial service on January 21, 1971, caught something of the larger meaning of Ben's achievement in lines adapted from Conrad Aiken.

But he shall have a name, though like us all
He was only one of millions, mostly silent,
Yet one who came with eyes and hands and a heart
To build his dream into the thing he loved.

ITHACA COLLEGE ANTHEM

WORDS BY
JOHN OGDEN
MARION MILLER

MUSIC BY
WARREN BENSON

Plate Series IV: Projected Campuses

Architect's rendering of proposed building in the Buffalo-Tioga Street Block

Tallman & Tallman

First model of South Hill Campus (west of Danby Road)

A more spacious model (still west of Danby Road)

Photo by: C. Hadley Smith

Site of proposed Quarry Campus (former Ithaca Hospital buildings, foreground and nurses' home top right)

VII.   The Dillingham Years 1957 - 1970 (2)

"A Time to Build Up . . . A Time to Tear Down"

EVEN before the decision to build on South Hill had been reached, Ithaca College was embarked upon a program of far-reaching curricular change — changes that would affect not only the humanities but the institution as a whole. A school that for more than half a century had dedicated its efforts to professional education in a variety of specialized areas had, on May 8, 1956, officially transformed its catch-all General College into the College of Arts and Sciences. This new entity would soon become the dominant member of the Ithaca College family, in influence as well as in numbers. The driving force behind so drastic a transformation of institutional identity was Dean Warren L. Hickman.

Hickman, as mentioned earlier, was brought to Ithaca by President Job in September 1954 to head the General College. The appointment was made in response to a crisis situation, just as Job himself had arrived as dean in 1931 at a time of similar curricular crisis. In 1931, the very validity of the College's degrees, particularly with regard to teacher certification, had been under fire. Now, in the mid-fifties, full recognition for certain of the professional curricula was being denied because the College as a whole was not accredited. The bid for accreditation in 1953 had been rejected after the scathingly critical report of the first Middle States team of visitors. Hickman was hired as an immediate consequence of that debacle; his first assignment was to make certain that the College should prove successful in its second try.

Accreditation was in fact achieved in May 1955, but with a number of stipulations and the obligation to submit periodic progress reports. No one was more aware than Dean Hickman that the problems of the College in general and of Arts and Sciences in particular had hardly begun to be resolved. By the following September, he had prepared a lengthy "Annual Report to the President and Vice-President" — forty-five pages of detailed analysis, plus four appendices. From this report, with its full complement of charts and statistics, we can learn much about the situation thirteen months after the arrival of the new dean.

He reported with satisfaction that his faculty had unanimously approved a statement of the objectives of the General College on December 1, 1954, and that similar statements for each of the thirteen departments now appeared in the Catalog. But moving down from that level of high pedagogical generalization, he found much to deplore.

The faculty was enthusiastic but not especially well qualified: there were far too few Ph.D.s and relatively little evidence of significant professional activity. Performance at faculty meetings and in the curriculum and grading committees attested to a growing sense of responsibility, but clearly the teachers were grossly overworked in an institution in which the faculty-student ratio was one to twenty-one. Noting that the average English professor taught three sections of composition (each with thirty students) and two sections of literature (one of fifty students, one smaller), he observed, quite reasonably:

> *I am convinced that it is a physical impossibility to grade more than twelve hundred essay-type papers in a semester while still devoting four to five hours a day to office interviews with hundreds of composition students, in addition to advising majors, supervising the newspaper, supervising a literary magazine, supervising playwriting contests, meeting with the literary club, handling committee assignments, preparing classes, etc. Some quality must be sacrificed somewhere.*

He disapproved of the tendency, in other departments, to eliminate written work altogether and to rely on easily scored objective testing.

His review of the curriculum exposed major deficiencies: a history course for which eight pages of reading per period were deemed adequate and which even then could not complete its syllabus within the semester; as the instructor explained, "a large number of the students were incapable of completing a college course." An analysis of the grading pattern as compared with the results of the newly instituted national testing program substantiated that allegation: the students were clearly below national norms, yet their grades were above any reasonable expectations derived from the objective data. It was difficult to find measurable differences in difficulty between freshman and upperclass courses, and efforts to upgrade the offerings in the major had met with student resistance: one business student "complained bitterly that it was unfair to require 'college work' of a senior if he had not been required to adopt college study habits during the first three years." An instructor reported that he had been directed, at some point in the past, to give the grade of incomplete rather than fail a student; the history department used a curious grading equation guaranteed to reduce the number of Fs almost to zero. Yet Hickman pointed out that in a department in which he had succeeded in stimulating a considerable upgrading of standards, the result was not a loss of students but rather more and better prepared students being directed to the College from the outside.

He was emphatic on the effects of the limitations in plant and equipment on curriculum. Enrollments in speech and in drama were falling, and those departments were being carried by the courses open to TV-radio students. Yet the TV-radio department was in imminent danger of collapse because of its total lack of television equipment: "shoe boxes are at present being cut up and utilized as substitutes for camera viewfinders." He also called attention to a perennial Ithaca College problem: the high walls of exclusivity that prevented General College students from entering classes offered by the professional schools, particularly so in the School of Music.

Hickman's immediate concerns were a strengthening of the departments and majors which he had inherited, an upgrading of the faculty, and a not always successful effort to sway the admissions office toward a consideration of the future of the College rather than immediate financial returns. A comparison of the Catalogs attests to his efforts to broaden the range of courses and majors open to the students. In the Catalog of 1955 - 1957, there was a dramatic increase in the number of biology courses, and two "Inter-Area Concentrations" were opened up in American civilization and social science — these were options at no additional cost. A department of chemistry and a department of physics were added in 1958 - 1959 (though still without real laboratories), and a considerable growth was observable in TV-radio — new and impressive facilities became available when the studios over the Library on Buffalo Street were dedicated on October 11, 1958. By 1959 - 1960, majors in general science and in philosophy were announced, and no less than six separate curricula in TV-radio were articulated. The Catalog of 1961 - 1962 included the biology major and two science options for prospective teachers: biology and general science and chemistry and general science. By this time, American civilization had dropped out, there having been few interested students.

But something far more impressive was being planned behind the scenes. Probably as early as 1956 - 1957, Hickman was quietly working with Dillingham and with a handful of faculty advisers on a radical rethinking of the curricular problems of the small liberal arts college. In October 1959, this would be announced to the world in a brochure and in a lengthy and approving article on the education page of the Sunday *New York Times* as the "Ithaca College Plan." Later, this curricular model would be familiarly known as the "Triplum" — an appellation for its three-strand, six-semester core in literature, history, and philosophy which had been retrieved out of the curriculum of the medieval universities by History Professor John MacInnes.

The launching of Sputnik on October 4, 1957, had powerfully influenced the building of the South Hill campus. The impact was equally great on the College's curriculum, indeed on American education in general. Widespread criticism of our inadequacies, especially in the sciences and in mathematics, had generated a wave of curricular reform — a trend against the "fragmentation" of curricula, against the "proliferation" of courses, against an elective system approaching an academic smorgasbord. Now the demand was for a return to required courses, to core curricula, to tougher standards, and to a streamlined and more efficient approach to education on every level. Fred Hechinger summarized it in the *Times* article on the Ithaca College Plan:

The new direction, which parallels a trend in high school reform, is toward a combination of a more carefully mapped out undergraduate program, a deepening of the content of general education, combined with a more direct lead-in to specialized work, an attempt to permit at least some students to speed up or intensify their efforts, and greater insistence on independent work.

Hechinger noted earlier moves in those directions — at Amherst, Colgate, Columbia, the University of Pittsburgh. But his prime example was Ithaca College and its "experiment in modern higher education."

Hickman had chosen as his starting point the observation that far too many graduate students were ill prepared for study and research on that level. The problem, he found, arose from overspecialization at the undergraduate level — intensive work in some area of the major which a professor had been personally interested in developing, with glaring gaps in other, perhaps more important, areas — and a general misuse of a highly diversified elective system. Addressing himself specifically to the liberal arts college of under 1,500 students, he discerned an overly ambitious deployment of courses which fell basically into two categories: terminal survey courses or narrowly specialized offerings. Not only was it ineffective, the resultant curriculum "has become too expensive for the average independent college to handle."

How, then, to provide a sound background for graduate work? Hickman outlined three basic programs. First, in the natural and physical sciences, he proposed "an integrated program without the limitations of integrated courses." That is to say, all science and mathematics majors would follow a common pattern of courses for their first three years (with a minor exception for physics majors). The courses they took would also be available to nonmajors, so that the entire interdepartmental program would require only fifteen or sixteen semester courses in biology, ten in chemistry, sixteen in mathematics, and ten in physics. Two semester courses each in Western civilization, American history, and literature, plus a second year of a foreign language, would complete the background work (restrictions of time had made it impossible completely to eliminate the "survey" courses). Writing skills would be handled by an expository writing course, different from the garden-variety of composition course in that the writing would be based on the content of other substantive courses. The fourth year, in each area, would be a year of intensive specialization, with one course mandated from outside the major area.

Similar patterns were prescribed for the social sciences and for the humanities, with intensive reading programs for the summer vacations following the freshman and sophomore years. As with the sciences, the students followed a common program for three years, that is, the Triplum, and then moved into their respective concentrations. Each semester of the Triplum focused on a chronological segment of Western civilization: in the first semester, three parallel courses in ancient history, ancient philosophy, and ancient literature, to be followed by a medieval semester, a Renaissance semester, and so on, reaching the twentieth century by the end of the junior year. Freshman Triplum courses were limited to forty students, the sophomore courses to sixty; then, in the third year, "history, literature, philosophy, and government will be taught as a theatre-type lecture to the entire junior year enrollment in these two divisions (that is, from 120 to 300 students)." The senior year utilized primarily seminars and tutorials, along with electives.

Hickman summarized the advantages of his Plan — a broader common background of supporting courses so that the senior courses could be taught at a far higher level, freedom to change the field of major after two or three years without loss, a saving of faculty of from 6.5 percent to 13 percent, a reduction of courses of up to 46 percent. And, from these impressive economies, he held forth the promise of substantial increases in the compensation of participating faculty members: much was said of the "Master Teacher" during this period.

The Ithaca College Plan was freely offered to any other college that might be interested. At Ithaca College, Hickman envisioned the admission of 60 students in each area every year until the full complement of 720 should have been reached. They would be carefully selected, but not merely on the basis of superior achievement or promise. Two-thirds of them would receive full scholarship aid. At the end of each year, a battery of standardized tests would compare their progress with that of students in other, less favored, institutions.

President Dillingham put it succinctly in his preface. The Ithaca College Plan was "an experiment in academic accomplishment, economy, and efficiency."

Hickman's "brainchild," as Dillingham approvingly referred to it, was a response to conditions specific to Ithaca College as well as to his awareness of the larger scene in American higher education. It reflected the College's pervasive sense of economic stringency — the concern for uniformity in scheduling as a function of budget planning. In the 1950s, it was deemed essential to survival to know at least a year ahead how many students would take what courses and at what hours — there was no other way to work out the logistics of staffing and space allocation within the confines of plant and budget. Even the bookstore insisted that it had no facilities for returning unpurchased books and so had to know, at least a year in advance, how many students would be enrolled for English 203 or Accounting 101. Faculty members scrambled to secure the predicted number of students for their sections; salaries were known to have been reduced to part-time levels after fall registration if the head count fell short. Yet on the positive side, the College of Arts and Sciences was so new a creation that no curricular patterns had hardened, so that extensive change was indeed possible, and the coincidence of the announcing of the Ithaca College Plan and the intent to move to a new campus (whether Quarry or South Hill) offered an unparalleled opportunity to build a campus as a totality, with curricular objectives, if not always foremost, at least held firmly within sight.

Looking back, one can easily discern the built-in biases of the Ithaca College Plan. Hickman's background had been in

history, especially in international relations; he had minored in philosophy at Colgate. History and English being the two relatively strong departments in the humanities at Ithaca College, he built his Plan upon them, and, because of personal conviction, he undertook to create a philosophy department virtually *ex nihilo* and to assign to it a role that was unusual, to say the least, in a nondenominational institution — the teaching of a mandated six-semester, eighteen-hour sequence in the history of philosophy for a projected 720 students. Sciences were weak at Ithaca College, but he had, in Professor Hal Yingling, a trusted biologist who had worked with him at Ohio Northern; hence, the atypical emphasis on biology courses for chemists, physicists, and mathematicians. (Indeed, this virtual marriage between mathematics and the physical sciences is reflected in the early plans for a science building.) Outside of history, government, and economics, the social sciences had only token representation: there were no majors in sociology or anthropology. Psychology was not so much as mentioned. It was tacitly assumed that the objective of a college of arts and sciences was primarily to prepare undergraduates to enter graduate schools in due course. The total program presupposed massive subsidies from foundations or from the government, so that qualified students could be attracted: among other things, the Ithaca College Plan was an effort (in large part surprisingly successful) to upgrade the quality of student admitted to Ithaca College — and not just within Arts and Sciences. But the financial aid was not forthcoming, the students were never so well prepared as the planners had hoped, and the heavy course loads (17 - 18 hours each semester) would eventually prove unmanageable.

But whatever the future might hold for the Ithaca College Plan, in 1959 the College had made educational history.

The financing of the Ithaca College Plan was closely tied in with the financing of the South Hill campus. In his memorandum to the Board of October 20, 1959, Dillingham had stated that "we have reason to believe that a grant from the Department of Health, Education, and Welfare will spark foundation grants for academic buildings to implement the project thus supported." Both the Ford and Carnegie Foundations had "expressed enthusiasm for the new concept," and application was being made to HEW for $498,000 for scholarships and faculty salaries. Dillingham had pointed out that an Arts building, a Science building, a Union that could temporarily house administrative offices, and a Library would have to be completed within two years if support for the Ithaca College Plan were to be forthcoming.

On August 29, 1959, the College had submitted a formal request to HEW, specifically for "an experiment in curriculum revision as applied to the natural and physical sciences." Pointing out that "seldom, if ever, has an experimental four-year curriculum, involving a complete revision of each course within the existing curriculum, been adopted by an American college or university," the application spelled out details as to the design of the experiment, the controls to determine its efficacy, and the provisions for the publication of the data thus obtained. HEW was asked to provide $360,000 (this application being just for the science component) to cover the cost of a coordinator of research, faculty salaries, and scholarships over a period from January 1, 1960, to December 31, 1968. The College would come up with $1,319,100 — mainly for a Science building and its equipment and for various administrative expenses — most of this, it was hoped, would actually come from foundation grants. The *Ithaca Journal* of September 30, 1959, announced that the College expected about a quarter million in grants for the Ithaca College Plan, which was to begin in 1961 when the $7 million building program was completed (the reporter still envisioned this as at the Quarry site and warily added, "the announcement did not mention how the seven million in building funds would be raised").

But by November, the president was forced to announce a setback to the faculty. HEW had rejected the application in its original form, because it was not really a statistical research project with provable outcomes; instead, it was recommended that the College submit an application for a "self-contained experiment in curricular revision," for total of $1,250,000. A new budget was drawn up, asking for $1,207,307 in government subsidy and predicating $2,928,000 from the College or from "other sources." As HEW pondered this second request, there was a flurry of excitement that economist and financier Beardsley Ruml might be helpfully interested (the Ithaca College Plan anticipated many of the ideas he expounded in his *Memo to a College Trustee* in 1959). There were also rumors that a research team from the *Reader's Digest* would be coming to Ithaca to do an article on the Plan. But Ruml died, no article appeared, and hope rapidly dwindled.

As the academic year 1960 - 1961 drew toward its completion, it became clear that no support was coming from any source. The decision was made to implement the Ithaca College Plan anyway — with whatever students happened to be on hand and with whatever South Hill facilities could be made even approximately ready by that time. A completely redesigned Catalog (October 1961) played up the new programs in substantially the language of the 1959 brochure, but with some accommodations to the realities of the situation: an option in international relations was added, and, in recognition of the needs of ordinary Ithaca College students, several curricula within the Ithaca College Plan structure that led toward teacher certification. The work "Triplum" occurs for the first time, defined as "a basic core or matrix, from which the student's knowledge of all areas of the social sciences and humanities can be developed." Summer reading lists still figure prominently.

The first Triplum classes accordingly began amid the mud and construction of South Hill in September 1962. From this point on, the operative word was Triplum. The sciences, never very firmly anchored in the Ithaca College Plan, began almost immediately to move away from the three years in common and to revert to more traditional models. But in the humanities, specifically, for English, history, and philosophy majors, something quite extraordinary was under way — a three-year study, in depth, of Western culture, chronologically organized, to a total of fifty-four credit hours. Thus that first September, freshmen were reading Homer, Greek drama, and Virgil while simultaneously studying Greco-Roman history and oriental religious philosophies — with assignments in expository writing drawing upon the content of the three Triplum courses and jointly graded by the Triplum faculty member and by someone from the writing staff.

The difficulties inherent in such an interdepartmental core curriculum were staggering. Under the best of circumstances, there would have been problems of coordination — how to dovetail the syllabi of three different disciplines so that on the one hand, no violence was done to the intrinsic logic of each and, on the other, sufficient correlations were established so that the entire Triplum concept was validated. The amount of paper shuffling involved in the dual evaluation of student essays was taxing in the extreme, and there were embarrassing moments, as when an expository writing instructor graded a paper F only to have the philosophy professor change the grade to A+ because he was impressed by its insights and not in the least put off by its deficiencies in form. The Triplum sequence was perhaps fatally disturbed from the very inception when the one-man philosophy department adamantly insisted that the first Triplum semester had to be devoted exclusively to oriental religious philosophies — a private conviction that threw philosophy out of synchronization for three whole semesters, for half of the Triplum sequence. Repeatedly, students complained that there were few meaningful intersections, while faculty members jealously guarded the integrity of their disciplines against what they sometimes felt to be an arbitrary and authoritarian interlocking of essentially incompatible materials. The Middle Ages, for example, stretched over a time span of a thousand years, but unfortunately the major literary masterpieces were written toward the very end of the millennium whereas the "history" was spread out more evenly — and philosophy, following its idiosyncratic timetable, was just getting to Plato and Aristotle. A bigger question was often raised: why philosophy in the first place — six required semesters of it — in a school historically strong in the fine arts? Why not a component in music, painting, and sculpture, at least as an alternative to Spinoza, Kant, and Hegel?

Despite these handicaps, enthusiasm for the Triplum ran high. It was certainly Ithaca College's most distinctive contribution to curricular theory; its public relations value was enormous. There can be no doubt that a number of superior students were attracted to the College precisely because of the Triplum or that its general effect was tonic for all the divisions of the school. Students and faculty members alike felt that Ithaca College was not only building a magnificent new campus, it was doing something truly exciting educationally. Returning alumni still ask about the fate of the Triplum, and many remember it as the most significant educational experience of their lives.

But the seeds of dissolution had been planted from the beginning and would flourish under the changing conditions of the mid-sixties. The sciences went their own way; so did TV-radio. The components of the Triplum sequence had represented the strengths of the College as of 1958 - 1959; the following decade saw the rapid development of important new disciplines. Between 1958 - 1959 and 1966 - 1967, the number of semesters of work offered in government increased from seven to eighteen (and the ambitious new department changed its name to political science); psychology courses went from seven to fourteen, and sociology from

six to fourteen (now becoming sociology-anthropology). The emerging departments, fiercely competing for students, protested strenuously against the "massiveness" of the Triplum — fifty-four hours, plus twenty-two more in expository writing, foreign language, and biology, plus the requirements of the major — and with physical education soon to be an added requirement. With seventy-six hours preempted apart from upper-level electives in the major, the undergraduate had precious few hours to use in tempting new areas like the government and politics of the Middle East or the sociology of minority relations. Interdepartmental rivalries broke out into open warfare after the resignation of Dean Hickman on August 31, 1963.

Hickman would go on to further educational experiments, first with the International Institute Foundation and later as vice-president for academic affairs at Eisenhower College. On campus, the acting dean, Frank Kolmin, strove to cope with mounting faculty unrest. Even within the Triplum area there were demands for change: the history department was finding insuperable difficulties in its social studies curriculum (which prepared students for teacher certification). The combination of the existing requirements and new mandates from Albany meant that some students might be taking 140 hours or more, and, ironically, social studies traditionally attracted those students for whom the straight history major was too arduous. The debate spread to the meetings of the Arts and Sciences faculty: could an individual department unilaterally alter a core curriculum? If the Triplum was dismantled, would Ithaca College's principal claim to curricular distinction have been destroyed? — why then should students not go more cheaply to a state college? Voices were raised in defense of "modern liberal studies"; one political scientist remarked caustically that the Triplum was a fine program — "for producing lovely nineteenth-century people." Its rigidity, its historical-chronological organization, its emphasis on the past in five out of six semesters, its limitations for the most part to Western culture — these were some of the objections raised against it.

The controversy became too intense for an acting dean to handle, and on April 16, 1964, President Dillingham was brought in to chair a meeting of the Arts faculty. All the arguments were rehearsed. The president seemed scrupulously concerned to balance the value of a prestigious program against real problems in student load and performance:

the Triplum class entering in 1962 had experienced a 59.6 percent attrition. The meeting ended inconclusively, and the debate dragged on for another year. Finally, on June 1, 1965, the new dean of Arts and Sciences, Robert M. Davies, conveyed the president's decision to the faculty: the Triplum curricula would have to be revised so that no student would be taking more than 16 hours a semester; the total number of hours for graduation could not exceed 128; and, as a token gesture to the Triplum defenders, all nonscience liberal arts departments must offer a Triplum option for those qualified students wishing it as an honors program. These modifications had to be effected within one week, in order that the new Catalog might go to press in time for the Middle States reevaluation scheduled for the spring of 1966.

The 1966 - 1967 Catalog was as different in content as in format from its predecessors in the Hickman years. The introductory prose for Arts and Sciences continued to present an abridged statement of the Ithaca College Plan, but the beginning of the end was clear enough from the paradigms for the specific majors. Only philosophy remained unchanged. English provided an escape hatch in a footnote, and other departments had worked out varying degrees of accommodation, ranging from a slight reduction in the number of Triplum courses to outright abolition (except for the perfunctory statement that a Triplum program might be worked out for an individual student upon request).

"The Report of Institutional Self-Study" (January 1966) attempted to describe this revolution as a generally peaceful and gradual process of curricular adjustment.

The occasional debates over details and possible procedures have served to focus faculty attention vitally upon the whole problem of what constitutes a good education, and have thus encouraged and re-enforced the characteristics of organized turbulence and intellectual ferment which are the appropriate features of a Liberal Arts faculty.

But this not totally candid report did not succeed in glossing over the widening gap between the distinct publicity values still inherent in the Triplum idea and the actualities of campus politics. Davies attempted to be suavely optimistic that somehow all would be well.

With the present reduced hour-load for students, the introduction of an option concerning the Triplum, the virtual completion of the construction of our academic buildings, the elimination of the necessity for commuting between South Hill and dormitories, there is ample reason to feel that the Triplum curricula will remain a badge of excellence and fulfill the high hopes entertained when the curricular revision was first undertaken.

No one believed it.

The Self-Study Report had also claimed that debate over the merits of the Triplum had involved even the students in an examination of the nature of their educational development and of "the respective roles of the institution and of the student himself in contributing to it." The quoted phrases were unconsciously prophetic of the remainder of the decade: students would indeed have much to say about the "relevance" of their educational experiences. For a highly vocal minority, the Triplum would come to symbolize the inadequacies of the genteel tradition in education — an education designed for the pre - World War I leisure classes, callously indifferent to slums and ghettoes, to racism and exploitation, to nuclear threat and the Vietnam war. In a survey article in September 1969, the *Ithaca Journal* would ask, "Triplum — Is It Innovation . . . or Anachronism?" A faculty member would take the matter even further.

Historically, the whole concept of liberal education has been a possession of the Tories. It's class oriented. We're the most snob-ridden country in the world, and I'm afraid that some of the biggest snobs are in the humanities.

The politics of relevancy will be explored more fully later in this history. Suffice it to say here that by the Catalog of 1970 - 1972, virtually all requirements — of whatever sort — within Arts and Sciences had been swept away, except for those determined by the faculty and students of a given department. Despite a half-page of copy still extolling the Triplum as "a broad and stimulating program" offered by the English, history, and philosophy departments, only the English department in fact mentioned it in its course descriptions — and even for the English majors, only the eighteen-hour literature sequence remained intact. What Hechinger had described in 1959 as the "self-service" curriculum was back again. Those who remained unrepentant in their conviction that a truly humanizing education must liberate from the prison of the here and now could only bide their time.

Just as the faculty and students of Arts and Sciences were shaking the foundations of the Triplum, the School of Music undertook to introduce a curriculum closely modeled on it — and indeed one that was in several significant ways a distinct improvement. This four-strand curriculum was essentially the creation of Dean Craig McHenry. Up to 1966 - 1967, the Music students largely devoted themselves to music: the Catalog for that year lists no electives at all for the applied music students, and only twenty-four hours outside their area — six in English composition, six in a foreign language, and twelve in surveys of world literature and Western civilization. Other options were scarcely more generous; from 1892 on, there had been a fairly continuous tradition that a conservatory should be engaged primarily in professional training. Dean Rawski had set up waves with his "European" emphasis on the humanities; he resigned before effecting significant changes. Even in the mid-fifties, instructors occasionally encountered students who had been told by their Music professors not to prepare their assignments in English or history, since such activities subtracted from the time needed for voice or violin.

In the larger world outside of Ithaca College, concepts of what a conservatory should be were changing, and Dean McHenry was keenly aware of the new winds of doctrine. The future, he was convinced, lay with an effective blending of general cultural background and rigorous specialized training. The four strands of his proposed curriculum were applied music and performance, music structure, music pedagogy, and the humanities — the last being itself a five-strand sequence spread over all eight semesters and comprising literature, history, philosophy, art, and the history of music.

The base for the curriculum is a chronological study of the philosophical, aesthetic and historical development of civilization from the earliest times to its present state — with the evolution and influence of music being specifically emphasized throughout.

More comprehensive in its coverage than the Triplum, it far more closely approximated the ideal of team teaching in a common course: the syllabus scheduled instructors speaking in their areas of specialization in a pattern determined by the logic of the period under consideration, not by the arbitrary boundaries of five independent courses. The program assumed the organic unity of Western culture and approached that unity holistically.

There were of course difficulties. No grants materialized, and so there was no money for a coordinator. The courses were offered in the early morning hours, so that departments in Arts and Sciences tended to view them as hardship assignments, to be reserved for the instructors with least seniority. But in fact, the Music Humanities Program foundered on the shoals of politics. McHenry had worked out the planning in consultation with a very small group of faculty members from Music and from Arts and Sciences. The new curriculum was revealed to the faculty at large during the summer of 1966 and went into effect that fall — so precipitously that no notice could be given of it in the Catalog for 1966 - 1967. The uproar was understandably loud, partly for reasons already familiar from the Triplum (some forty-one to fifty-four hours were being consumed), partly on grounds that would become increasingly cogent as the sixties wore on — the right of the faculty to make major determinations of curricular policy. The program attracted considerable attention from the outside and was commended by a team of examiners from the State Education Department in December 1968 as "a most imaginative and unusual approach" to the problem of "the integration of the humanities and the literature and materials of music." But after 1969 - 1970, the will of the faculty prevailed: if they had not been invited to vote Music Humanities in, they at least had the satisfaction of voting it out.

This was not the only innovation in the School of Music. During the sixties, Professor Don Wells organized a highly original course rather curiously titled The Semantics of Music — in it, he confronted graduate students who had at least one year of teaching experience with the (for them) devastating question, What is music? By a skillful interweaving of music, painting, and poetry, with guest professors for the last two portions of the course, he attempted a critical resolution of that question. In 1963 - 1964, the College received a grant from the Ford Foundation for a seminar in contemporary music; this work, under Composer-in-Residence, Warren

Benson, was continued by an additional grant from the Music Education National Conference. In 1966 - 1967, a two-year experimental program was initiated "to promote creativity and a better understanding of contemporary music" among both college and high school students: again, the project was assisted by the Ford Foundation. Further, by the end of the decade, Ithaca College had become, as it still is, one of the nation's largest centers for the teaching of violin to children by the Suzuki method.

The School of Health and Physical Education also involved itself in a curricular adventure during this period. As early as 1932, Commissioner Cooper had commented on the irony that a school famous for its programs in physical education did not make work in that area mandatory for all students (and also require courses in music of the Physical Education students). The inadequacies of the existing facilities precluded any move in that direction — until the opening of the new gymnasium on South Hill. By May 1964, the faculty was considering a required course in physical education for all students. Discussions were heated, and curiously Manichaean in tone: collegiate institutions, one gathered, were expected to attend to the concerns of the spirit, but the needs of the body were beneath formal notice. In the background lurked the unspoken fact of declining enrollments in Physical Education majors, down each year from 512 in 1964 to 450 in 1969, as the total student population rose from 2,330 to 3,695. The course was approved, but without academic credit. The Physical Education faculty sensed a snub in that decision: why were their professional efforts not on a par with those of a trombone teacher, or of a physicist, for that matter? The curriculum committee wrestled with the problem, and, in a gesture of colleagual amity, recommended credit for GIPPE, as the General Instruction Program in Physical Education was called. The faculty acquiesced in May 1965. Thus freshmen and sophomores were scheduled for a one-hour course each semester.

> *GIPPE is planned and conducted in cooperation with the College Health Center physicians and other health professionals, utilizing the clinical facilities of the Division of Physical Therapy. Thus, this program not only effectively promotes the general health of students and carry-over skills, but prescribes modified courses on an individual basis for students with specific handicaps or problems.*

But GIPPE was not fundamentally remedial in purpose: it was soundly predicated on a concept of man as an indissoluble psychosomatic entity and aimed to establish an appreciation of the ideal of physical fitness that would continue not just for the college years but for an entire lifetime.

For all of that, GIPPE encountered strenuous resistance, both from students and from faculty members. The GIPPE classes were all too often scheduled for 8:00 on cold Ithaca mornings; the one hour a semester sounded nominal enough, but classes met several times a week, and additional time was required for dressing and undressing, to say nothing of recovering from the trauma of early-morning archery. The musicians led the attack, even though their dean had already wangled a concession: members of the marching band were granted a dispensation, presumably because they got their exercise while in uniform and carrying their tubas. In October 1969, the faculty council of the School of Music petitioned the educational policies committee to make GIPPE elective: they leaned heavily on the argument that only the faculty of the School of Music should prescribe the curriculum for Music students. That was dubious doctrine: there was nothing novel about the idea of all-College requirements set by the faculty as a whole. But 1969 - 1970 was a good year for causes, and, after extended discussions, lengthy letters and editorials in the *Ithacan,* a barrage of memoranda, and rumblings reaching even to the Board, the Physical Education faculty capitulated — in April 1970. Recognizing the right of departments and schools to govern themselves and affirming the need to promote "continuing harmony," they voted that GIPPE should indeed be elective.

There were other curricular innovations throughout the College.

Long before black rights became a campus issue, Ithaca College had pioneered in a program to bring African students to small colleges like itself — a program parallel to Harvard's effort to achieve the same goals within the larger universities. Frank Kolmin, professor of accounting and later to become assistant dean of Arts and Sciences (and acting dean for the year following Hickman's resignation), had not only reconstructed the department of business on modern foundations; drawing upon his own prolonged sojourn in Africa before coming to the United States (as education officer for the British colonial government in Tanganyika), he almost immediately began to move toward recruiting African students. The first two arrived in 1959, a scholarship program was set up, and in 1960 - 1961, the *Ithaca Journal* could picture six students from East Africa reveling in the novel experience of snow. This Cooperative African Scholarship Program (CASP) flourished; a grant of $1,200,000 was obtained from the federal government, and Kolmin directed the efforts of some thirty small colleges in the Northeast which were beneficiaries of the grant. He was soon elected to the American Council on African Education. The College hosted the Scholarship Advisory Board, visiting dignitaries arrived from Tanganyika and Malawi, the first anniversary of Tanganyika's independence was duly celebrated with a dinner, dance, and lecture. Harvard's African scholarship program and CASP merged early in 1962, but African students, including some from Ethiopia and Liberia, continued to be a presence on the Ithaca College campus.

Another novelty out of which the College derived some considerable press coverage was the "Dial-A-Course" program. South Hill construction provided opportunity for extensive wiring for projected electronic facilities, and the new classrooms and lecture halls, as well as the Library and Health Center, were connected with the control panel in the modern language laboratory. This alarming capability was broken to the faculty in October 1964: what if they were to tape their lectures as they delivered them, so that students sick in the infirmary, absent for some other reason, or merely desirous of refreshing their memories or correcting their notes, could play them back from a variety of stations spread throughout the campus? The educational advantages were undeniable, but the more paranoid segment of faculty response was quickly alerted to danger. The administration, as well as the students, could tune in at will — and with what dark motives? Even one's departmental colleagues were hardly to be trusted; lectures, it transpired, were confidential transactions between professor and students. A few instructors were genuinely interested in the applications of technology to education, and the experiment was initiated, for the most part quite successfully, with some 120 stations in operation. Eventually, even limited faculty participation proved a strain on the resources of the language laboratory, and by the late 1960s there were few lectures to tape. Formal classroom presentations had given way to "rap" sessions, and since the College could never bring itself to install microphones that could pick up voices other than the instructor's, "Dial-A-Course" disappeared.

"Study Abroad" would prove more durable. Its beginnings went back to 1956, when Dean Clarke escorted a summer study group to the Caribbean; the following year, Dean McHenry initiated the first of many summer European music tours. These programs were immensely popular with teachers who wished to combine travel with academic credit: others were scheduled for Mexico, Africa, the U.S.S.R., Peru, and Ecuador. By 1966 - 1967, the College was actively participating in the summer school program of the British universities. By the mid-sixties, much thought was given to a year abroad for Ithaca College undergraduates: such an arrangement would permit an even larger enrollment without putting additional strain on campus facilities — and it might add materially to the attractiveness of the Triplum. At first, a freshman year abroad was considered — the first semester in Athens for a firsthand view of classical civilization, followed by a medieval semester in Spain. But ideology roared its protest. Study in Castro's Cuba, one heard, would be truly rewarding, but Ithaca College could hardly contribute to the economic well-being of the Greece of the generals or of Franco's Spain. English Professor E. W. Terwilliger worked indefatigably to realize the objective of undergraduate study abroad, however, and by the fall of 1969, his efforts were successful. Seven Arts and Sciences students went to Rome as part of a program developed in cooperation with Loyola University. A study abroad committee came into existence during that semester, and by spring, arrangements were being made in conjunction with Schiller College. The full implementation of such a program would be deferred to the 1970s.

Many long-established programs experienced dramatic growth spurts in the 1960s, so much so that they soon threatened to burst forth from their defined institutional boundaries. Physical Therapy, newly accredited by the American Medical Association, could boast, by the end of the decade, that it was graduating more physical therapists than any other college or university in the nation. In ten years, it had more than doubled in size, brought in some $760,000 in outside financial support, and had developed "a new approach to professional and liberal education" for Physical Therapy majors, which "introduces clinical orientation in the freshman year, provides extensive opportunities for independent study and research, offers a broad range of electives, and strengthens the laboratory phases of professional courses."

Speech pathology and audiology, especially after the dedicatory visit of Sir Alexander Ewing, became a highly visible operation, expecially with its work with speech-and-hearing-handicapped children in the area. Its graduate program was accredited by the State Education Department in 1969; by 1969 - 1970, it was operating the only mobile audiology unit in New York State — purchased with the aid of a $50,000 grant from the Gebbie Foundation. In September 1969, the first Ralph W. Jones Public School Fellowship was awarded — in honor of a man associated with the College curriculum and for more than forty years a prime mover in the speech and hearing programs of the Ithaca public schools. With each new development, this complex department seemed less and less appropriately classified as a unit within the School of Arts and Sciences.

The same kind of tension — the presence of an energetically developing professional curriculum located, by historical accident, within Arts and Sciences — was being felt in the case of TV-radio. On July 20, 1957, the Board, meeting at Lake George, heard an impassioned plea from Trustee Jay Kennedy: not only was new equipment needed to end the shoe-box era, the College should undertake to create nothing less than "a showplace." The Board authorized new facilities in a second floor to be added to the downtown Library building. The year 1957 - 1958 buzzed with preparations for expanded activities, especially through the transmission of TV programs over the local TV cable franchise. The gala opening was scheduled for March 1, 1958, with Jay Kennedy, appropriately, as the principal speaker: the studios were toured and seminars were held. TV programs began to be transmitted to the Ithaca community on March 3. Professor Kolmin considered "Your Tax Problems," Professor Yingling began a series "Biology and You," John Ogden's show was "Speaking of Poets." Also, there were "Controversy," "Tempo" (musical and other performances by members of the College community), and "Community Spotlight" to fill in a week of vigorous programming — of inestimable value to viewers in the area in those days before educational TV had become a public reality. The fall of 1958 - 1959 added "Show Case" (with such features as "A Tribute to Cole Porter") and the first graduate course to be offered for academic credit over WICB-TV — "The Twentieth Century American Novel," which was followed in the spring semester by "Masterpieces of Ancient Literature." The studios were formally dedicated on October 11, 1958, with Robert F. Lewine, vice-president of NBC, as speaker. Early in 1959, there were disquieting reports that the New York

Telephone Company would drive Ithaca College off the air: the Ceracche Cable Corporation strung its wires on telephone poles, and the utilities company felt that the College was competing with network presentations. But the matter was satisfactorily resolved, and WICB continued its transmissions. A play by Barrie was aired in May, and, in the same month, the first outdoor remote telecast done live in the area brought the I.C.- RPI baseball game to thousands of viewers.

The early 1960s were the golden years of Ithaca College television. Roy Colle had succeeded Robert Earle, who would go on to College Bowl fame (an I.C. team, coached by History Professor Harold Emery, appeared on College Bowl on May 9, 1965). Colle brought energy, creative imagination, and a clear sense of educationally significant objectives to a rapidly expanding curriculum that was simultaneously a major community service. A succession of leaders in communications came to observe and to conduct seminars; later in the decade, the College would establish an immensely fruitful relationship with Rod Serling, who became a visiting professor in the fall of 1967. The number of programs shot up from five to ten (even though credit courses proved an unsuccessful undertaking). "Controversy" continued to tackle such problems as "Are Fallout Shelters Feasible?" and "Fluoridate — Or Wait?" Murray Abend, professor of political science, busily devised special programs, some of them original creative works; a panel of I.C. and Cornell faculty members analyzed "Goals for Americans" in March 1962; other programs were written and produced entirely by students. Local activities, such as meetings of the County Board of Supervisors, the Common Council, the County Planning Board, and the School Board, were aired for the first time in the history of Ithaca, and anyone of importance passing through town was certain to be interviewed. By the spring of 1963, the College was seriously interested in an educational-TV pilot project. Broadcast institutes were held each year beginning in 1963, students were taken to Europe in the summer of 1965 for a study of "Comparative Mass Media." Internships were set up to include fifteen major network stations and an important advertising agency; the College cooperated with Cornell in the training of Peace Corps volunteers for work in educational TV in Peru: a half-hour videotape, produced as a public service class project for the Peace Corps, was highly commended.

"We're home-grown, corny TV," Colle once told a local

reporter. In a more serious vein, he defined the role of WICB-TV in its relationship to the community: to help people relate to their "unseen world — literature, art, politics, philosophy, religion, commerce, social conflict"; to stimulate self-expression by local talent in the creative and performing arts; and to provide essential information about the community in its "business, social, labor, educational, and civic structure." Colle (who also established the sociology curriculum at the College) left at the end of 1965 - 1966 to accept a professorship at Cornell; there was, in fact, a complete turnover in staff within a five-year period. George Hoerner, of the drama department, served as chairman for a year, and then Ronald Nicoson took charge in September 1967. One of the last units to leave the downtown campus, TV-radio moved into its new quarters in the performing arts building in 1968 - 1969.

Toward the end of the sixties, filmmaking emerged as an important interest. Two students had been making a movie on their own in March 1963, and a full-length production, *Without Getting,* premiered at the Strand Theater in the spring of 1967. This also was undertaken without official College involvement, but a program leading to the Bachelor of Fine Arts degree in a department of cinema was under discussion in September 1967. The curriculum committee discouraged such a development, which would be deferred until the seventies.

As public broadcasting stations began operations in upstate New York, the emphasis shifted from community service to the more immediate tasks of preparing students to enter the communications industry. TV-radio, eventually becoming the School of Communications under John Keshishoglou, would remain one of the College's strongest and most prestigious divisions. "Kesh" had established an effective instructional resources center: he was keenly interested in "hardware" and in the "systems" approach to education. Many who fondly recall the imaginative thrust and intellectual stimulation of Ithaca College television in the earlier sixties must feel, however, that a certain slick professionalism had taken the place of that pioneer verve, creativity, and daring.

TV-radio, speech pathology and audiology, business were clearly outgrowing their status as departments within the College of Arts and Sciences. Similarly, another new curriculum was sprouting within the School of Health and Physical Education, which would also contribute to the drift toward the proliferation of semiautonomous administrative entities.

On July 1, 1968, the Department of Health, Education, and Welfare granted the College $260,000, to be spread over a five-year period, during which the only four-year program in health services administration in an American undergraduate institution would be set up. The driving force was Stephen Schneeweiss (later president of Cazenovia College), who would become director of the curriculum, at first within HPER, then as an independent School of Allied Health Professions. Building on existing programs, especially those in Physical Therapy and in speech pathology and audiology, Schneeweiss constructed a professional curriculum geared to the anticipated shortage of personnel to administer hospitals, medical centers, public health agencies, and nursing homes. After two years of general education, with summer internships after the sophomore and junior years, the student continued with further field work in administration, with a novel feature in the senior year — forty-five hours of "management simulation" — a "complicated game something like Monopoly," which "will require the students to draw upon everything they have learned previously and to apply it to real situations which arise in the administration of health service." The first twenty-eight students were enrolled in September 1969.

Our chronicle of curricular innovation and achievement might well suggest that Ithaca College had indeed done what it set out to do — to devise educational programs that would match the splendor of its buildings. In many important respects, that is a just appraisal. But candor requires us to acknowledge that not all outside observers were fully convinced that educational miracles had in fact occurred.

The accreditation of 1955 had been a shaky business at best, with periodic progress reports to be submitted to the Middle States Association (in 1956, 1958, 1960, and 1962). The next big test was scheduled for 1966: that March, joint evaluation teams from Middle States, from the National Council for the Accreditation of Teacher Education (NCATE), and from the State Education Department were on campus. The visitation had been carefully prepared for. The faculty were apprised of the fact in December 1963, and the following fall, a two-year self-study project was launched, with a number of faculty-administrative committees reporting to the coordinator, John MacInnes. Newsletters were issued from time to time; the president wrote glowingly about the challenge of institutional self-evaluation in his annual report for 1964 - 1965. The upshot of this activity was the "Report of Institutional Self-Study for the Middle States Association of Colleges and Secondary Schools," dated January 1966. This report is a bland, even complacent, document, deploying an impressive array of statistical data to the advantage of the College and deftly masking those areas of serious weakness which everyone knew to exist. The physical plant and various quantitative measures were flaunted at every opportunity.

The figures that follow will indicate how in various ways the student body has approximately tripled in a decade, how the quality of admitted students has rapidly risen, how the faculty has tripled to meet this need, how the physical plant has grown with dramatically arresting speed, and how throughout the institution there has been the visible evidence of a school moving from its congested living quarters downtown to its present spacious eminence.

The preface betrays a certain nervousness in its concern that cold statistics may not fully reveal the true dimensions of the inward transformation.

Readers of these pages may miss that spirit of change and improvement, and enlarged opportunity for service to modern American youth, that is so clearly felt by every faculty member, administrator, and supporting person on the campus. It is this spirit, we believe, which charges all of the accompanying statistics and analyses with a vibrant life that is not perhaps readily apparent to the casual reader.

But the visitors were not casual readers or perfunctory observers, and they were not taken in by this smooth presentation. At first, the introductory paragraphs of *their* report affect a tone of amusement tempered by wonder.

Ithaca College has caught the educational boldness . . . that would cause even a Paul Bunyan to pale, and out of this mixture of nerve and verve an institution is emerging that justifies use of education's probably most overworked expression.

Ithaca College is an exciting institution. . . . It is

exciting for the reason every circus goer knows — danger.

There is a direct similarity in holding one's breath to watch the high-wire artist as he seeks the security of the other end and watching an institution with a current equity of approximately $3,500,000 coolly borrow $30 million more and start to cross to the eventual security of full amortization. . . .

In any review of the assets of the College [the president] heads the list, with his daring and boldness happily tempered by his equally manifest resources of skill, taste, educational know-how, experience, a touch of P. T. Barnum, and a deep, abiding desire to leave the educational world just a little bit better because he was once one of it.

Then they got down to the hard details.

Their evident affection for Howard Dillingham did not weaken their conviction that he was too much of a one-man show, with fourteen administrators reporting directly to him. They urged the immediate creation of a new position — that of chief academic officer — preferably from one of the traditional liberal arts disciplines, and to be chosen with faculty involvement.

They were singularly unimpressed by the historical rationalization for the existence of the three "semi-autonomous" schools. Whatever may or may not have been true in the past, such a structure now suggested "a house divided against itself."

Not only loyalties to professions and past achievement, but grim determination to maintain and widen separate empires can hamper opportunities for even greater achievement possible only as a unified Ithaca College.

The examiners had high praise for the traditionally strong areas of Music and Physical Education, but Arts and Sciences revealed glaring weaknesses. The evidence suggested "high faculty enthusiasms, with a more erratic evaluation of competence which might well be summarized as average plus." Standards were generally low, especially with regard to *cum laude* degrees. Exciting things were undoubtedly happening, and many students were clearly inspired to significant achievement. Yet many departments came in for pungent criticism. Chemistry was promising, but physics "represents some promise but very little present fulfillment." Biology was stagnant. The drama department was carrying "rapport" with the students to the point of becoming "soapy and slippery," and the faculty there seemed "anti-intellectual in their approach to the training of the students and to the drama." Speech correction was urged to move quickly toward a graduate program; those completing the curriculum in TV-radio were found to be deficient in general education. Teacher training reflected the general problem of the semi-autonomous schools: there was no centralized effort.

The extension program — William Grimshaw's far-flung empire — was categorically rejected, for reasons noted in an earlier chapter. It was further to be deplored that no faculty members whatever were serving on the committee on graduate studies.

There were additional difficulties: retirement benefits, the role of the departmental chairmen, faculty and student involvement in College governance, faculty evaluation for tenure and promotion. But the report ended on a note of shocked incredulity at the College's financial prospects:

> *. . . probably there is no college in the nation with so few assets in relation to such high indebtedness as Ithaca College.*

The examiners could hardly bring themselves to contemplate a future in which, by the year 2012, the debt service would be reduced to a mere $450,000. The mandate was clear: the Board must endorse a major capital campaign for operating funds, preferably with the aid of a professional fund-raising firm.

On balance, this was bad news indeed, giving little assurance that the College's accreditation would be renewed. The president could refer to the report in public as "both encouraging and challenging"; in a letter to the executive secretary of the Middle States Association, he would state:

> *Though criticism is rarely solicited, it is rarely useless. The administration and faculty of the College have read the report of the Visitation Team with sober gratitude for the measured judgment and useful advice they have given us.*

It was obvious, however, that swift remedial action afforded the only hope of salvation, in order that an unsolicited progress report could be submitted before the Middle States Association had a chance formally to vote on the College's status.

On July 1, 1966, Robert M. Davies, dean of the College of Arts and Sciences, became the first provost of Ithaca College — without faculty involvement in the appointment and, it would appear, without consultation with other members of the administration. Grimshaw was given two years' retirement pay in consideration of his failing health, and Hushang Bahar (later to become president of the Tompkins-Cortland Community College) was brought in from the Corning Community College to preside over the liquidation of most of the off-campus extension centers. The College scrapped its old retirement plan in favor of TIAA-CREF, and the Board "voted to initiate during its 75th Anniversary Year (1967 - 1968) a major fund-raising campaign with a goal of $10,000,000." Faculty members were appointed to the committee on graduate study, and the graduate Catalog was completely revamped. Other improvements included a greater recognition of the role of the departmental chairmen, a new chairman for biology ("with a national reputation in teaching and research"), the establishment of all-College faculty committees, and the strengthening of internal communication through the appointment of a director of information services. Two new members broadened the range of the Board of Trustees.

These sweeping reforms elicited the desired result. On January 18, 1967, the College was informed that its accreditation had been reaffirmed — although, once again, a further progress report would be required by March 1969. Looking back over the year, Provost Davies, in a gem of understatement, could apprise the faculty on May 10 that "something of a crisis concerning the academic programs" had occurred.

The National Council for the Accreditation of Teacher Education, visiting the campus at the same time, also emerged with only qualified approval. The undergraduate programs in teacher training received a provisional accreditation, but action on the graduate program was deferred for one year. Upon their return in April 1967, they found a radically changed situation, with much to commend — a provost, a new director of Graduate Studies, a functioning graduate committee. As to the disgraceful extension programs, "it is the sentiment of the visitors that the drastic cutbacks . . . have been accomplished with a singleness of purpose which approaches the heroic." Provisional accreditation of the graduate teaching curricula was granted in October 1967.

The progress report to Middle States dated February 25, 1969, is essentially a chronological survey of Provost Davies's work in implementing the recommended changes. It is rich in details of administrative reorganization, following in part from a study made by the management consultant firm of Cresap, McCormick, and Paget. It describes the setting up of a complex system of faculty committees and councils, with emphasis given to the educational policies committee and to the campus life committee. A new role for students was represented by the fact that "by the end of 1969 a strong Student Congress had begun to replace the fairly loose forum that had previously existed under the title of Leaders Group." All of this "fairly complex activity" was presented in a chart of almost Byzantine obscurity. But Davies candidly described how he managed to make it work. The provost, by virtue of his office and his access to information from all quarters, had "a certain platform from which to bring about unity through the powers of example, persuasion, and to some extent, through budgetary discretion." The report did not mention the $10 million capital funds campaign, of which no more is ever heard.

NCATE was temporarily mollified, Middle States required no further action until the time should come for its next ten-year reevaluation. But another chasm quite unexpectedly yawned open. In December 1968, a team from the New York State Department of Education arrived for the purpose of reviewing, for registration purposes, all of the College's academic programs. Their report, dated March 28, 1969, was a blockbuster. The financial status of the College no longer gave them pause, and their appraisal of President Dillingham continued to be highly laudatory. There was still little evidence of communication among the three schools, however, and the state of the faculty was deplorable in the extreme.

> *Where three years ago, the faculty was excited, the current faculty, for the most part, seems to have resigned both from any aspirations to fulfill scholarly expectations, and from hopes for advancement at Ithaca College. The faculty is doing its job of teaching, nothing more.*

The high hopes for the Triplum had faded; individual programs came in for withering criticism. Mathematics was "weak academically and shows little promise of improvement"; although the new chairman of the biology department, Louis DeLanney, had a fine research laboratory for his own work on axolotls, "the equipment for student use is minimal and reflects purchases made by a scientifically unsophisticated faculty"; chemistry, as always, was something of a showpiece, but physics should be phased out as a major at the earliest possible moment. Music continued to win high praises, but the examiners expressed grave doubts about the future of the school — endowment funds and the recruiting of first-rate teacher talent were essential to survival. TV-radio was lacking in leadership; teacher education was still a morass of duplication and overlapping. And while the extension programs had been subjected to radical surgery, it could be argued that those programs that had survived were vulnerable to the same criticisms that had resulted in the elimination of the others.

Reluctantly, the Bureau of College Evaluation extended registration of the undergraduate programs for five years — with the exception of mathematics, biology, and physics, which would have to be reappraised in two years. The on-campus graduate programs were accepted; the others had to be studied further before a decision could be made. The president spluttered with rage — "a completely irresponsible report" — and his response was in part justified by the arrogant superficiality of the document. After a cooling-off period, the author wrote to explain that Albany was not *demanding* the abolition of the physics major if the College did not mind "the exorbitant cost." The graduate studies committee abolished the very termed "Extension" and reduced the off-campus programs to two "Graduate Centers" — one in the Albany district, the other in the Triple Cities.

The academic year 1969 - 1970 thus opened with a kind of uneasy armistice established on the various curricular fronts. In other respects, the campus was ready to burst into flames — in fact, combustible materials had been smoldering for some time. One might even say that most of the faculty and student body were hardly aware of the high-level crises in the acceptance of the College's academic programs, so great had become their involvement in the political and ideological controversies of the later sixties.

The annual report of the dean of students for 1956 - 1957 is highly instructive as an estimate of the temper of the student body, at least as seen by an administrator, at the beginning of Dillingham's presidency. Big Brothers (140 fraternity men) duly indoctrinated the freshmen, especially at freshman camp. But, Clarke reported, the student council accomplished "much less than is desirable" (mainly recommendations for reducing noise in the Library). The interfraternity council, he claimed, had eliminated "much of the childish hazing of the past," and the honor societies were more or less routinely doing what they had always done. Interest in class affairs, however, was at a low ebb; both the *Cayugan* and the *Ithacan* had "very unsatisfactory" years; the student literary magazine, the *Camerata,* had been discontinued. The campus scene was dominated by the fraternities, still in a period of growth; the liveliest activity came from the Catholic, Episcopal, and Jewish religious groups. The dean found that "our disciplinary problems are much less serious than are usually found at colleges of comparable size" (possibly because all the men lived off campus, and the strictest of parietal rules still governed the women's dormitories — curfews would not be completely abolished until December 1969). The College, we learn, "assumes no financial responsibility for the treatment of mental health cases." The overall impression is one of almost complacent satisfaction that nothing was really happening at all.

> *Each year the writer attends a two-day meeting of Deans of Students from upstate private colleges and universities . . . . when [he] returns from this conference, he is more than ever thankful that he has his own problems to deal with instead of the more numerous and serious problems which seem to face his colleagues in similar positions.*

Matters of editorial concern to the *Ithacan* reveal much about the changing moods of the student body. "Food Stink Raised by Frosh Students" is of course a perennial theme; complaints about "apathy" are also chronic. The early sixties reflected considerable concern over "the cheating problem" and the possibility of an honors system; the faculty, committed to a belief in original sin if not total depravity, stoutly resisted the latter. The year 1966 was apparently much agitated over "P.D.A." — the public display of affection: the

Ithacan approved of such display, which it carefully distinguished from "D.S.S." (Deliberate Sexual Deviancy). By the spring of 1967, contraception had become a topic of public discussion, especially insofar as the Health Center was concerned; questions of venereal disease and abortion likewise became newsworthy. "The New Morality" earned editorial comment, as did "God is Dead." In December 1968, the alarm was raised that "poisonous love beads were on sale at the College Bookstore"; this was not viewed as an administrative conspiracy, however. And, as tuition rose each year, the plaintive cry was heard, "Must Parents Pay and Pay?"

Changing attitudes toward liquor form an important part of the record. The campus in the late fifties was still officially dry: before each social function, two students were appointed to assume responsibility that no drinking would occur anywhere in the area. There were ugly situations such as a prom at which all or most of the students abandoned the dance floor to the president and the chaperones while they remained defiantly in the adjacent bar. A faculty member was scratched temporarily from the promotion list because, it was claimed, he had been lax in enforcing the liquor code at a dance. But the South Hill campus soon acquired a pub, even though students could still be dismissed for possessing liquor elsewhere on campus. In 1966 - 1967, the administration accepted an interfraternity council recommendation that each Greek unit be permitted one official cocktail party on a weekend in the spring semester. The campus went wet in the fall of 1970, as we shall see, but the ban on drinking at athletic events was still "to be strictly enforced" in 1969 - 1970 and after.

A closely related issue was intervisitation — the entertaining of a member of the opposite sex in one's dormitory room. In the earliest days of South Hill, women were disciplined for communicating with men in adjacent dormitories through the windows, and if there was to be any "P.D.A.", it was to be confined to those areas in the Union and the West Tower "Dating Lounge" set aside in concession to the frailties of the flesh. A chaplain would protest that sex in a Volkswagon was dehumanizing.

In 1963, in a move of unusual daring, the second-floor lounges in the women's dormitories were opened to men each Sunday from 7:00 to 9:00P.M. (older faculty members recall that earlier in the downtown campus, even on the occasion of the annual open house, at least one chaperone was stationed in every room). By October 1965, an *Ithacan* columnist posed the inevitable question: "Should girls be permitted in men's rooms on campus?" — and, surprisingly, the response was three to one against. But by the following fall, intervisitation was authorized in the Greek units between 3:00 and 5:00 on Sunday afternoons. Thereafter, the topic became a lively one. The student congress appointed a committee; recommendations were made to the Board. A "Coeducation Dorm" (separate wings for each sex) had proved successful — and decidedly anaphrodisiac. By February 1969, the Board was prepared to sanction for one year both relaxed liquor regulations and extended intervisitation (it being assumed that the latter would of course not involve SEX); each living unit would be authorized to determine its own policies in such matters, within a general framework designed to protect the rights of individual students. Not all the trustees were happy about "open dormitories": one resigned because he declined to serve, the word went round, as "a member of the governing board of a bawdy house." One student writer wondered why Board approval was sought in the first place — "It's none of the trustees' business."

The drug culture manifested its presence on the campus by the mid-sixties. Even tobacco smoking took on a new ominousness. Earlier, the College proudly announced its singular good fortune in having been chosen for the distribution of sample packages of cigarettes in a promotional scheme. Now, attention was paid to the warnings of the surgeon general; two faculty members offered to help students stop smoking; the efficacy of worry beads to combat the symptoms of withdrawal from nicotine was publicly recommended. Marijuana arrests soon became fairly common. An illegal drug control committee was established, although the president could still insist, in his report of 1966 - 1967, that addiction on campus "was not a serious problem." The author of *The Varieties of Psychedelic Experience* lectured in the Union on February 14, 1967. For the most part, the College's approach to the problem was rational. The director of the Health Center, Dr. J. David Hammond, could justly claim, in September 1967, that "as far as we know, we're the only college in the U.S. approaching drugs as a health problem." The *Ithacan* thought in broader terms: in February 1970, it published a full page of marijuana recipes, including one for "Alice B. Toklas brownies."

Student self-government went through an endless series of revisions during the sixties. As early as February 1959, an editorial denounced "Phony Democracy," especially as regarded the powers of the student court: the jurisdiction of that body was a continuing cause for dissension, the students claiming "judicial sovereignty over all matters pertaining to student conduct," the administration and trustees unwilling to surrender their ultimate authority, and the faculty concerned lest their discretion in assigning penalties for cheating be undercut. Student government itself evolved from an ineffectual "Leaders Group" to a student congress more than ready to throw itself into the political frays of the late sixties. Even then, the radicals eyed it warily: it might all too easily be co-opted by the administration.

Sooner or later, the student movement is going to solidly clash with the administration. Perhaps our Student Government will side with the administration. This would be a pity since it's serving the students. That is the proper role of the student organization. In such a case, we'd have to abolish it.

Despite all the writing and rewriting of constitutions, the proliferation of committees, the making of recommendations, and the issuing of manifestoes, the fact remained (as the *Ithacan* editorial put it, not disapprovingly), Ithaca College was "a benevolent dictatorship."

The political self-consciousness of the faculty approximately paralleled that of the student body, with considerable reciprocal incitement. Salaries increased, but hardly proportionately to the increase in total budget or in tuition: after 1962 - 1963, the annual reports disguised this unpleasant truth in the ten-year comparisons by giving the figures for the total payroll instead of the median faculty salary. The spectacular increase in numbers (which permitted this juggling trick) steadily pushed up the remuneration of the lower ranks, but the associate professors and the professors lagged far behind, so that the College's overall rating in the annual surveys published by the American Association of University Professors remained distressingly low. The tenure battle had been won in fact if not in theory before Dillingham became president, though as late as May 1959, the trustees were still maintaining that a given Board could not commit future Boards by any promise of continuous employment (and this at a time when they were preparing to commit future Boards to a staggering debt that would not be liquidated until well into the twenty-first century!). They came round on February 21, 1969. Throughout the sixties (and after), tenure was a haphazard affair: at first three, then five, then seven years of survival were the primary requisites — guidelines were hazy to the point of uselessness.

There were important gains in fringe benefits. Sabbaticals were approved by the trustees in June 1961; the older retirement plan (which provided a maximum of $210 a month after thirty years of service) gave way to TIAA-CREF; teaching loads, in Arts and Sciences at least, gradually dropped back to twelve hours (with some possibility of an occasional reduction to nine); insurance benefits improved; free tuition for faculty children and a tuition exchange with other colleges (later a direct grant) became effective; support was provided for attendance at meetings of learned and professional societies.

Faculty self-government proceeded at differing rates, rapidly in Arts and Sciences, far more slowly in the other schools, fitfully for the College as a whole. One of the first actions in Dillingham's administration was the appointment of a committee to draw up a Faculty Handbook. This committee was soon dissolved and was succeeded by a "Faculty By-Laws" committee. But a Handbook, which could merely be descriptive of existing policies but not necessarily binding in any legal sense, proved safer, and, after much discussion and with suggestions from the newly formed A.A.U.P. chapter, was approved by the faculty on February 19, 1959. This early Handbook is an insufferably preachy document, which for the most part could have been written by a paternalistic administration without any faculty involvement at all: "when notices and requests are sent, care should be taken to read them *all the way* through and follow instructions," "displays of irritation and anger, verbal abuse and sarcasm should be avoided in all faculty-student relationships," "history discloses that the greatest teachers have been those who inspired love and admiration in their students," "the teacher is expected to serve in the role of gracious host." A section on bell-shaped curves attempted, rather generally, to address the question of the discrepancy between College grading patterns and national norms. More significantly, a first groping effort to set up guidelines for the various faculty ranks was included (however ineffective in application), and the statement on tenure was close to revolutionary in providing for review before a committee of the A.A.U.P. chapter, with full steno-

graphic record, in the event of the dismissal of a professor with tenure. The trustees, we remember, would not commit themselves to the principle of tenure for another ten years.

The revision of September 1965, attractively printed and bound, updated the informational sections, especially with reference to the newly acquired fringe benefits. Its salient addition is Section XII: "Academic Freedom and Professional Responsibility" — substantially A.A.U.P. orthodoxy, but with some pointed local expansions.

> *Faculty members will generally be expected to preserve that distance between student and instructor that experience has proved most conducive to learning. . . . The faculty member will strive at all times to make his institution a genuine community of scholars, not just an accidental association of teachers. . . . The faculty member will avoid making anonymous accusations concerning his colleagues to those in authority. . . . No faculty member is employed merely to "teach his subject"; all good teaching is witness to a man's total commitment. Yet the faculty member is expected to avoid rigid dogmatism and irrelevant digression.*

The Handbook conceded, however, that to distinguish "rigid dogmatism" from "intense conviction" and "irrelevant digression" from "fruitful excursus" might "in practice call for more than Solomonic wisdom." It wryly noted that "when a faculty member is accused of 'getting off the subject,' the real issue is often the unpopularity of the views he is expressing; those who in class defend 'proper' views, however irrelevant, are rarely so charged."

Insofar as each fresh edition of the Handbook offered an opportunity for more daring claims of faculty authority, the events of the late sixties inevitably prompted further revision: Professor Terwilliger was by then an old hand at the compilation of such documents. Changes were coming so fast that the edition of September 1968 frankly describes itself as a stopgap measure until all suggestions should have been received and acted upon. It contained novel features, however. For the first time, the College Charter and By-Laws were printed in full, and, although the title Faculty Handbook was retained, a long section now gave exhaustive details about administrative organization and officers. Part III, "Faculty Organizations,

Responsibilities, Rights, and Benefits," presented much new doctrine: the very word *rights* was portentous. Nine areas of faculty responsibility were defined, from the determination of curriculum to the acquisition of Library books, with a cautious proviso that

> *the faculty as a corporate entity is not an absolutely autonomous body, but is responsible to the President and, therefore, may be overruled by him.*

In such a contingency, the president would "for their guidance present to the faculty his reasons for doing so."

An elaborate committee structure was described, both for the College as a whole and for the three schools. The Handbook, now seventy-three pages long, included lengthy statements by the national A.A.U.P. on academic freedom and professional ethics and is remarkable for a section on procedures for dismissing a faculty member with tenure which, in legal complexity, far surpassed anything ever contemplated by the national A.A.U.P. or, some would claim, anything adopted by any other American college or university. September 1969 saw yet another Handbook (still described as under continuous revision). This edition is notable for a more detailed statement on the awarding of tenure — still entirely a matter of timetable and notification, with a complete bypassing of the vexatious problem of criteria, except for a linking of tenure appointments with promotion to the associate professorship (itself defined in only the most general of terms). The faculty had rather begrudgingly approved this document on December 12, 1968, as describing adequately enough the present policies of the College, but without implying "faculty approval of these policies and procedures." The situation was fraught with difficulty for the future.

Faculty meetings being largely informational sessions organized by the president, additional governmental structures were bound to arise. Some indication of the need can be seen in a "Liaison Committee" created in 1961 because it had come to the president's attention that some faculty members were "unhappy over certain circumstances affecting their work." It is mind-boggling to read how much time and energy were devoted in those days to the problem of getting chalk to the blackboard ledges. Not all the rumblings of discontent were allayed, however. In February 1962, the faculty of Arts and Sciences took the unusual step — indeed, the unprece-

dented step — of sending a letter directly to the members of the Board. No one remembers just what the letter was about, but only that the president and the trustees were livid with rage.

By the spring of 1961, a movement was afoot to create a faculty senate. A Constitution and By-Laws were drafted early in the academic year 1961 - 1962. These have not survived, but it is well remembered that the president, upon receiving his copy, returned it with two principal criticisms: the document was longer than the Constitution of the United States and it was unreadable. He then sent to each member of the faculty, with his compliments, a copy of Strunk and White's *The Elements of Style*.

A revised text was adopted in January 1962 and reworked again the following November. Essentially, it defined broad areas in which faculty opinion should be determined and forwarded to the administration as recommendations. The committee structure included an executive committee, a committee on academic policies, a committee on public functions and administrative procedures, a committee on faculty welfare (which would assume responsibility for revising the Handbook), and a committee on student welfare (with of course no student members). The last named would formally commend the student council for its resolution mandating proper dress for the Sunday noon meal and banning "bathing suits, football jerseys, bare feet, shower sandals, and short shorts" from the Union. (Offenders would be denied food on Sunday afternoons and, if contumacious, hauled before the student court.) It should be noted that, unlike any subsequent faculty governmental body, the senate was actively concerned with stimulating the professional development of the faculty and the intellectual and cultural life of the campus. A substantial amount of its energies and resources, under Terwilliger as president, went to the setting up of concert and lecture series and the obtaining of grants to support various scholarly endeavors.

Eventually, Dillingham was persuaded that the much revised constitution was reasonably brief and more or less readable, and so he agreed, in December 1962, to forward it to the Board for their acceptance. The Board approved "in principle" the following May but haggled over details; in October 1963, they returned the document to the senate for further study. The record breaks off about that time, and in May 1965, the faculty summarily abolished the senate, apparently without debate. No one recalls why an organization so broadly conceived and functioning so energetically during its first year languished to the point of having to be put out of its misery.

After 1966, efforts to organize the faculty of the entire College proved ineffectual: it was difficult even to secure attendance at faculty meetings — probably because their agenda was empty of significant content. The educational policies committee — surely the most tedious debating society that Ithaca College has ever known — produced some recommendations on fairly routine matters of academic housekeeping, but mainly confined itself to high-level discussions of educational philosophy or to an agonized questioning of its own reason for being. In the final years of the decade, the initiative passed to the Arts and Sciences faculty council, easily the most politicized faculty group on campus at the time. One of its more conspicuous actions was the sending out of a questionnaire on faculty morale, not only to its own constituency but (to the provost's annoyance) to the faculty of the other schools. It contained such items as:

> 30. (It bothers me) (It does not bother me) that contrary to the recommendation of the Middle States Evaluation Team, the Provost was appointed without consulting the faculty.
> 32. (It bothers me) (It does not bother me) that the main activity in the General Faculty Meetings is the making of announcements.
> 34. (It bothers me) (It does not bother me) that a faculty member at Ithaca College seems to have about the same rights and privileges as a white collar worker in business or industry.

The provost denounced the questionnaire as divisive and arrogant (the results revealed a widespread lack of confidence in president and provost, but considerable support for the deans). To his criticism that some of the questions were tendentiously worded, a faculty member responded, disingenuously, "Certainly some of the questions were loaded, but we are dealing with a loaded situation."

The rallying cry for faculty rights was given impetus by an article by McGeorge Bundy in the *Atlantic Monthly* for September 1968 (which, curiously, the president commended to the faculty for its perusal). Bundy asserted that "when it comes to a crunch, in a first-class university, it is the faculty which must decide"; he defined the president as "the agent of the university faculty." The faculty council created in 1969 - 1970 certainly shared those views, but its full operation had of necessity to wait until a new decade and a new president.

There may indeed have been political "tension within the Ivory Tower," as an *Ithacan* columnist phrased it. But the story of the late sixties must expand to focus on the College's response to national and international developments. From this point, the history of Ithaca College becomes inextricably bound up with that of Cornell, the nation, and the world.

Concern for racial equality on the Ithaca College campus and elsewhere goes back to the years immediately following World War II and of course markedly intensified in the sixties. A committee against segregation was formed in February 1961, with considerable faculty encouragement; it was very much in evidence when Martin Luther King, Jr., visited Cornell that April. A year later, WICB-TV devoted a special broadcast to the Congress on Racial Equality (CORE) and the Black Muslims. Discrimination became a matter for lively editorial comment, local black leaders spoke on campus, and joint meetings were held with equivalent groups at Cornell. President Dillingham assured the faculty of "the happy situation on this campus with regard to minority groups in the past," and for a while, the agitation was directed primarily against discrimination in local barber shops, housing, and employment. But the pull of larger issues was strong by the spring of 1964. Ithaca College students were urged to march on Washington in February in support of the Civil Rights Bill, and the United Christian Fellowship sponsored a voter education and registration project in Greensboro, North Carolina. In September 1967, the *Ithacan* produced a special civil rights issue. Doctor King's murder on April 4, 1968, brought the racial issue to a sharp focus. There was an on-campus memorial service; the Protestant chaplain declared, "There is no need for many words, only actions." The *Ithacan* registered some concern as it asked, "A Leader Is Slain, but How Is He Mourned?" and went on to decry the consequent rioting and looting. On April 17, 1968, the College experienced its first organized teach-in on "Racism: Past, Present, and Future." Dillingham attended, some faculty members were actively involved, but the rhetoric came largely from the Cornell representatives. Cornell's Andrew Hacker proclaimed that "all whites are racists and by culture are incapable of regarding the Negro as a full human being"; the Negro question, he insisted, was not a "problem" because problems by definition have solutions. The Ithaca College Afro-American Society took a less despairing view as it launched a program "designed to provide scholarships for Negro students as well as to broaden student and faculty awareness of Negro culture and history." The administration pledged to match dollar for dollar the funds raised for the Martin Luther King Memorial Fund.

At approximately the same time, Spring Weekend was celebrated with the traditional rites; the float parades were organized, somewhat nostalgically, under the theme of "the Gay Nineties."

The war in Vietnam loomed larger than the racial question because it directly affected more students. At first, the interest was more curious, more fact-oriented; a former South Vietnam ambassador to the United States spoke in the Union in April 1964. In February 1965, the *Ithacan*'s "Roving Eye" column asked students what they thought of the "Vietnam situation": their replies were serious, well informed, literate — and blessedly free of slogans. Petitions began to circulate by the following November — notably, a petition backing President Johnson's policies in Southeast Asia. In fact, a student committee was organized to support the government's position — "to dispel, in part, the very misleading theory that all college students are blind, draft-card-burning, idealists who have no idea of the real conflicts in Vietnam." In a debate, "Resolved: that the current military involvement of the United States in the war in Vietnam is justified," it was the College team that took the affirmative position. In April 1966, an anti-Vietnam war demonstration and march held in DeWitt Park drew mainly Cornellians, but the press reported that "many of the most active hecklers were from Ithaca College, and two of the speakers who took the microphone to speak against the march were from the College."

By November 1966, the *Ithacan* was taking a less approving look at Johnson's visit to the Far East, printing a syndicated parody of the Gettysburg Address:

I promise that this nation, under me, shall have a new birth of conformity (boy, will we shut up those peaceniks) and that government by consensus, by manipulation, for the sake of saving face, shall not perish from the earth, although admittedly the population might.

In February 1967, a Syracuse newspaper headlined "Ithaca College Group Raps Vietnam Policy" — a reference to a Cornell-sponsored meeting which Ithaca College delegates attended. In April, an on-campus forum on Vietnam was heavily attended; later that month, the campus learned that a former Ithaca College student had been killed in action.

Thereafter anger mounted. A community teach-in during the summer of 1967 heard a spirited defense of civil disobedience as well as Professor John Ryan's more reasoned presentation, "Alternatives to Escalation." By October, the *Ithacan* had succumbed to the prevailing rhetoric ("Imperialist War Becomes Genocidal"), and the coverage of Vietnam overshadowed the reporting of the College's seventy-fifth anniversary party. Students were informed that "The Office" had opened in downtown Ithaca — a storefront with "a complete line of anti-war literature." A student printed her "Reflections on the D.C. March"; a College physician, Adib Karam, left for Vietnam; the "I.C. Students and Faculty against the War in Vietnam" sent Christmas gifts to the GIs, who presumably were serving involuntarily in that distant and unhappy conflict. The pro-government party had not of course disappeared. In December 1967, the *Ithacan* featured an article by "hawk" Andrew Ezergailis (history) as well as a counterstatement by "dove" John Ryan (political science). In February 1968, the doves undertook to issue their own publication, *Peace;* by 1969 - 1970, *Nexus* would serve as the organ for conservative opinion.

Opposition to the war in Vietnam was never a totally disinterested humanitarian concern: it took its edge from the imminency of the draft for many college students. The draft-deferment tests, administered first in April 1966, brought sheriffs to Egbert Union against an anticipated demonstration which in fact did not materialize. The *Ithacan* in 1966 - 1967 and 1967 - 1968 contains much on the subject, including a regular feature on how students on other campuses were responding. Discussions of the conscientious objector became frequent; the "draftee migration" to Canada included some Ithaca College students; the *Ithacan* luridly caught the mood of many in "The Draft: First Link in a Chain of Death." In April 1968, simultaneously with the response to King's assassination, students and demonstrators marched and chanted outside of the Union following a three-day teach-in on "The Draft and You." The *Ithacan* noted that there were more spectators than protesters, but the College had had its first "demonstration."

There had been lengthy preparations for such an eventuality. Back in April 1961, the student council, aided by the Knights of Columbus, had arranged for a showing of the film "Operation Abolition," produced by the House Committee on Un-American Activities and purporting to prove that student demonstrations in San Francisco had been communist-instigated. The matter took on some urgency in October 1965: the trustees, viewing the national scene with alarm, directed the president to formulate a policy on "student unrest." In February 1966, the Board voted to continue "the firm policy of discipline" in such circumstances. At a Forum meeting in March 1967, Dillingham hedged when asked just what he would do in the event of a nonviolent demonstration on campus. But in April, he felt able to assure the trustees that there was no significant unrest on campus.

The students, meanwhile, were carefully following the patterns of behavior on other campuses, and the *Ithacan* gave full attention to student riots in Spain in January 1967. Throughout 1967 - 1968, student "demands" became increasingly insistent, but the official attitude was still that good communications existed, especially through the work of the campus life committee. On February 22, 1968, Provost Davies preached a homily to the faculty, with texts chosen from an article by Wayne Booth urging "rational discourse on the College campus and the importance of 'sweet reasonableness.'" After the "Draft and You" demonstration, the Arts and Sciences faculty felt impelled to forward to the Board an A.A.U.P. statement on faculty responsibility for the academic freedom of students, which the Board discussed, without action, on May 17, 1968.

The era of "sweet reasonableness," if indeed it had ever existed, was fast coming to a close.

In 1967 - 1968, the most clearly evident tensions within the College community had to do with student participation in College governance. The previous year, a small victory had been won: representatives of the press were admitted to a faculty meeting. By October 1967, the *Ithacan* was calling for student participation in the work of all campus committees, especially those concerned with faculty evaluation and personnel decisions — a stand arising directly out of the non-reappointment of an English instructor with a devoted following. An article attempted to explain "How Ithaca Selects Faculty" — most capriciously, it was implied. By November, the students were ready to present ten proposals (not yet "demands"), in a still conciliatory and irenic mood — "not in the Berkeley tradition of dictating to educators what must be but . . . suggesting to one another ways in which Ithaca College can become a stimulating educational center." The proposals included the formation of the campus life committee, student representation on curriculum committees, the formation of intradepartmental committees composed equally of students and faculty members "to discuss courses and methods of instruction," a greater student role in the affairs of the Library, student presence "at some point" in faculty meetings to present their views, attendance of both student and faculty members at Board meetings "to participate in long-range planning decisions and the formulation of college policy," and student attendance at administrative staff meetings. The president responded sympathetically, reporting to the alumni that the students' "justifiable fear [was] that in education, as in many other areas of our national life, the individual is being relegated to the role of a statistic." The first proposal was easily accepted, and the campus life committee was functioning by the spring of 1968.

The *Ithacan* conducted its own poll to determine just what students wanted. The responses ranged widely — student power, unlimited cuts, legal abortion, withdrawal from Vietnam, more premarital sex, legal marijuana, a wet campus, intervisitation, national fraternities. The same issue hardly helped to foster the spirit of consensus by reprinting a cheap journalistic tantrum entitled "The Student as Nigger" (this setpiece would be dragged out upon occasion for the next few years).

Other minor concessions were made, though there were setbacks: the faculty tabled a motion to allow the editor of the *Ithacan* to attend faculty meetings on a regular basis. The student leadership showed some signs of restiveness; Ithaca, one of them complained, was just "a safe school" — "we are seventy-five years old only because we hang onto the memory of the ladies' violin club of 1892." But the year closed without serious incident. It was the last year that the Davies policy of defusing through discussion would prove even moderately efficacious.

The year 1968 - 1969 opened on a note of optimistic faith that gradualism and peaceful reform would still work. The *Ithacan* headline "Class of 1972: Welcome to the Problem" was meant to be challenging, not cynically despairing. As the president of the student body put it:

> *The Ithaca College Student Government pledges to continue the quiet revolution begun last year. There can be no denial that the role of the modern student is to help reconstruct American education and by so doing reconstruct America.*

The previous May, the *Ithacan* had reviewed the year just closing as one of substantive accomplishment in a variety of areas:

> *Students pressuring the administration to offer courses on Negro history and black cultures, demonstrating against the War, the draft, and the administration of the college itself, are events remarkably new to the Ithaca College campus. This was the year of the first college demonstration, everyone was set for the worst, but it was peaceful and orderly.*

The new year continued that momentum, and, one by one, many of the goals defined in 1967 - 1968 were realized. Representatives of the student body began attending the weekly meetings of the administrative staff; students became voting members of the Library committee, and the educational policies committee recommended that all departments seat students either as voting or nonvoting members whenever student matters were under discussion; students on the presidential search committee were accorded voting power; two student leaders were invited to attend a faculty meeting, although their right to do so regularly was not conceded (by April 1969, students came anyway, en masse, and were not ejected). Not all of the ten proposals were accepted, and new ones were added from time to time, such as the right to examine the budget. But progress was unmistakable, and for most students, liquor and intervisitation were its most obvious manifestations.

Yet not everyone was committed to gradual transformation through the established machinery. Some perceived such an approach as slow and at bottom phony; others found it more exciting to play at being revolutionaries, especially as word arrived about the suspended classes at Stony Brook and about Mark Rudd's antics at Columbia. And in the spring of 1969, Ithaca College students joined the nation and the world in watching on TV as the Cornell campus was turned into an armed camp. A speaker at the dedication of the performing arts building contributed to the growing interest in direct action by suggesting that rioting in the ghettoes of American cities could best be understood as a form of communication.

An "underground" newspaper, *The Scimitar,* appeared — on sale, with no risk to anyone above or below ground, in the Union; an *Ithacan* editor dismissed this competition as "a hippie faggot newspaper with leftist overtones, basically trying to appeal to the psychotic community, which, I believe, is very large." FUSA (the "Free" University for Social Action) organized noncredit courses on a variety of topics — William Styron's *The Confessions of Nat Turner,* Black Protest, The Liberal Arts or Reactionary Arts: An Examination, The Exploitation of Students and the Poor in Housing. One faculty member denounced FUSA as "intellectually pretentious and professionally insulting" in its naive faith that "all social problems can be solved by rational means." A branch of SDS (Students for a Democratic Society) was organized, and held a rally in April 1969.

For a while, the campus floundered in search of a really hot issue. Picketing a local supermarket in defense of the California grape-pickers was of limited usefulness. Some indignant reaction followed when the chairman of the psychology-sociology department dismissed requests for change by remarking, "You women will only get married anyway," but the issue had little staying power at that time. Steps toward establishing a link with the ROTC unit at Cornell would not become an issue until the following year, and barring military recruiters from "our Union" did not prove difficult — at one point, sound equipment was brought in to play protest songs at ear-splitting volume.

The explosion came over the issue of black power.

In October 1968, James Farmer arrived to speak on "The Negro in America: What Must Be Done." By the end of January 1969, black students were blasting "our Ivory Tower College," where it was impossible "to get more than

20% of the student body to participate in a demonstration." That estimate was really far too high: in February, only forty-five students turned out in front of the Job Hall to back the demands of the blacks. These included the admission of eighty black students by September 1969, the appointment of two black professors by September 1969, an office of black affairs with a black assistant dean by September 1969, at least seven additional courses "dealing with Blackness" by the same date, a full Afro-American studies program by 1972, and a summer program and tutorial assistance for Educational Opportunity Program students. These demands were approved by the student congress, but the College, some felt, was moving far too slowly. In April 1969, a new kind of demonstration occurred. Some thirty blacks held a fifteen-minute rally at which President Dillingham was burned in effigy.

The SDS rushed in: "The Ithaca College Students for a Democratic Society fully support the Afro-American Society's demands and actions in their fight against this administration," and the Cornell Afro-American Society, very much a presence on the Ithaca College campus, proclaimed, "Let it be clear to everyone that the blacks of Cornell and the blacks of Ithaca College are a community." The hope was expressed — it was also a threat — that Ithaca College would not have to go through "the same traumatic experience of Cornell."

Some results were achieved: the appointment of a graduating senior as coordinator of the black studies program; one full-time black professor; some expansion in courses and support programs, and a commitment to at least forty new black students. At the direction of the faculty, the president appointed the inevitable committee "to explore and determine the feasibility of the Afro-American and Economic Opportunity proposals for increasing aid to minority or underprivileged student." By then, it was May, so that the issue would remain as unfinished business for the following academic year.

Disorders on other campuses and in particular the awareness of a great university in turmoil on the opposite hill focused concern on the formulation of a policy to cope with such emergencies. In September 1968, the Board had been told that despite "some unrest" among junior faculty members, no "revolt" need be expected in the current year. In December, the *Ithacan* was calling for rules for the conduct of campus demonstrations; the primary concern was that the educational process not be interrupted. In March 1969, the department of economics and business administration formally requested administrative action for the maintenance of order. The educational policies committee debated the matter in April, but deferred action when the student members persuaded the others that to issue a statement might in fact precipitate precisely what it was attempting to avoid. But after being burned in effigy, the president, understandably, concluded that the time for action had indeed come. His statement of April 22, 1969, put the campus on notice that the administration would not condone

> *any action on the part of students, faculty, and/or staff which constitutes a potential hazard to life and property; which is designed to disrupt academic or social life on campus; which is accompanied by arbitrary demands or threats; or which is calculated to provoke or encourage unlawful seizure or assembly.*

Asserting that prompt action would be taken to assure the integrity of the classroom, academic freedom and the life and property of all concerned, he pledged that "for this purpose, the administration will employ any or all resources available to it." Many read the most sinister of implications into the last sentence. Two days later, Dillingham assured the community that he would take no arbitrary action, that a restraining order would be invoked only after reasonable approaches had failed, and that the police would be called in only as a last resort.

On April 28, approximately one thousand persons attended an all-day teach-in on "What Education Should Be and How Ithaca College Fits into the Educational Process." Provost Davies strove valiantly to keep the discussion on a high plane of ideality, but the shadow of Cornell and the armed occupation of its Union hung heavily over the sessions. "Don't make your revolution here," a professor of Music pleaded; "Go make your revolution in the cities, in the ghettoes, in the factories." Faculty concern centered not so much on the disturbance policy as such as on the fact that it had been proclaimed without faculty involvement: there was much discussion of the need for a committee on campus disorders to counsel the president in an hour of crisis. Another teach-in on May 2 attracted a somewhat smaller crowd and again heard a warning, this time from Dean Paul

Givens, that the very existence of the College as a center of objective inquiry was in danger. He saw "a new kind of tyranny in academic life — a tyranny of militant confrontation." Even in such tense circumstances, faculty meetings had difficulty maintaining a quorum. Nevertheless, the committee to advise the president was approved, and the demands of the Afro-American Society accepted in principle, along with the committee to attempt their implementation.

The annual float parade was held, in much the usual fashion, and the semester ended.

The State of New York, through the Henderson Law, by then required the filing of a statement of "Rules and Regulations for the Maintenance of Public Order." A document was drafted by those members of the campus life committee who were available in June and put in final form by the administration, the trustees, and the College attorney. This statement was dispatched to Albany on July 14. The campus would then be quiet until the return of the students, at which time 1968 - 1969 would seem only a pallid preview of the year about to begin.

The City of Ithaca used the summer to convert the bath-house at Stewart Park into a detention center — just in case.

For several years, protest had been mainly a springtime ritual, but in 1969 - 1970, the excitement began to mount as soon as the students arrived. Early in the summer, the English department had done it again: Beatrice Goldman, a young instructor, who, with her husband, was prominently identified with the radical left, had been informed that her appointment would not be renewed for 1970 - 1971. The chairman offered assurance that the decision had been reached for professional reasons that had nothing to do with "considerations of politics, race, religion, and sex," and, in accordance with the practice of the period, no public explanation was given. Mrs. Goldman had a great deal to say in public, the Arts and Sciences faculty council chose to involve itself in the issue, and the "Goldman case" was well on its way to being one of the principal causes of the year. "Shafted" was the *Ithacan*'s caption to a front-page picture-story. (The *Ithacan,* incidentally, was now "independent" — that is, its only official tie to the College was a hefty financial subsidy, without which it could not continue to exist.)

The two divergent approaches of gradualism and direct action continued to be in evidence. The campus life committee moved forward with a request to the Board for faculty and student trustees and for an open budget; a leader of the student left predicted that the movement was pausing only before a new burst of activity which might include "the seizing of property, the shutting down of classes, and the provoking of confrontations through the making of threats." "Underground" (an unearned adjective that insulted the work of every real Resistance fighter) movies were scheduled; FUSA moved into its second year, still seeking to demonstrate "how pleasant life can be if [one is] allowed to live it in freedom." Courses in black culture, black politics, minority relations, and Afro-American history were added to the curriculum of the College of Arts and Sciences. Black speakers related the "white man's indifference" to the "black man's violence"; a guest editorial blustered "Wise Up, White Man!"; Dick Gregory arrived to provide a rationale for revolution:

> *Whenever any form of government becomes destructive of those ends [the principles of the Declaration of Independence], it is the right and duty of the people to destroy or abolish it*

and to contribute his distinctive brand of rhetoric:

> *I hate your stinking American white racist society with its stinking American white racist institutions.*

The big event of October 1969 was the "Moratorium" on the fifteenth. This was to be a national effort. "On October 15, students and faculty all over America will leave their classes for one day to ring doorbells and talk to their fellow Americans about the madness of Vietnam." Some talked of a two-day interruption in November, three days in December, and on in an escalating progression throughout the school year. Elaborate programs were prepared for both Cornell and Ithaca College; I.C. students were granted cuts without penalty; and instructors were left free to cancel their classes. There was an on-campus rally, at which President Dillingham spoke of his Quaker background and of his sympathies for students "trying to do something to actively promote the cause of peace." Then the canvassers assembled in DeWitt Park before fanning out throughout the city. Most classes were held and most of the student body attended them; only 500 turned out for the rally, and a mere 125 participated in the canvassing (during which they were greeted with obscenities and threatened with a wrecking bar by one irate citizen). "The Blot" was the *Ithacan*'s description of the massive indifference of the campus; in part it blamed student congress for withholding its official blessing of the Moratorium. There was no follow-up in November. Instead, buses took interested students to Washington for what was described as the largest antiwar demonstration in the history of the United States.

By November, the attention of the campus was riveted on a distressing incident much closer to home. In a party celebrating the end of the football season, a fight occurred between two students, one white, one black — the epithet *nigger* was used. Immediately, the Afro-Latin Society issued an ultimatum demanding the expulsion of the white student; reports circulated that the blacks were about to bring guns onto the campus for their self-protection. Blacks armed with razor blades burst into the room of the student who had precipitated the crisis. The president roundly condemned racism in any form but the Afro-Latin Society accused him of handling their grievance in "a subversive and insulting manner" and demanded an apology from him as well as the expulsion of the student. There were mass meetings and emergency sessions of the campus life committee, which called for a board on racism, mainly composed of students, with jurisdiction over any case involving the charge of racism. The faculty expressed its horror at the thought of being hauled before a student-dominated court. The impasse was broken when a national mediator was brought in: tensions subsided, and a shaky peace between the president and the Afro-Latin Society was negotiated — as between two sovereign powers. Black students would be allowed to have their own living area; students were given the right to appeal a suspension or expulsion to final and binding impartial arbitration; the board on racism was set up, but without any judicial authority.

The *Ithacan* had signalized the new year by announcing that it was officially abandoning the distinction between reporting the news and editorial comment (a distinction it had found shaky enough in the best of times). Before the month was over, it had full opportunity to act on its new policy. By January 1970, a history professor, also the faculty adviser to the SDS, was in trouble with his department for dropping from his class a student who had criticized Dick Gregory in a letter to the editor and for making, in a seminar, a scatological comment about the quality of a colleague's interpretation of the American Revolution. Two hundred students turned out for a rally, not to protest Professor Taber's behavior but to denounce the history department for presuming to censure him for unprofessional conduct. The *Ithacan* proposed yet another plan for making faculty personnel decisions, this time with final authority resting with all the faculty members of a department and its student majors voting together as equals. A radical dropout wrote back that "students should call a teach-in and assume governmental powers to run the school"; he even volunteered to return to help in the takeover.

On the night of February 9, 1970, some 150 students acted upon these calls for militant action by occupying the third and fourth floors of the Muller Faculty Center. By 1:15 A.M., they were ready to issue four demands: that all faculty personnel committees have equal numbers of faculty members and students; that all candidates for appointment respond to a student questionnaire probing their attitudes toward students; that dossiers contain letters of recommendation from students; and that Taber and Goldman be rehired pending reevaluation under this new dispensation. The occupation was a model of orderliness: faculty members wishing access to their offices were solemnly escorted by student marshalls. It was ended by mid-morning on February 10, by which time the students agreed that their presence was proving inconvenient.

The provost made the gymnasium available on February 11 for workshops to discuss the four demands; the faculties of each school were instructed to meet for the same purpose. It was estimated that some four hundred students wandered in and out at various hours while the cadre prepared an ultimatum for mimeographing and distribution — "By three o'clock today, February 11, 1970, we want an affirmation in principle that students have a say in the hiring and firing of faculty." The faculties of Arts and Sciences, Physical Therapy, and Allied Health did what they were told to do. The Board, meeting simultaneously in New York City, voted to accept two faculty members, two students, and two alumni as trustees.

The *Cornell Sun,* in an unprecedented action, issued a South Hill edition to provide complete coverage of these developments in a neighboring institution. In it, Taber chirped his delight: "there was an explosion coming at Ithaca College. I was happy to be the catalyst." The mood of many others was one of exultation. The provost hailed "the apparent victory for reason and moderation in handling sensitive issues," although a few day later, he allowed that the demand for equal faculty-student representation on personnel committees was "not entirely and exclusively logical in all cases." John Ryan summed it up in the *Ithacan* of February 13.

Revolutions are made by patient men — Lenin, Mao, Ho — whatever else they were, they waited to act. . . . You have established yourself as a vital political force on campus. Now wait, and if the final proposal takes a week, wow, you've done a great thing.

The editorial, "Right On," strained for words to describe the situation: "On Monday night an almost intangible momentum sucked up Ithaca College."

Ryan's reference to "a week" referred to the other clause in the student ultimatum: specific implementation of student participation in personnel matters by February 18. To be sure, some 150 nonradicalized students signed an open letter to the trustees denouncing the "Liberation Group" as being unrepresentative of the student body (as it certainly was) and protesting the unseemly haste in which the faculty was stampeded toward compliance with the demands of the minority. Nonetheless, the principle of student involvement in faculty appointments had come into its own, where it would remain for a least a decade. One by one, the departments trouped into the recreation room on February 18 and dutifully reported their "progress" to some 300 "concerned" students and faculty members. It transpired that in some departments, notably in the School of Music, in philosophy, and in biology, the majors were not in the least interested in altering the status quo.

While the College was assimilating these far-reaching changes, some minor brush fires broke out. The Physical Education students, who, the year before, could find nothing more epochal to protest than crowded lockers and a too chilly swimming pool, now asserted their right to "freedom in personal appearance" as an inalienable form of self-expression: some of their number, sprouting mustaches, had been barred from registration. By early April, the P.E. students had won "The Battle of the Hair." And an unexpected uprising of the art majors resulted in a one-day boycott of classes, largely because of dissatisfaction with the departmental chairman.

By April, the action had moved once again to the other hill, as Cornell celebrated its "America Is Hard To Find" weekend, with a sensational appearance, in Barton Hall, of fugitive

Daniel Berrigan, S.J., while the FBI men looked on in frustration and rage. The fire at the Africana Studies and Research Center and the sacking of the University bookstore sent shock waves across the valley. Smoldering discontent over the lagging Educational Opportunity Program and rumors of a reduction in its budget resulted in an ugly incident on April 13. A black delegation of about fifty, with perhaps as many more SDS supporters, barricaded the president and an aide in his office, overturned a desk and filing cabinet, destroyed some *objets d'art,* and threw the potted plants down the stairwell of Job Hall. After this brief occupation, the protesters marched to the Union to "trash" the bookstore. The civil authorities were alerted, an injunction was obtained (though not used), the campus life committee was hastily convened, several dozen faculty members were mustered as a fire watch in the academic buildings. In the end, the usual concessions were granted — amnesty for the trashers, an increased budget and other improvements in the EOP, College transportation to and from the Cornell black community. In the aftermath, the provisions of the Henderson Law were sternly quoted, and the campus life committee went on record as deploring "all forms of violence and destruction" and urged all to exercise "understanding and restraint." It was lost on no one that violence and destruction had in fact carried the day.

There had been a few lighter touches in 1969 - 1970. In October, forty gallons of detergent were poured into the reflecting pool, so that billows of foam, caught in a brisk breeze from the south, cascaded down the steps adjacent to the performing arts building. In March, a fraternity pledge was dumped in a women's dormitory in his underwear, with his hands taped behind his back. And even in this troubled April, Spring Weekend brought out the usual floats (this time on campus, since downtown Ithaca was busy with "America Is Hard To Find"). But May 1970 would prove to be not the festive ending of the academic year, but a time of the most bitter confrontation.

On May 3, the editors of eleven Eastern college newspapers agreed to run a common editorial asking "the entire academic community of this country to engage in a nationwide university strike" to protest the escalation of the war. The heads of thirty-seven colleges and universities (including Howard Dillingham) sent a telegram to President Nixon warning him of "the incalculable dangers of an unprecedented alienation of America's youth." The Ithaca College leftists responded almost immediately. A flyer addressed to the administration, faculty, and staff brusquely offered those groups the privilege of joining them in their strike against Nixon, but only on the acceptance of three demands: the release of all political prisoners (such as Bobby Seale and the Black Panthers), unilateral and immediate withdrawal of all U.S. forces from Southeast Asia, and the termination of all "complicity with the U.S. war machine" (such as defense research, ROTC, counterinsurgency research, and so on). Specifically, Ithaca College was directed to terminate its ROTC contract with Cornell, to cancel all classes and final examinations. "'Business as usual' at I.C. must come to a halt." Should any feel inclined to resist this invitation, the flyer warned that the students would then strike against them as well as against Nixon. During this week of striking, workshops would be scheduled, culminating in a march on Washington on May 9.

The massacre at Kent State on May 4 exacerbated feelings both of anger and of helplessness. Another flyer reviewed the history of political assassination in recent American history and pictured every student as facing the loaded rifles of the National Guardsmen. Gas masks, at least, could be obtained for $8.00 from the "Strike Headquarters" in Syracuse. And precisely at this unpropitious moment, there was a severe setback at the faculty meeting on the evening of May 4.

It was a faculty meeting long to be remembered: on what previous occasion had the professors ever attempted debate with at least five hundred students jamming the lobby and entrances of the Main Theatre and stationed in the boxes and balcony? The faculty endorsed the president's telegram and abolished the GIPPE requirement; then, after some routine business, it turned to a really explosive agenda item — an honorary degree for Governor Rockefeller, who was scheduled to give the commencement address. Much rhetoric flowed — "he has been part and parcel of the military-industrial complex which will destroy the earth if it is not stopped." Dillingham pointed out that at least it could be said that Rockefeller was a patron of the arts and an ardent conservationist. The honorary degree was voted — by the slimmest of margins.

It was then moved that the College join in the nationwide strike. An attempt to sidestep the question by a motion to adjourn was defeated in rather an unusual manner — the students blocked all the exits. Many faculty members expressed their objection to this detention, pointing out that

the democratic process was less than perfectly manifested in such action. One member of the Physical Education faculty, sturdily built, lowered his head and successfully charged through the student guards. Others merely worried about their staying power. Happily, a member of the student government soon announced that the barricades were being lifted, and discussion was resumed (after the inevitable quorum count).

The question at last had to be faced — no strike? a strike for a single day? one for a few days or possibly for the entire week? The faculty dissolved itself into a committee of the whole; the predictable range of opinions was expressed — the dangers of politicizing an educational institution, the urgent need for a symbolic gesture of protest. Students pointed out that *they* were striking anyway, so that the question was purely academic. The provost, rather tactlessly, asked the students whether they were against the war or merely afraid of getting killed in it. But after two hours, the meeting was reconvened. A motion was made for a strike from May 5 to May 9. To the vast annoyance of many, a secret ballot was demanded: students equipped with binoculars peered down from the boxes to see how individual faculty members were voting. The motion failed, 50 to 53, and at approximately 11:00 P.M., the meeting was adjourned — but not without a final fillip of drama. A history professor, turning to leave after an exchange with a student perched on the stage, was shocked to hear "Watch out . . . or you'll end up with a bullet in your back." Upon complaint, the safety division unaccountably delegated an active SDS student to investigate: his report, not surprisingly, was that "the threat was of a general nature and not directed specifically" at the professor to whom it was addressed by name. Even so, a flyer was hastily prepared and circulated by morning, in which the student insisted that he had meant nothing unfriendly.

The next day, another student would write that it was a time of "the most bitter pessimism, the most utter dejection." Blaming those "Long Island miniature revolutionaries," the "little Che's," who bogged down in endless subcommittes, he conceded that the strike had failed.

Classes were being held and business was just as usual. Those protesters whose expressed purpose was to discourage those students going to classes or taking examinations failed as well. Yes, a symbolic handful of students walked out of their classes, but only a pitifully small number. A number of professors made their finals optional, but even this was not enough. And for the most part, except for a few shaggy heads meandering along the sidewalks and a few posters in the Union, one would never have known that there was a Strike on, or, for that matter, that anyone had really heard about it.

There was a bomb scare at 2 Fountain Place; ROTC was suspended indefinitely (because, it was discovered, the Cornell faculty had never approved the arrangement with Ithaca College). Some students went to Washington anyway, and the president shared his gloomy ruminations with the Board.

. . . he sees the quality of education being slowly eroded along with the value of the degrees that students are receiving from their institutions. For the present, he sees no viable way of reversing the trend.

Recognizing the helplessness of a college like Ithaca College "in the face of violence and destruction," he drew comfort from the fact that the professional students at least were "too busy with their studies to become involved in campus turmoil."

He was hardly looking forward to commencement on May 16.

From the time the choice of speaker had been announced, the rhetorical big guns had been moved into position and the volleys began. The campus was soon plastered with a leaflet summarizing "The Case Against Nelson Rockefeller" — a hawk, a friend of dictators, an exploiter of the working classes both at home and in South America, and filthy rich. Despite the rumblings, Dillingham held firm: commencement occurred as scheduled and the governor became a Doctor of Fine Arts. But not everyone heard his address (in which he proposed to serve as intermediary between the students of New York and President Nixon). About two hundred persons — including students, faculty members, a few parents, and one member of the administration — walked out in protest (about half the protesters were in fact visitors from Cornell).

The dissidents marched to the recreation room in Egbert Union, where they held "The First Annual Ithaca College [Alternate] Commencement." This ceremony was designed as an expression of "repulsion and disgust for the values celebrated at the traditional ceremony," as a protest against Rockefeller, but mostly as "an affirmation of life" and of those who had "taken a stand for life."

The war against Blacks, Vietnamese, Cambodians, and all other people who have life in their veins is intolerable. The institutions of higher learning in America support the slaughter of life by their myopic and insulated pursuit of wisdom or by their lucrative defense contracts and research projects. We have complained and protested against irrelevancy and university complicity with the war. We now must graduate from it.

Douglas Dowd, professor of economics at Cornell and just back from Hanoi, and Jerry Zilg, "movement worker, expert on the military," were the scheduled speakers. Entertainment was provided by the Peace Theatre Ensemble from Syracuse University; there were wine and cheese (for this was "a celebration of life") and an afternoon of workshops on such topics as Rockefeller, Vietnam, women's liberation, political repression, and Third World peoples.

Back at the Hill Physical Education Center, Rockefeller, good-humored throughout, seized the occasion to comment on the strengths of a political system that could gracefully tolerate dissent. But the bland optimism of these remarks and of his prepared speech was movingly counterpointed by two appeals from members of the College community. Professor Frank Darrow pledged unremitting efforts to encompass the goal of peace; John McGhan, president of the senior class, spoke for the graduates of 1970.

We have listened — now we must speak. We leave Ithaca College with no great optimism. We are far too aware that we now enter a world plagued with conflict and tremendous sadness. We see the shape of America — and we grieve for her. Therefore, we cannot leave today without publicly committing ourselves — each and every one of us — to change. . . . We want peace — we will work for peace — each in his own way.

We beg you — give peace a chance.

And so, at the last, everyone had spoken, all the chords had been sounded — although no one, on that May 16, could have heard them in any coherent relationship to one another. The crucial principle of free expression of mutually incompatible views had met and survived a major challenge — at the cost of the most bitterly divided campus in the history of Ithaca College.

Surely President Dillingham must have thought, many times, how much pleasanter it would have been to have retired in May 1968, after the triumph of the seventy-fifth anniversary year. Those who know him well remember the occasional moods of dark depression that followed May 1970 and his official departure on August 31 of that year. But his thirteenth and final annual report, written after the fall 1970 honors convocation, put it all into perspective, even to its title, "Ithaca College Today."

The survey of what had been accomplished in those thirteen years was breathtaking even in its simplest chronological and statistical statement. But Dillingham chose to look forward rather than backward, however flattering the retrospective view might be.

> *In my youth academic institutions prided themselves upon being aloof from the world. The ivory tower was regarded as the best possible abode. When we left it, distinguished commencement speakers assured us that we were going forth into a brave new world and that, with perseverance, we would find the pot at the end of the rainbow. Times have changed. The ivory tower is not where the action is. Pot has a new connotation, and the knowledgeable aren't looking for it under a rainbow. This isn't really a brave new world, but a troubled old one. Fortunately its problems are being attacked by a new generation,*

> *better educated than its predecessors, and having in its hands a technology non-existent a few years ago.*

Picking up, perhaps without being aware that he was doing so, a major theme of his inaugural address in 1957, he reaffirmed his faith in the capabilities and concerns of college students.

> *Our problems as a nation loom ever larger because the pressure for their resolution is becoming stronger and is being applied by the young and college-educated, who have the courage and idealism to persevere.*

Contemplating education in its largest compass, he saw even the humanities only at the very beginning of their exploration of man's nature and destiny: vast uncharted areas of non-Western thought and experience remained to be discovered. His charge to his successor was to continue working toward that goal which he had always cherished as a vital part of his heritage — the transformation of the campus into a "community-in-miniature."

The faculty tribute likewise stressed Dillingham's contribution to the emerging ideal of community.

> *. . . although you will always be known as the Builder-President . . . we would stress your ability to create a kind of spiritual elbow-room, an atmosphere in which new ideas could get a hearing, in which far-reaching decisions could be made, in which the College community could experience the crises of change without demoralization or irrevocable loss.*

The trustees, on October 17, 1970, bestowed upon Howard Dillingham the highest accolade which it lay in their power to confer — the title of president emeritus of Ithaca College.

Plate Series V: **Building the South Hill Campus**

The South Hill site

First model of present campus (note chapel in center, tent-like field house and gym at right)

Photo by: C. Hadley Smith

Phase I - five dormitories and Union

Five more dormitories and the Health Center, Friends Hall in center

Photo by: C. Hadley Smith

Added: The Science Building, the Gymnasium, and the Music Building

Photo by: C. Hadley Smith

Faculty Office Building and classrooms, Administration Building, Tower Dormitories and Dining Hall

Lecture Halls, Library, Terrace Dormitories, Performing Arts Building

Photos by: J. P. Harcourt

The College Farm

The Center Quad of the Campus

The Garden Apartments (center section of photo)

The Caroline Werner Gannett Center

Photo by: Jon Chrispin

The Herman E. and Florence S. Muller Memorial Chapel

Photo by: Jon Chrispin

VIII.   The Phillips Years 1970 - 1975

"A Time to Breathe Out . . ."

WILLIAM Grant Egbert — farmboy-violinist from Danby, New York. George C. Williams — son of a stonecutter from Dryden, New York. Leonard B. Job — raised on an Indiana farm. Howard Dillingham — educated in his early years in a one-room schoolhouse near Auburn, New York. The first four presidents of Ithaca College were products of rural America. They were essentially self-made men, the first of their families to achieve distinction by the time-honored American route of educational opportunity.

The fifth president of Ithaca College, Ellis L. Phillips, Jr., could hardly have been more different. He had been born to affluence and secure social status; his education had followed the pattern appropriate to his class — Deerfield Academy (*cum laude*, 1938), Princeton (with a degree *summa cum laude* in history in 1942), a law degree from Columbia (where he was a Harlan Fiske Stone Scholar) in 1948. After a period with a New York City law firm, he had returned to Columbia in 1953 as associate professor of law and assistant dean, becoming professor in 1956. Since 1959, he had served as president of the Ellis L. Phillips Foundation, where one of his particular interests had been a program of internship in academic administration. The man who had made it possible for more than forty men and women to take a year's leave of absence to observe collegiate administration in depth and who had described this far-reaching experiment in *A New Approach to Academic Administration* finally decided to take on the challenges of a college presidency himself.

I have accepted the position partly because I am intrigued by the problems of how to run colleges and universities. So naturally, one would at some point like to have the opportunity to test one's theories.

The appointment, announced after the May 1970 Board meeting and effective September 1, 1970, was greeted with general enthusiasm. A few students and faculty members muttered darkly about the new president's "elitist" background and about Marion Grumman Phillips's connections with Grumman Aircraft. But Professor Ashur Baizer, chairman of the presidential search committee, articulated the prevailing view: "The appointment of Dr. Phillips is a great relief and an exhilarating climax to the exhaustingly difficult challenge of the past fifteen months." Student response was equally positive: "He's a very, very fine gentleman"; "His relationships with people are very good and he is a very direct speaker. . . . I think he'll be sympathetic to activist students." In short, after a prolonged period of searching marked by some disgraceful infighting, the College had found new leadership and had renewed its hope that tensions within the academic community were amenable to reasonable and civilized solutions.

Yet for all his urbanity, his ingratiating manner, his perennial smile, Phillips made it clear that he would resist encroachments upon the powers of the presidential office. From the beginning, he expressed his opposition in principle to having students and faculty members as voting trustees. He told a faculty group that he could not accept the idea that a college president was merely the executive officer appointed to carry out the will of the faculty: "That wouldn't be any fun," he concluded, with a disarming grin. At the end of the first month in office, he spelled out his conception of academic administration in some detail before the Ithaca Rotary Club. After remarking that in former times, when a group of students was seen going to the president's office, *they* were in trouble, he rejected the notion of "participatory democracy" as a mode of college governance. A college, he pointed out, was not "a finishing school, a social ticketing agency, a refuge for dilettantes, a service station for government or industry, a political training ground or staging area." Rather, institutions of higher learning were organized for public purposes on behalf of society as a whole: the trustees, to whom the destiny of Ithaca College was legally entrusted, derived their authority from the people of the State of New York. The president, as the chief administrative officer of the Board, "must inspire and lead those who are presently on campus participating in the academic work of the institution, but he does not receive his authority from them." He stressed the importance of "input" from all the constituencies within the academic community. Nevertheless, the "Trustees' Trustee, the President, must assume responsibility for decisions which affect the vital interests of the college on a long-range basis. . . . This responsibility cannot be delegated." In the last analysis, trustees and president must "legislate for the silent constituency to whom they are ultimately responsible — society at large."

The fall of 1970 was reserved for farewells to President Emeritus Dillingham — chief among them, the festive honors convocation on October 17, 1970. The inauguration of President Phillips followed as the principal event of the spring semester. Scheduled as an all-day celebration on Wednesday, April 7, 1971, the "Academic Festival," organized by Professor Robert Pasternack, had chosen for its theme "Man In Control."

> *Our purpose is to involve the College Community and guests in a day of self-discovery and rededication to education in the service of mankind.*

Representatives of sixty-seven colleges (including seven presidents) and of twenty-one learned societies, professional organizations, and foundations attended.

The morning program consisted of a series of demonstrations of the festival theme — computer presentations, a variety of scientific experiments, a participation clinic on bowling techniques, hearing tests in the mobile audiology unit, a clinic on the relief of pain, a viewing of the operations of the TV-radio studios and the film studio, a panel discussion by members of the department of political science on "critical political and social issues related to man's control of his environment." Music gamely attempted to fit its offerings into the pattern of "Man In Control of His Musical Heritage" with open rehearsals of a Brahms quartet and by the symphonic band and the College choir. The afternoon convocation continued with a multi-media presentation by students and faculty members and a "Festive Ode for an Academic Occasion" with words by Eric Blackall and music by Karel Husa. Another College tradition was established as David J. Laub, chairman of the Board of Trustees, invested the president with a presidential medallion designed for this and subsequent inaugurations. Phillips, as principal speaker, entitled his address "We Can Control. Let's Start." Optimistically, he predicted "more respect for the law and order of society," a renaissance of the family and neighborhood, and a reintegration of home and work; more immediately, he expressed his support for "the establishment of a consultative body of students, faculty, and staff with which I and my colleagues in the administration may share our perception of the path Ithaca College should follow." The *Ithacan* could not bring itself to share this confidence in the inevitability of progress: "We can always go backwards," an editorial observed. But the "Day of Self-Discovery" ended on an up beat with a concert by the jazz-soul singer Roberta Flack.

Shock waves from the student activism of the 1960s continued to reverberate, though in diminishing intensity, during the first years of the new administration. Incredibly, the responsibility for freshman orientation in September 1970 had been entrusted to a group of SDS - dominated students. Beanies, cheers, school songs, and all similar bourgeois symbols were declared abolished; instead, the incoming students were assigned summer readings in Eldridge Cleaver's *Soul on Ice* and Theodore Roszak's *Making of a Counter Culture;* orientation sessions were explicitly designed to shock them loose from their middle-class backgrounds and to begin the process of radicalization. "This Is Orientation?" the Syracuse *Herald American* asked in an indignant editorial, which went on to recommend that any prospective Ithaca College freshmen seriously consider attending some other institution.

Also before the new president took office on September 1, another group of leftist students had been spending the summer drawing up plans for the improvement of "the quality of life" at Ithaca College. Student elections in the previous academic year had resulted in a sweeping victory for the "Change Party," whose platform centered on the inalienable right of students "to determine their own destiny, and what is and is not relevant to them, both inside and outside the classroom." The College had been induced to support eleven student leaders as "summer research interns"; they remained on campus for nine weeks (at $80 per week). One project was a complete revision of the judicial system, on the principle that students could be prosecuted for the violation only of those rules which they themselves had made. A "Student Bill of Rights" was also drawn up, with emphasis on freedom from unreasonable search and seizure and on the confidentiality of all student records. The interns further recommended exclusive student control of all student activities and of the Union, including the College funds budgeted for such purposes; a bookstore essentially operated by the students; new academic programs in public education, public service, and community and policy studies; "behavioral modification" programs for the safety patrol personnel; and twenty-four-hour intervisitation in the dormitories. A proposal that would have immediate impact on campus was for a referendum to be held in September 1970 on the question of whether or not instruction should be suspended for two weeks so that students could participate in the campaigns preliminary to the November state and national elections.

The impetus for this last proposal came clearly from the "Princeton Plan," which stipulated for that institution a two-week recess just before the November elections. The interns, to their credit, provided a balanced statement of the pros and cons of such an arrangement, with due attention to the possible adverse effects of a political recess on the tax-exempt status of a private college. They outlined seven possible courses of action, ranging from "business as usual" to a preelection moratorium. The educational policies committee took the initiative early in September and recommended that those students who wished to campaign be allowed to do so without penalty and with every opportunity to make up the work that they would miss; it further recommended the

establishment of an appeals committee to adjudicate any allegations of unfair treatment by hostile faculty members. The faculty itself voted a slightly amended version of these recommendations. But after all the rhetoric, little actually happened. In the referendum, 636 students out of 1,000 voting favored participation in the campaign, but only 321 stated that they themselves would in fact be involved. By November, Provost Davies announced the cold statistics: only 12 of the College's 3,849 students had availed themselves of the opportunity to be absent from campus for political purposes. Later in the year, a proposed debate on U.S. involvement in Indochina likewise failed significantly to affect the programs of the College.

The era of the teach-in was over.

But there was other unfinished business from the sixties. On May 5, 1970, at the peak of campus confrontation, a group of students headed by Nadine Cohen had entered the classroom of a history professor, Donald Niewyck, and attempted to divert him from his scheduled lecture to a discussion of the American invasion of Cambodia. There were angry words; then Niewyck peremptorily dismissed the class. The repercussions from this occurrence climaxed in November 1970. Niewyck filed charges against Cohen and appeared before the student court to defend his right "to hold classes without disruption from moral absolutists or political fanatics." He further characterized the invading students as "fascist thugs"; Cohen retorted that Niewyck himself was a fascist thug. The student court, hardly unbiased, exonerated Cohen on the grounds that the instructor had not explicitly informed her that her behavior was in violation of the Henderson Law. Later that semester, the chief justice of the student court would label the Henderson Law "inane" and announce his refusal to hear any further appeals based upon it.

Several faculty members asked the faculty council to investigate an apparent infringement upon Professor Niewyck's academic freedom. E. W. Terwilliger submitted a motion for adoption by the faculty.

> *Solemnly, with full awareness of the gravity of its action, this faculty condemns Miss Cohen and her companions for behavior incompatible with the life of an institution devoted to free intellectual inquiry, justice, and tolerance. . . . they set a precedent which, if not denounced unequivocally for its lawlessness, has destroyed academic freedom at Ithaca College.*

But an ad hoc committee of the faculty council could find Cohen guilty of nothing more serious than "rudeness," and by the year's end, the Niewyck affair had sputtered out.

"Jocks Join the Revolution," the *Ithacan* of December 10, 1971, noted, and that belated national response was not without its impact on the South Hill campus. In the fall of 1970, there had been an altercation between the Physical Education administration and the Egbert Union board over the use of the gymnasium for rock concerts: the political overtones could be heard clearly enough in this dispute. Hairstyles within the School of Physical Education had already become an issue the previous spring. Now, in September 1970, five members of the gymnastics team announced that, in reaction to a "no beard, short hair" ruling by their coach, they would not return. Solemn debate ensued as to the precise relationship between length of hair and intellectual and personal freedom. Eventually, the athletic council left the matter in the hands of the individual coaches, with the proviso that "neatness in appearance shall not prevent an individual from having his own style of dress and hair if such a style will not interfere with his successful participation in the sport."

And throughout the early seventies, the trustees were treated to a new and no doubt disturbing experience of activism in the form of lengthy harangues from the student representatives who now sat with them at Board meetings. In the spring of 1970, the By-Laws of the College had been amended to permit two students (without vote), two faculty members, and two alumni to be elected to the Board. By the following September, the campus was engaged in heated debate over the precise status of these representatives. President Phillips branded student-faculty participation as "a bastardizing of the decision-making process"; in his view, students might conceivably be present to express their point of view, but should exit before discussion, have no vote, and leave no trace of their presence in the official minutes. A student leader responded in kind: the Board was "the least legitimate body" in all of College governance and should be supplanted by a faculty-student senate with responsibility for corporate as well as academic decisions. The student congress defiantly elected two representatives (Arthur Badavas and Peter Orville) as *voting* trustees and summoned a representative of the Board to render an accounting to the students, to be broadcast live over the College radio station.

If either or both of these requests are denied by the Board of Trustees, the Student Congress Executive Board will take necessary action to implement said requests by its own authority.

Just what that necessary action might be was left unspecified.

The faculty were likewise concerned about their role as trustees: the Board's action in May had apparently granted them a vote, but the executive committee had subsequently rescinded that privilege. Even so, two temporary representatives, Mary Arlin and Willard Daetsch, were chosen. The Board agreed to record the votes of the on-campus representatives without considering such votes legally binding and to review the entire question after a year.

In any event, the students became a lively presence beginning with the October 1970 Board meeting. Badavas and Orville regaled the readers of the *Ithacan* with their less that wholly objective accounts of what went on at those hitherto secret conclaves. Trustees would henceforth hear explosive and lengthy outbursts in support of the proposals of the summer research interns, on the need for women, blacks, educators, and staff representatives on the Board, on faculty personnel procedures, and on what would later be known as "divestiture" of stocks held in politically reprehensible corporations. Some trustees still recall, with a shudder, the appearance in their midst of tieless, jacketless, long-haired "agitators," but it is safe to say that the Board became aware, as never before, of the mood of at least a certain segment of the campus. The eventual upshot was a series of "Trustee Days" or "Days of Inquiry" in 1971 - 1972, and, in May 1972, the election of Gloria Hobbs brought to the Board a distinguished woman who was also a black and an educator. The total number of trustees was at that time increased to thirty, to permit of greater variety. Full voting rights had been conceded to both students and faculty members in February 1972.

Trustee Orville could still play the old record at full decibels ("Whoever pays for the College runs it"), but he soon vanished from the scene, and more irenic voices began to be heard. The Board was apprised that an "era of cooperation, not confrontation" had begun, and the *Ithacan* of September 24, 1971, made it official: demonstrations were now proclaimed to be anachronistic, having "at best no effect and at the worst, a negative effect." The campus blacks became noticeably less militant, focusing their energies on celebrations of black culture and black womanhood. Phillips refused to jump on the bandwagon with the expected ritual condemnations of the authorities at Kent State or Attica — and got away with it without being burned in effigy or losing his potted plants down the stairwell of Job Hall. Even the old whipping-boys, the military recruiters, had lost their power to mobilize campus indignation and quietly resumed activities. By April 1975, that venerable tradition, the senior prom, would be reinstituted; its announcement in the *Ithacan* ("Here is a last chance to capture your youth") pointed unmistakably to the graying of America.

With the exception of the Berrigan fracas in the spring of 1974, student causes during the Phillips years were less concerned with politics than with the problems of campus living. Some of these concerns were the traditional ones — the improvement of institutional food, expanded facilities for the Egbert Union, more egalitarian parking rights, better counseling, increased attention to career planning, and, of course, in a time of spiraling inflation, lower tuition costs. Drugs continued to be discussed in elaborate detail. The Health Center established a highly effective informational program. The students themselves inaugurated a twenty-four-hour "Drug Line" for those in difficulties; they lobbied for the modification of laws concerning the use of marijuana; there were sporadic on-campus "busts." Abortion rights and rape became focal issues. The setting up of a "Crisis Center" in February 1972 provided the campus with a staff of carefully trained students and guaranteed assistance in an atmosphere of the strictest confidentiality.

A sense of growing insecurity was reflected in concern over the presence of firearms on campus even if carried by safety division personnel and in the establishment of SASP, the Student Auxiliary Security Patrol, in the spring of 1972. The vexatious "pet problem" probably stemmed from the same underlying psychological causes. Many students acquired pets, particularly those irresistible puppies; their presence in the dormitories created innumerable problems, especially when the animals were merely abandoned at vacation time or at the end of the school year, and the sanitation issue became the subject of unending and tedious debate. A policy prohibiting pets except in the Garden Apartments became effective from 1973 - 1974 on.

The "quality of campus life" became the cliché of the era.

One of Phillips's early acts was to arrange a meeting of students and administrators at the Aurora Inn on November 10, 1970; the *Ithacan* enthusiastically reported that this conference had "planted the seed of love." The following May, the faculty held a two-day colloquium on the subject, at which J. B. Lon Hefferlin, who codirected an academic administration project for the Phillips foundation, confidently predicted that "Ithaca College will be in the lead of the ferment of reform and experimentation of the seventies." Some concrete proposals for administrative reorganization and for curricular reform emerged from these discussions, but it is safe to say that for most students the "quality of campus life" meant two things: the right to have liquor in the dormitories and the right to entertain members of the opposite sex in their rooms. After extended preparation in campus committees, the Board reaffirmed its limited approval to both demands in October 1970, and complex processes of implementation were established to guarantee the rights of all concerned. Throughout the seventies, various patterns of "coeducational dorms" were instituted, whether by wing, by floor, or by alternate rooms. Some highly unpleasant publicity ensued when a Communications student filed a story about "SWAP" with a national wire service. Landon Hall, it transpired, had adopted a plan of assigning roommates of opposite sex by lot for one-week periods — SWAP was the acronym for "Switch With Another Person." Since Landon was a "Living-Learning" dormitory, this exchange was deemed a useful experiment in interpersonal relationships, but the newspapers of the country saw it as a program of College-authorized cohabitation. The uproar was so great that one local observer wrote that "the sound and the fury behind the coverage of this experiment . . . would lead an outsider to believe that Adolf Hitler had been found alive and well on the second floor of Dorm Six." The trustees, noting that the story had appeared even in the *China Times* of Taipei, were not amused. Nor did strenuous denials by the vice-president for student affairs that the College was sanctioning promiscuity wholly satisfy them that the "quality of life" at Ithaca College was all that might be desired. Oddly enough, the ban on alcoholic beverages at athletic functions continued to be enforced throughout this era of permissiveness.

The after-tremors from the sixties had perhaps their most devastating effect on the curriculum. The programs of the professional schools, largely mandated by the State of New

York or by the various accrediting agencies, were not significantly affected; indeed, several of them were extended and strengthened. Physical Therapy and the Administration of Health Services experienced growth spurts; the latter produced its first graduates in May 1971. The TV-radio curricula were supplemented by majors in educational communications and in cinema studies and photography, and summer film institutes were held. The first color TV cameras were purchased, and a graduate degree in Communications was authorized in 1974 - 1975. The School of Health, Physical Education and Recreation celebrated the fiftieth anniversary of Physical Education at Ithaca College throughout the spring of 1972; its recreation major was restored to the curriculum in the following fall. The College's teacher-training programs received full accreditation in May 1971. Offerings in jazz were now listed in the School of Music; the more traditional strengths in that area were enthusiastically described in a 1971 issue of the London *Times Educational Supplement*.

But within the College of Arts and Sciences, the old stabilities were being swept away and the rallying cry was "relevance." We earlier noted that the platform of the "Change" party had arrogated to the students themselves the right to determine what was or was not appropriate to their education, and this principle was espoused by more than a few faculty members. In the spring of 1970, all requirements for graduation outside of those imposed by the major had been abolished: a student no longer needed to enroll for a science course, learn a foreign language, take freshman composition, or satisfy any pattern of distribution requirements. And if even the now democratically relaxed demands of the various majors proved onerous, a program in "General Studies" was initiated: all that was needed for such a degree was the consent of a faculty adviser to whatever combination of courses suited a student's fancy.

The proliferation of new courses may indicate what was deemed "relevant" in the early seventies: among them were Chess for Credit, Death, Sincerity and Authenticity, Politics in Children's Literature, Freud and Einstein, The Image and Role of Women in the Judaeo-Christian Church, Dynamics of Black Family Life, The Teacher-Brain Interface, Popular Culture. Some of these were developed within departments, some were interdisciplinary (Time and Future Studies; What Is the Twentieth Century?), most eventually found a home in the Center for Individual and Interdisciplinary Studies. The sciences, deprived of their captive audiences in the introductory courses, reached out imaginatively for their share of the students with courses like Why the Sky Is Blue and All That. For those to whom even the CIIS was too restrictive, the Free University was revived in the spring of 1974 to offer such noncredit courses as Ripple Afghans, Bikeology, Beginning Billiards, Massage for Relaxation. The nadir of curricular disintegration was reached when, in the summer of 1975, the College lent its institutional prestige to a continuing education course in astrology.

Extensive curricular revisions were of course inevitable at this point in the evolution of the College. The Triplum had long since ceased to be an educational reality, whatever the Catalogs and the admissions brochures might say, and the faculty discussions on graduation requirements revealed a pathetic lack of any coherent educational philosophy: most of the pleas for the continuation of the traditional patterns amounted to little more than "this is the way it has always been done." A freeing-up of the curriculum was overdue; a fresh consideration of the meaning of liberal education for our time was essential if the steadily growing pretensions of departmental territoriality were to be effectively challenged. Along with much nonsense, fresh breezes were stirring.

The word *innovative* carried magical power in those days; *traditional* almost immediately became a wholly pejorative term. But despite the tendency of either side to contrast the best of its own with the worst of the other, debate on fundamental curricular principles was lively and sustained. By the spring of 1974, this debate took formal shape under the rubric "Change in Liberal Education." But discussion soon polarized into two rival groups and eventually petered into insignificance. The problem remained unresolved.

Along with rethinking the curriculum, new approaches to teaching itself loomed large in the debates of the period. The sciences sponsored seminars on the Keller Plan; workshops in "Cognitive Mapping" were held; there was considerable interest in programmed learning and in learning laboratories; education moved from the classroom to the residential units through a Living-Learning dormitory, the members of which pursued common studies, such as Time and Future Studies, sometimes with a faculty member living in their midst. A more demanding "Planned Studies" program supplemented the anarchic "General Studies" approach.

Emphasis on the "experiential" as opposed to the "cognitive" led to an attack on the grading system. How could mere letters or numbers do justice to the mysteries of personality growth? *Intra-College*, the official College bulletin, published a definition of a grade as "an inadequate report of an inaccurate judgment by a biased and variable judge of the extent to which a student has attained an undefined level of mastery of an unknown proportion of an indefinite amount of material." Failing grades were denounced with particular violence: a failure, permanently recorded, was, one was told, brutally damaging to the student's self-esteem. By May 1972, the all-College faculty set up two grading options: first, Pass, Incomplete, or Not For Transcript (which replaced the former D's and F's, was abbreviated to NFT, and pronounced "Nifty") and, alternatively, A, B, C, NFT, and Inc. Pluses and minuses were restored the following year for the grades of A, B, and C. So soft-headed an approach inevitably backfired: by the mid-seventies, students would have discovered that they were in fact being severely penalized by an academic record so phony that prospective employers and graduate schools refused to credit transcripts.

Concern for the "practical" led to an expansion of work with migrant agricultural help; the department of politics set up a Washington internship program; anthropology, to be accepted as a major in 1975, had initiated an immensely successful annual project in San Salvador in 1972; there were field-work projects in community problems and on-site biology studies in Florida. This concern for education as a total experience gave fresh impetus to study abroad. After several years of affiliation with Schiller College and other universities with overseas programs, Ithaca College in 1972 - 1973 set up its own London Center in a handsome town house in South Kensington. Under Director Edward Vincent, its offerings rapidly expanded to include programs in many of the divisions of the College: in addition to work in literature, history, and art, a seminar on the Common Market was sponsored by the politics department; TV-radio studied communications both in the British Isles and on the continent; Music students took advantage of the unrivaled opportunities for attending concerts and recitals in a major cultural center. The *Ithacan* correctly observed that the London Center was utilizing the city itself for its classroom. By February 1975, students were participating in an "Experiment in International Living" in Ghana, Japan, and Nepal.

Closer to home, one of the immediate problems confronting Phillips in 1970 - 1971 was the reorganization of the administrative structure of the College. The original Conservatory had gradually acquired its constellation of affiliated schools; after some trial and error, these had settled down into the basic tripartite divisions of Music, Speech-Drama, and Physical Education. Then the General College had subsumed Speech-Drama, the loose collection of "academic" courses, and such new creations as business and radio, and had become eventually the College of Arts and Sciences. But by 1970, a major rearrangement was in order. Business and speech pathology were not easily accommodated within Arts and Sciences; Administration of Health Services, under Schneeweiss's ambitious direction, clamored for increased recognition; and something had to be done for the growing number of "innovative" offerings spawned by the unrest of the late sixties. The irrationalities of history, the largely unplanned, pragmatic, if not opportunistic, directions that the College's growth had taken, cried out for some degree of rationalization.

Philosophical coherence would of course prove unattainable. Functionally, Ithaca College could be reduced to two major divisions: the professional curricula and the humanities and sciences. But the long tradition of the Conservatory of Music made it impossible that music, queen of the humanities, could be absorbed into a School of Arts and Sciences, and not everyone was agreed that the programs in drama and speech were essentially professional in nature. The best that could be hoped for was a reshuffling that would be at least a bit more orderly — and more congruent with that thrust for greater autonomy for the administrative subdivisions which was also the College's legacy from the sixties.

Ithaca College, in short, was ready to transform itself into a mini-university.

The concept of long-range planning had had a long history at the College. Indeed, institutional self-study in the past twenty years had proceeded with an intensity that would suggest, in the case of an individual, a narcissistic fixation of truly alarming proportions. References to long-range planning begin to appear in the faculty minutes for 1959 - 1960; the periodic reaccreditation visits intensified the effort; outside consultants were brought in from time to time to aid administration and Board in understanding the past and present, if not the future, of the College. Not infrequently, these self-examinations suggested something approaching an identity crisis: "Is Ithaca College a college, or is it three colleges?" an educational consultant, F. Taylor Jones, had asked in 1965.

By 1968 - 1969, it was clear that the Ithaca College Plan had collapsed. As Provost Davies observed, "We no longer had a plan. We were drifting." Demographic predictions of a diminishing student population generated concern for the College's survival; as, one by one, private colleges began to go under, educational drifting could hardly be tolerated. News releases in the summer of 1969 suggested a stepped-up activity: "This is our opportunity and our only real chance for bringing together discordant parts of the College and developing a unified conception of what the College can become." The Board assumed responsibility for a rethinking of institutional philosophy and structure at its fall meeting in 1969 and charged Provost Davies with the task of working within the campus community to prepare appropriate recommendations for Board action.

The academic year 1969 - 1970 had thus begun with an urgent call to action. Turnout for the first general meeting was disappointingly small, however; inevitably, the impetus had to come from the provost and his steering committee, and the work would be done through a proliferation of committees. By February 1970, the personnel of nine working committees was announced; administrators, professors, and students would address themselves to the problems of admissions, curriculum, instruction, student life, faculty welfare, academic organization and governance, alumni and continuing education, physical plant, and financial resources. Retrospectively surveying this effort in June 1973, Provost Davies (by then consultant to the College) defined the key questions the working committees were created to consider:

> *Who will, and who should, come to Ithaca College?*
>
> *What will they study?*
>
> *How will they learn?*
>
> *What will be the quality of their lives in this kind of environment?*
>
> *What kind of environment and policies will best sustain a strong faculty?*

> *What kind of relationships will the college develop and sustain for assuring just and fair dealings among its members (the* living *community); for providing appropriate learning opportunities (the* academic *community); and for providing financial responsibility (the* corporate *community). . . ?*

The months of concerted activity began to make headlines in 1970 - 1971. The urgency of the problem had been brought home to President Phillips in his first semester at the College through a confidential memorandum from the firm of Franzrep and Prey Associates, which mercilessly pinpointed the weaknesses of the institution and concluded that what was required was "a breathing period from major growth, expansion, and debt increases; consolidation and unification; programmatic rationalization and improvement."

The committee on academic reorganization and campus governance was the first to release its report, in November 1970. This contained two possible statements of the College's mission, a list of seven academic objectives, and, most importantly, a plan for reorganizing the institution into six academic units. The proposal envisioned a Center of Individual and Interdisciplinary Studies (which would include the department of education); a School of Humanities and Sciences divided into three faculties (humanities, physical sciences, and social and behavioral sciences, including speech pathology, each headed by a director under the dean); a School of Music, unchanged; a School of Physical Arts (embracing physical education and physical therapy); a Division of Business Administration (which included health administration as well as accounting and business); and a Division of Communication Arts (which would annex the departments of art and speech-drama to TV-radio). Public hearings were held; written comments were solicited and received, both from individuals and from departments. Spirited discussion pinpointed the weaknesses: no provision had been made for graduate studies and continuing education; the programs in health administration did not wish to be relegated to a Division of Business Administration; art and speech-drama were uneasy about being incorporated into a Division of Communication Arts; and speech pathology was not exactly a social or behavioral science.

The proposal was ready for a revised edition by January 1971. Now, the School of Humanities had only two faculties:

the humanities and the natural and social sciences; speech pathology had been moved to the School of Health Professions, with two subdivisions (allied health professions and physical education); Music and the CIIS continued much the same; Communications was restored to its status as a professional curriculum with the removal of art and speech-drama; Business Administration was reduced to the areas of business and accounting; and due recognition was accorded to a Division of Graduate Studies and Continuing Education. Earlier, the provost had expressed the hope that the recommendations could be considered "with respect to the educational objectives of the College rather than to individual aspirations or to campus political maneuvering." But if Music refused to budge from its traditional pride of autonomy, why should physical education be any more willing to assume a subordinate status within a School of Health Professions? It successfully survived the challenge, becoming the School of Health, Physical Education, and Recreation, while the administration of health services, speech pathology and audiology, and physical therapy were merged into a new School of Allied Health Professions.

In February 1971, the provost urged the trustees to accept these revised proposals, which, he estimated, would cost from $90,000 to $100,000 to implement. A "mission statement" piously invoked the College's perennial claim to represent a unique blending of professional and liberal studies; a new low in jargon was reached in references to "this synergistic academic mixture." The shadow of the sixties could be discerned in an announced intention

> *to encourage students to develop their own balanced programs of professional and liberal emphasis to meet best their individual life goals and to develop an awareness of their lifetime responsibilities as active and involved citizens.*

Much was made of the objective of creating "one" College — not "in the sense of homogeneity, but in the senses of unity in diversity and facility of movement and communication." Hence, the strong emphasis on service courses, on enhanced opportunities for interdisciplinary course offerings. The report acknowledged that the intransigence of the School of Music made impossible the creation of a School of Fine Arts that would comprise music, drama, and art; instead, it rather

lamely proposed a council on the arts, which would attempt that kind of integrated effort that seemed unattainable in any other structural pattern.

The ensuing months saw a sustained effort to convince the Board of the practicality of the proposed reorganization. The provost pointed out the advantages: it would help the admissions office maintain full enrollment in the face of declining student population by providing a number of strong programs rationally organized; it would provide a management system "which can control costs while guaranteeing quality throughout the institution." President Phillips, in his inaugural speech (April 7, 1971) lent his enthusiastic support and concluded with a call to action — "Let's Start!" The Board voted its approval on May 14, 1971, an action described by one trustee as being "the second most historical decision" that body had ever made (the first being the move to South Hill).

Acting deans and directors were appointed for the new administrative units late in August 1971. Theodore Baker had already been named dean of the School of Humanities and Sciences, and Craig McHenry continued as dean of the School of Music. The designation "acting" dean or director for the others reflected faculty concern that both they and the students be involved in the process of selecting permanent appointees. A similar demand for faculty participation in administrative personnel decisions was articulated when the president announced his proposals for restructuring the central administration. But mostly, 1971 - 1972 was given over to working out the details of reorganization and to assuring alumni and the public at large that the College had not radically changed its nature. "We are building logging trails through the forest of learning." Provost Davies wrote to the alumni in an unusual burst of metaphor; and again, less pyrotechnically to the same constituency, "Ithaca College has created what might be called a blueprint for a relevant educational environment." The transitional report of the long-range planning committee outlined a number of refinements, with much attention being given to Living-Learning units within the dormitories (including provision for the resident faculty members):

> *The overall theme of the residential experience would be "Dimensions of Man." This would be translated into four topic areas equivalent to the four residential units of the upper quad, lower quad,*

Towers, and Terrace residences. Each residential unit would focus on a dimension of man: "Creative Man," "Concerned Man," "Reflective Man," and "Pragmatic Man."

The 1972 - 1973 budget would include funds for a pilot "cluster college," and, as we have already noted, the beginnings of such a program were established in the fall of 1972 under the rubric of the team-taught Time and Future Studies. These efforts would continue for several years, without attracting widespread student support.

Much of this reorganization was little more than a regrouping of existing programs. One distinctively new entity had emerged from it, however — the Center for Individual and Interdisciplinary Studies, directed by Professor Willard T. Daetsch and largely the result of his devoted efforts. The Center assumed responsibility for the work of the General Studies students and also, somewhat later, for the Planned Studies programs; the latter were put into effect in 1972 - 1973 with the aid of a $40,000 grant from the Merrill Foundation. The Center was also charged with the responsibility for developing interdisciplinary courses and programs, for working out new patterns for gaining academic credit outside of the traditional context of the classroom, and for focusing the efforts of the faculty in the development of new approaches to education.

The Center was staffed by interested faculty members and also by many part-time appointees from outside the College community. Its course listings each semester were certainly the most exciting portion of the curriculum: some were ephemeral, others immensely successful, such as Popular Culture, which attracted an enrollment of some five hundred students. Inevitably, opposition developed, both to some of the courses, parodied as being of the "fun-and-games" or "touchie-feelie" variety, and to the academic qualifications of some of the part-time instructors. In the spring of 1973, this hostility found a focus in a course, The U.S. Military, which appeared to be taught by a sophomore politics major. Thereafter, the Center would show an almost defensive concern for the credentials of its faculty members.

But while all innovative programs have their aberrations, these should not obscure the real contributions made by the Center. As the dream of a department of black studies faded, courses in the Center were able partly to meet that need. By

1974 - 1975, feminist studies would become a staple in its offerings. A program in policy studies, one in community service, opened up new areas for Ithaca College students; a minor in social work was in operation by 1975. The Center sponsored College and community workshops on such topics as cognitive mapping and the work of William G. Perry on the intellectual and ethical development of undergraduates. Courses that the traditional departments were at first unwilling to risk were often tried out in the Center and, if successful, later incorporated into the permanent curriculum.

By the fall of 1978, the Center ceased to exist as a division and became instead a department within the School of Humanities and Sciences. Along with the Ithaca College Plan of the late 1950s, it will be remembered as an important, and on the whole surprisingly effective, contribution of Ithaca College to educational theory and practice.

Any issue, however burning, has a limited claim on the attention of an academic community; academic reorganization had had its day. By January 1972, the *Ithacan* was reporting that a disappointingly small number of faculty members had turned out for a "non-meeting" under the sponsorship of the long-range planning committee. By that time, the question of College governance had captured the headlines.

Informal discussions on the topic had been under way before President Phillips took office. The concept — indeed, the mystique — of "community" proved profoundly appealing to many. In some sense, never clearly defined, the College was to be viewed, not as a business operation in which students paid to be taught by their instructors, but rather as a community of scholars, professors and students alike, all involved in the educational process in a total and largely self-contained academic society. In this egalitarianism, little attention was given to the possible ontological significance of the fact that the students paid tuition while the faculty members received salaries, and it was all too easy to speak as though the College were a community unto itself — something between a monastery and a commune — an enclave independent of the surrounding world and quite possibly a model for some more nearly perfect emergent society for America as a whole. An idealism of the highest order, a rhetoric of easy abstractions, and some patently self-serving motives (such as keeping law-enforcement bodies off the campus, especially in drug cases) all contributed to the prevailing ethos, which quickly produced the most extraordinarily complex governmental machinery that Ithaca College had ever known.

In his annual report for 1970 - 1971, President Phillips posed the question, "How best to run a college?" Reacting to the ongoing debate, he conceded that there were no easy answers, but held forth the hope that somehow, perhaps through the establishment of a college council, it would prove possible to affirm the authority of the trustees and the accountability of administrators, while at the same time to "keep initiatives close to the teaching and the living processes and still benefit the whole institution."

> *The president will not be the principal decision-maker as I see it, but instead will be responsible for the effective functioning of the decision-making process.*

At Phillips's request, the long-range planning committee addressed itself to the problem at the very beginning of his administration, with the assistance of a consultant, J. B. Lon Hefferlin of the University of California. By September 1971, it circulated the text of its proposal for campus consideration. This document defined the committee's understanding of the "criteria of a good governance system" — acceptance by the majority of those affected, review of grievances by one's peers, and, most significantly, the power of "governing bodies of academic units . . . to enact their decisions." This is to say, a policy originating from the chief academic officer of a given unit must receive majority approval by the members of that unit. Policy thus determined by majority vote, administrators would be left free "to make their own decisions regarding the day-to-day operations of the units for which they are responsible," subject always to reveiw "for legitimacy." Much attention was given to the role of the faculty and the students in the work of search committees, particularly for vacancies at the highest administrative levels.

The proposal further envisioned an all-College council, containing students, faculty members, and administrators, and under it, an administrative council, a faculty council, and a student council. The College council would have veto powers over the decisions of any body subordinate to it; its own enactments might be vetoed by the president, in which case, if the veto were to be overridden, the issue would be referred to the trustees. The College council would reserve the right to review all actions taken by its administrative members — that is, all top-level administrators.

Strenuous opposition developed almost immediately, to the surprise of the committee that had drafted the proposal. "Governance Proposal Battered," the *Ithacan* reported. The College council was grossly nonrepresentative, it was alleged; there was much citing of the principle of one-man, one-vote. The staff members expressed their outrage at being excluded from the "community"; faculty members worried whether the College council, on which they were a minority, would have ultimate jurisdiction over matters such as curriculum traditionally reserved to professors. The faculty members of the School of Humanities and Sciences (the thirty of them who bothered to attend the meeting) overwhelmingly rejected the proposal, and the student congress could not muster a single affirmative vote for the document as presented. Certainly there was concern from administrators and Board members that altogether too much authority was being delegated to the faculty and to the student body.

So it was back to the drawing boards. A revised proposal was circulated in December 1971. Specific criticisms, such as the number of representatives from each unit on the community council (its new name) and the need for a staff council, were met. What most impresses, however, is the backing away from the earlier assertion of all but complete autonomy for the community council:

> *By recommending a council form of governance we are recommending that normally College policies shall be developed by groups, but that final responsibility and authority shall rest with the administrators of the College.*

That is to say, the community council shall "participate" in "the developing of policies and the making of decisions for the College as a whole." The operative concept is now "consultation," although the faculty council is still described as "the decision-making body for the All-College Faculty." Balloting by the College community on this modest document produced 70 percent support from those voting (only 23 percent of the faculty cast ballots, with 35 percent of these negative).

The modified governance proposal, marginally ratified,

was submitted to the Board of Trustees at their February 1972 meeting and approved in principle, although there were objections to requiring the Board to arbitrate a disagreement between the president and the community council. During that spring semester, the document was further edited and details of implementation worked out. The authority of the student congress (it was decided to retain that name) was strengthened, at least on paper, by a vague but ominous statement that it "retained the right to act on its own conclusions." Also new was a detailed description of some fifteen all-College standing committees, including a "committee on committees" to keep all this complex machinery in good running order. (The criterion, formulated earlier, that a good system of governance would be "economical in terms of its demands upon the finances of the College and the time of its members" appears to have been quickly forgotten.) In May 1972, the Board voted the requisite changes in the By-Laws of the College, and in the following September a publication *Governance and Committee Structure* was officially printed and distributed, and the community council began its functioning. A new *Judicial Code* had been issued a month before (comparable to the governance document in length and complexity). In his annual report for 1971-1972, President Phillips could summarize the long and tortuous evolution of "How We Administer Ithaca College" and conclude:

> *I view the governance and committee structure, and the Code and its court system, as important steps in establishing and maintaining a stable academic community in which scholarship will flourish.*

Revising these two documents and trying to make them workable would keep the campus busy for the remainder of the decade.

As the College strove to articulate its concept of community in appropriate institutional forms, its work was punctuated by the usual milestones and crises of academic life.

A number of trustees resigned and were elected to honorary membership on the Board: Harold Allen, Robert Boothroyd, Roland G. Fowler; Gustave Haenschen, Carroll Newsom, Harold Smiddy. Edward R. Eastman, a trustee since 1956 and long known as counselor to Ithaca College students, died on

December 29, 1970. One of the College's principal benefactors, Walter B. Ford, died in 1971 at the age of ninety-six.

Changes in the administration were numerous. Provost Davies resigned in 1972; he would stay on for a year as consultant and author one of the most thoughtful of the many appraisals of the College — the "Davies Report." Stanley Davis, psychologist, who had rendered invaluable service during the difficult times of the late sixties and who had been named vice-president for student affairs in 1970, returned to Cornell in 1972. Paul Givens, dean of the College of Arts and Sciences and then the first director of institutional research, left for Millikin University in 1972. Phil Langan relocated at Princeton in 1973 after six years as director of sports information. John McConnell, former president of the University of New Hampshire, served as counselor to the College from 1971 until 1975. Craig McHenry, whose association with the College dated back to 1926, retired as dean of Music in 1973, only to return as acting dean in 1974 - 1975. Stephen Schneeweiss, vice-provost, director of Graduate Studies, and pioneer in the development of the administration of health services programs, was named president of Cazenovia College in 1975. Marylouise Potter, administrative assistant in the School of Music, retired at the end of 1970 - 1971, setting the record for the longest tenure of any nonteaching employee with her forty-five years of service. The year 1972 saw the death of Neva Mattocks, longtime secretary to President Dillingham and described by him as "the unsung hero" during the building of the South Hill campus.

Deaths also reduced the ranks of the faculty: John MacInnes, professor of history, in 1969; Ralph Jones, visiting professor of speech pathology, in 1971; Walter Beeler ("Mr. Band") in 1973, after more than forty years with the College; Lawrence Grant, founder of the philosophy department, also in 1973; and, in 1975, Rod Serling, who for many years had given helpful guidance and creative impetus to TV-radio.

In October 1967, the Board had created the rank of professor emeritus, and the first three faculty members to be so honored had been Lynn Bogart and Celia Slocum, both of Music and retiring that year, and Marguerite Rowland, history, who had retired in 1965. Now, in 1971, the list grew: Carlton Worth, who had established the mathematics department in the fifties, and some of the greatest names from the earlier days of Physical Education — Isadore ("Doe") Yavits, James ("Bucky") Freeman, and Elsie Hugger Erwin.

Helen Blauvelt, longtime professor of anatomy, would join this distinguished group in 1973.*

Resignations, retirements, deaths must be expected; certain other events, precisely because they are unanticipated, prove more dramatic in their impact. In October 1972, it was discovered that there was not enough money to get through the year:

> *We called a one-day meeting of all concerned administrators, including academic deans and directors, and we faced the questions squarely. A cutback of all the budgets of the College by an agreed percentage was approved.*

More nearly cataclysmic was the sudden failure of the transformer that supplied electricity to the College — at 1:45 P.M. on Wednesday, March 27, 1974. A darkened, cold campus contemplated the stark facts. The three smaller transformers that were hastily installed could provide only 55 percent of the power needs. If these became overloaded and failed, the College would have to close for the semester — a move that might force it to suspend operations indefinitely. Emergency bulletins, couched in language that, rather unflatteringly, was assumed to register best on student minds, spelled out the gravity of the situation: minimal lighting and heating, the danger of food spoilage, increased likelihood of thefts, of mugging. . . .

> *It is true that one stereo system uses little power. If two thousand of us decide that just one stereo won't hurt things — THE BALL GAME IS OVER!*

Within a few days, an alternate transformer was unexpectedly located and a road bulldozed to get it to its site. By early April, the crisis was over, and, in the last "Emergency Bulletin" (April 5, 1974), President Phillips paid tribute to the extraordinary spirit of cooperation which had pulled the College through what was literally its darkest hour.

Some of the most painful crises involved personnel decisions. Provost Davies's resignation on February 22, 1972, had been requested by the president; it touched off some faculty

---

*The list would be augmented in 1976 (Craig McHenry, music) in 1979 (George Hoerner, drama), in 1981 (Carlton Wood, who in 1974 had been named Coach of the Year by the Association of American College Baseball Coaches), and in 1982 (Joseph Hamilton and Arnold Wilhelm, physical education).

protests and intensified demands for a greater faculty role in decisions relating to high-level administrators. In 1972 - 1973, Phillips dismissed a tenured faculty member, after extended discussions with the dean and faculty council of the College of Arts and Sciences. This decision was appealed both in the civil courts and through campus review boards; eventually, the dismissal was commuted to a letter of warning.

But these were minor skirmishes in comparison with the Berrigan affair.

The Reverend Daniel Berrigan, S.J., had been well known in Ithaca since 1967, when he had become associate director of the Cornell University United Religious Work. Convicted in 1969 of burning the records of a Maryland draft board, he had made a dramatic appearance at the massive rally held in Cornell's Barton Hall as part of the "American Is Hard To Find" weekend in the spring of 1970. Subsequently, he had been apprehended, jailed, and paroled. Even before his release, supporters at the College had been exploring the possibility of Berrigan's being appointed to a visiting professorship. A small group of faculty members, mostly in the departments of politics, sociology, philosophy and religion, and education, worked toward that end, and, in late December 1973, at a time when most members of the academic community were away from the campus, Berrigan arrived for an interview. An offer was made, without any general knowledge of the fact; then, over the weekend of January 4 - 5, 1974, the news was leaked to a local radio station and picked up by the Associated Press.

Angry protests began to pour in, some from parents, some from townspeople and alumni, but most of them from the trustees. The reactions of the trustees preclude easy formulation: shock at reading the headlines in their local papers without prior briefing, deep-seated objections to Berrigan's political stance, concern over a "jailbird" as a faculty member, disturbance over his announced conviction that it was justifiable "on occasion of crisis [to] destroy property in favor of human life," fear that once on campus, he might prove impossible to remove. Mostly, the difficulties arose from a notorious speech Berrigan had delivered on October 19, 1973, before the Association of Arab University Graduates, in which he had denounced Israel as "an Orwellian nightmare of double talk, racism, fifth-rate sociological jargon, aiming to prove its racial superiority to the peoples it had crushed." The student population at Ithaca College was heavily Jewish.

Would their parents be willing to pay high tuition to an institution that harbored the likes of Dan Berrigan? Yet even with all these reservations, the trustees from the beginning left the door at least slightly ajar. Let Berrigan come to Ithaca College for a day, for a week; let him speak his piece, under the aegis of a free exchange of ideas, then go away. But not for two semesters or even for one — and not with the status of a visiting professor.

The upshot of intense behind-scenes activity was the withdrawal of the offer on January 29, 1974. By that time, the campus had found its liveliest issue since the Rockefeller Commencement of 1970. The *Ithacan* fulminated; student and faculty groups met and passed motions; an assistant dean proclaimed that by its action, "the College has agreed that Socrates should have drunk the hemlock." A motion censuring President Phillips was introduced at a meeting of the community council; it failed to pass.

But no one was really interested in a strike or sit-in, and by February, the issue had moved from the public arena to the committee rooms. Among other things, the hubbub had revealed that there were no accepted guidelines for the appointment of a visiting professor; such guidelines were quickly drawn up and ratified. The faculty council of the School of Humanities and Sciences appointed an ad hoc committee "to explore with the President, Provost, and Dean Baker the real possibility of bringing Father Berrigan to the campus, preferably for the Spring semester of 1975." This committee, made up of five faculty members and four students, was from the beginning unanimously and unabashedly in favor of the appointment. What it undertook was essentially a process of legitimization: resubmitting the recommendation within the provisions of the new guidelines, with a clear statement of just what Berrigan was supposed to do on campus and appropriate documentation that he was in fact competent to do what he proposed. By late April, a new rash of headlines reflected an optimism that Berrigan would indeed come to teach courses in Prison Culture and on the Book of Revelation. The description of "Prison Culture" at least escaped the drabness of most Catalog prose.

You can refer to it maybe as an exegesis in wrung soul. . . . I would like to go with a miner's lamp into that darkness, which is really a voyage to the other side of our soul, a descent into original sin and its

hideous secular structures of expiation. I would like to go there . . . not as a tourist, but almost like a Hopi novice, seeking rebirth by enacting birth.

A positive recommendation, approved by three committees, by the department of philosophy and religion, by the dean of Humanities and Sciences, and by the director of the CIIS, was forwarded to the all-College committee on visiting professors, which also gave its blessing. And so, on May 24, 1974, the initiative passed to the provost and the president. All this intense activity by Berrigan's supporters had been carried out in the belief that there was a genuine possibility that the Berrigan appointment might receive favorable consideration. In retrospect, it is clear that they were misled: Board opposition from the beginning was almost unanimous — and unyielding. Once again, letters, both pro and con, began to pour into Job Hall. And, as the central administration agonized in its impossible position between faculty and trustees, Berrigan himself was pleased to deliver an ultimatum.

. . . the university [sic] is making such a mockery of academic freedom. They've held this thing up so long I finally wrote some friends in Ithaca and told them July 1 is it.

Even some of his supporters were angered by this arrogance. One professor wrote the provost that "we will have attained our majority as an educational institution when, as a matter of fixed policy, we send anyone who threatens to take his wagon and go home off with our blessing."

It would have been easy, of course, for Provost Frank Darrow simply to let the July deadline pass without action — exit Berrigan. But, to his credit, he refused to shirk the responsibility for administrative decision. On June 26, he wrote to the president, summarizing the arguments of both sides and concluding that Berrigan should not be appointed. The president concurred. There were further angry meetings, and a flood of rhetoric and motions that continued well into the following academic year. But although the *Ithacan* did its best with the headline "Berrigan Quake Rumbles On," the intensity of the seismic waves soon diminished. The provost, frankly acknowledging mistakes, strove to bind up the wounds and to redirect the energies of the College to more urgent problems.

During the months ahead, Ithaca College will be making many critical decisions. We will be finding a new president. We will be preparing for the Middle States reaccreditation visit scheduled for the spring of 1976. We will be wrestling with the College budget. It is my hope that we will be able to bring lessons learned from last year to bear on these important problems.

With that, the Berrigan affair became history.

As in earlier chapters, we must remind ourselves that while the day-to-day activities of the College seldom make the biggest headlines, the real life of the institution is to be found precisely there. Provost Darrow, in the memorandum just quoted, alerted the campus to a prospective reaccreditation by the Middle States Association. Throughout the earlier seventies, there were unremitting efforts to bring all the various components of the College into full accreditation. In May 1971, the programs in teacher education were accorded recognition by the National Council for Accreditation of Teacher Education. In 1973 - 1974, the Division of Physical Therapy received approval for reaccreditation by the American Physical Therapy Association, the Council on Medical Education of the A.M.A., and the New York State Education Department. The Ewing Clinic of Speech Pathology received interim accreditation by the professional services board of the American Speech and Hearing Association early in 1973 (its mobile unit had been chosen as the Easter Seal symbol for New York in 1972).

Visitors, distinguished, notorious, or both, continued to arrive on campus for lectures — "Yippie" Abbie Hoffman, Ralph Nader, poet William Snodgrass, Denise Oliver (minister of finance for the Young Lords, speaking on behalf of a "Free Puerto Rico"), Alvin Toffler of *Future Shock* fame, Otto Preminger, Art Buchwald, Dick Gregory (now proclaiming that "beautiful cats turn to animals when they get involved in party politics"), Eunice Shriver, transsexual Christine Jorgensen, Norman Mailer (who "began with a poem and ended with a dirty joke"), Philip Berrigan. The number of speakers on the women's liberation movement and allied topics steadily increased. On October 10 - 11, 1974, the College sponsored a Gertrude Stein Centennial Festival, organized by Professor of Spanish Kevin Schmelter.

The tradition of memorable concerts continued. On April 22, 1972, the College orchestra, under Thomas Michalak, dazzled a full house at Lincoln Center's Alice Tully Hall: the *New York Times* review concluded that "it must be assumed that they know how to get things done, and done well, at Ithaca College." On May 2, 1973, retiring Dean Craig McHenry and Walter Beeler were honored by a concert given by the College madrigal singers and women's chorale, directed by James Porterfield, and the College chorus, under Roland Bentley: the major presentation was Professor Malcolm Lewis's composition "A Farewell," written for the occasion and narrated by English professor and poet John Ogden. Cellists, under Einar Holm, were active, with a program in homage to Pablo Casals in April 1974. In the fall of 1974, Peter and Elizabeth Hedrick (shawms, oboes, and recorders) and Mary Ann Covert (harpsichord and percussion) offered a program of eighteenth-century music, "The Muse's Delight," at Carnegie Hall.

Other on-campus concerts included two operas, Puccini's *Il Tabarro* and, on April 6 - 7, 1973, the world première of *Doña Rosita,* composed by Charles F. Hockett, Cornell's Goldwin Smith Professor of Anthropology and Linguistics. A Verdi *Requiem* in the spring of 1974 saw the Ithaca College orchestra and the Cornell University glee club and chorus in a combined activity reminiscent of the early days of the Ithaca Conservatory of Music. A lost Haydn Mass, discovered by Professor Edward Swenson, was first heard in 1975; another College musicologist, Mary Arlin, restored an unpublished concerto by Michael Haydn to the repertory.

Physical Education's fiftieth anniversary observance in the spring of 1972 was soon followed by a banner year for sports in 1974 - 1975. The Bombers (there had been some protest that the team's name was too militaristic) were the Lambert Bowl winners, defeating Slippery Rock College 27 - 14 at a memorable semifinals game at Schoellkopf Field on November 30, 1974. (They would fall just short of the national title in a game played against Central College of Iowa at Phenix City, Alabama.) Coach Jim Butterfield was named Eastern College Athletic Conference Division III football coach of the year. In the same time span, the women's teams distinguished themselves in field hockey, swimming, softball, and volleyball; the men's, in tennis and golf. Lacrosse and baseball did well, and the crew, after an undefeated season, placed third in the Dad Vail Regatta in Philadelphia.

Drama during the seventies moved far from its Ithaca base. Students from the College continued to play a prominent part in the Vineyard Players, now a private nonprofit corporation. Others went during the summer months to Monmouth, Maine, where professor of drama, Earl McCarroll's Shakespearean productions were inviting international attention. *How To Succeed in Business Without Really Trying* went overseas for the Department of Defense in May - June 1972 and played before enthusiastic military audiences in Iceland, Greenland, Newfoundland, and Labrador. In 1973 - 1974, another College group toured the Azores and Europe under the same auspices. In the Ithaca area, summer repertory theater provided entertainment for both local residents and innumerable visitors to the Finger Lakes area.

In 1972 - 1973, drama chose to celebrate its diamond jubilee, somewhat broadly dating its existence from the arrival of George C. Williams in 1897. *The Prime of Miss Jean Brodie, Company* and *Romeo and Juliet* were presented in a year-long festival of drama, culminating in a May convocation at which actress Julie Harris was honored. Other unforgettable performances of the seventies were *Hair* and *The Merchant of Venice*; scenes from the latter (1971 - 1972) have been effectively preserved on film.

The new major in cinema studies was busily producing films of its own making. *Who Will Keep Them?* was a prize-winning study of the problems of geriatric patients; the stages in the development of an exhibition of Thai paintings and sculpture at the Boardman House Museum were recorded; another award-winning venture, *Take My Hand*, was a documentary on a children's home. The most ambitious effort was *They Made Movies in Ithaca*, a documentary on the pioneering days of filmmaking on the shores of Lake Cayuga, produced as part of a film institute held in the summer of 1974. The council on the arts was also interested in funding films, among them a version of D. H. Lawrence's short story "The Horse Dealer's Daughter"; "Inside Bucky's Head," a series of ten half-hour films on the work of Buckminster Fuller; a rock musical, *On the Other Hand*; and a musical produced by Ithaca College Public Theater, *Canterbury Tales*.

And of course, each succeeding academic year concluded with its commencement and attendant festivities. The commencement eve concerts continued to be gala events, although after 1974, death had removed the genial presence of Milton Cross from these occasions. For several years, the graduating students honored faculty members distinguished for their teaching: David McKeith, Professor of History, and Carl Sgrecci, Professor of Accounting, at the 1973 commencement; Ray Kaaret, Professor of Politics, and Rita LaRock, Professor of Physical Education, in 1974. At the 1974 commencement, Robert S. Boothroyd and Lillian Speakman Vail were the first to receive the Alumni Service Award.

That spring, at the Board meeting on May 17, 1974, President Phillips informed his trustees that illness in his immediate family necessitated his resignation. He agreed to serve until his successor should be named and in fact remained through the following academic year. He gave the address at his final commencement as president in May 1975.

Looking back over five years, Phillips could find much to note with satisfaction. Although a campus is never finished and new buildings are always desirable, the South Hill campus was for all practical purposes completed during these years. The Garden Apartments were occupied; maintenance and the safety division had new headquarters; the Herman E. and Florence S. Muller Memorial Chapel was under construction; the addition of two floors was transforming the Library into the Caroline Werner Gannett Center; several dormitories and Friends Hall had been renovated; a new transmission tower crowned the hill south of the campus. The London Center had been opened, and the Haskell S. Davidson Boathouse on Cayuga inlet had been dedicated on April 20, 1974. The College had been reorganized; the governance document and the judicial code were in effect; several crises of some magnitude had been weathered; the institution was effectively discharging its educational responsibilities to the largest enrollment in its history.

Even before submitting his resignation, Phillips had warned the Board that an era was drawing toward its close. Now, "imagination must take the place of growth. . . . the end of the quantitative phase has come, and we must do more with what we have." This fact was of course to be viewed essentially as a challenge.

We are not limited in our capability to develop the human mind, however, and we should not fear the end of the economic boom, but concentrate on new means of developing our most important source of power — the human spirit.

Speaking to the freshmen in the fall of 1974, he had noted that a time "to hunker down a bit" was fast approaching.

In retrospect, the 1940's were years of survival, the 1950's were years of Catching Up with the Good Life, and the 1960's were the years of Tackling the Infinite.

The later seventies, he felt certain, would require rigorous self-scrutiny and a sorting out of priorities in the face of diminishing economic resources.

In the 60's, we went too fast, and now in the mid-70's, we seem to have run out of breath. College is the place where we can catch our breath and see things clearly.

Summing up his experience in his final annual report, he wrote:

The experience of serving for five years with an institution as dynamic as Ithaca College is unforgettable. The College is in microcosm this nation with its capacity for individual initiative, for settling internal disputes in fair, open, and orderly fashion, engaged in a never-diminishing quest for more and better knowledge and the means to apply knowledge to practical problems, and prepared to finance all this on merit in a free and competitive market.

Surely the academic achievements which the successive annual reports had chronicled and, most of all, the spirit of community and colleagual harmony which the new governance documents attempted to embody represented an infusion of Phillips's spirit into the very life of the College — his reliance on the values of civilized men and women and on the great traditions that had made civilization itself possible, his conviction that reasonableness and freedom were infinitely preferable to their opposites, and a patience and a humility rooted in faith. The final paragraph of the December 1975 report summed it all up.

When I first came to Ithaca College, I was criticized by some students and faculty members for being too optimistic. I had to be cautioned before meetings to refrain from levity and to curb my natural inclination to grin. My experience in the past five years has not changed my hopeful outlook on the future, provided we recognize our dependence "under heaven" and retain our sense of humor. I am grateful for the opportunity of serving as the fifth president of Ithaca College.

For his predecessors, leaving the presidential office had meant the effective ending of their active careers. For Ellis Laurimore Phillips, Jr., an important chapter in a rich and varied life had drawn gracefully to its conclusion.

The regnal years of the first five presidents of Ithaca College have provided convenient termini for the major division of this history. Each president, in his own way and his own style, has decisively shaped the course of our institutional destiny. Yet in a larger sense, there is only one beginning and, ultimately, only one ending in the history of an institution. Authority is transferred in more or less orderly fashion; leadership emerges and recedes; the balance of power, the centers of initiative, shift; men and women — trustees, administrators, faculty and staff members, student leaders — come and go. These occurrences in part determine, in part merely punctuate, the larger narrative. From W. Grant Egbert's brave adventure in those four rented rooms through to the present and onward toward a still unknown future, Ithaca College lives in vital rhythms that transcend any individual person or event.

In this perspective, the Phillips years looked both forward and backward. In many ways, they were suffused with the afterglow of the sixties — minimally with the troubles of that era, far more significantly with its optimism, its idealism, its naiveté. But "there is a time to breathe out — and also a time to breathe in," President Phillips was fond of remarking; and he was certainly aware of the sharp, indeed painful, constrictions not only of resources but also of goals that would be experienced by those who would follow him. "Community" was the noblest of aspirations, but what if many, even most, of the faculty and student body declined to accept the heavy burden of responsibility imposed upon them by the governance document and the judicial code? This machinery would in fact soon prove too cumbersome for the institution to sustain: councils became cliques, committee after committee would go unstaffed despite the efforts of the "committee on committees." There were unfaced problems within the documents themselves — the relationship of the community council to the other councils, of the By-Laws of the College to the new legislation, with its vaunts of divisional autonomy and its arrogation of "decision-making powers" to various constituencies. For all of its acceptance of the governance proposals "in principle," the Board had never for a moment intended to surrender its ultimate authority over every aspect of the College's activity. Year by year, the percentage of tenured faculty members had been increasing and, by 1975, had already reached 100 percent in some departments; tenure was too easily conferred, yet every effort to establish more sensitive criteria had been defeated by the faculty. The first faculty vote on collective bargaining occurred on May 2, 1975; the defeat of the bid for unionization at that time ("Let's wait and see what the new President will do") only set the stage for further efforts. And, with each passing year, the warnings of the demographers became more and more insistent: given the birth rate, given the shrinking high school graduation classes, the pool of college applicants must necessarily diminish, and at some time, Ithaca College must be prepared to adjust to a freshman class smaller than its expectations — smaller, perhaps, than its budget can comfortably sustain.

Yet this history has been a chronicle of crises successfully surmounted quite as much as it has been a record of memorable achievement in so many areas. The sixth president of Ithaca College arrived with no illusions concerning the magnitude of his task, but with an unshakable conviction that strong and courageous leadership, however unpopular it might prove at times, would safely propel the institution toward its future. The solutions to the problems of this or any other private college in the last decades of the twentieth century would require more than managerial skills, more than "consensus leadership."

> *Perhaps it will require genius — maybe a little madness — but certainly the kind of executive who is ready to take on everybody. This executive will know when to confront and when to bide his time and tread water while others catch up. And even when he is not sure, he will show confidence and optimism, for he will understand well the fact that nobody appreciates a scout who is lost. And there will be evidence that he presided, and there will be signs that he passed that way.*

In those lines, James Joseph Whalen was generalizing about "The Future College Executive" in an address delivered before a conference of higher education in 1973. Yet his words may serve to define the mood of the new administration which he began on July 1, 1975.

Its story must be entrusted to the historian of some future date.

Index of Names

Snow, C.P., 92, 95, 97
Sousa, John Philip, 30
Spencer, Phyllis, 38
Spinoza, Baruch, 106
Squier, Jack, 94
Stalin, Joseph, 48
Stallman, Arthur, 89
Steber, Eleanor, 59, 61
Stein, Gertrude, 145
Steinhaus, Arthur, 90
Stevenson, Adlai, 48
Stokowski, Leopold, 96
Stowell, Leon, 59
Stravinsky, Igor, 66, 96
Strayer, George D., 53
Stringfellow, George E., 56, 59
Strunk, William, 119
Stutz, Harry, 42
Styron, William, 123
Suzuki, Shinichi, 96
Swartwood, C.J., 18
Swenson, Edward, 145
Sykes, William L., 5

Taber, Ronald, 126
Taft, William Howard, 31
Tague, Joseph, 67
Talbott, Mrs. H.E., 31, 49
Tallcott, Rollo Anson, 31, 33, 38
Tallcott, Mrs. Rollo Anson (Jennie Witmer), 31, 38, 97
Tallman and Tallman, 84, 86
Tatascore, Joseph, 41
Tchaikovsky, Peter, 23, 40
Terwilliger, E. William, 110, 118, 119, 133
Textor, George C., 61, 87, 95, 98
Thant, U, 95
Theobald, John J., 79
Thomas, R.J., 48
Thompson, Harold W., 71
Thomson, César, 32
Thoreau, Henry D., 47
Toffler, Alvin, 145
Toklas, Alice B., 117
Treman, Allan H., 84
Treman, Mrs. Allan H., 84
Treman, Charles E., 5, 13
Tunney, Gene, 59, 61

Vail, Mrs. Carl (Lillian Speakman), 24n, 40, 58, 59, 89, 146
VanDyne, Nellie, 32, 62
Venitt, S.S., 61, 94
Verdi, Giuseppe, 40, 53, 66, 145
Vincent, Edward, 136
Virgil, 105

Wallace, Marcelite (Mrs. Leonard Bliss Job), 75
Walton, Henry, 94
Wanzer, Esther M., 8
Warburton, Mr., 16
Warhol, Andy, 94
Washburn, Kenneth, 36
Watson, Thomas J., 52
Weill, Kurt, 66
Weinberger, Jaromir, 32
Wells, Donald, 96, 108
West, Cecil, 70, 96, 97
Whalen, James Joseph, 47, 148
White, Andrew Dickson, 1, 57
White, E.B., 119
Whitney, Maurice, 38
Wickstrom, Carl, 67
Wickstrom, Mrs. Carl (Helene), 67
Wilcox, F.A., 52
Wilhelm, Arnold, 70, 90, 143n
Will, Mr., 14
Williams, Ernest S., 30
Williams, Mrs. Ernest S., 30
Williams, George C., Chs. I, II, and III, 45, 49, 62, 65, 79-80, 131, 146
Williams, Mrs. George C. (Ruth Robertson), 6
Williams, Louise, 75
Willamson, John Finley, 30-31, 49
Willkie, Wendell, 53
Winter, James, 76
Witherspoon, Herbert, 32
Wood, Carlton, 70, 143n
Woods, Mark, 59
Worth, Carlton, 142
Wuest, Christopher, 70

Yavits, Isadore, 26, 26n, 41, 68, 69, 90, 98, 142
Yingling, Hal, 104, 111

Ziegler, Oscar, 32
Zilg, Jerry, 129